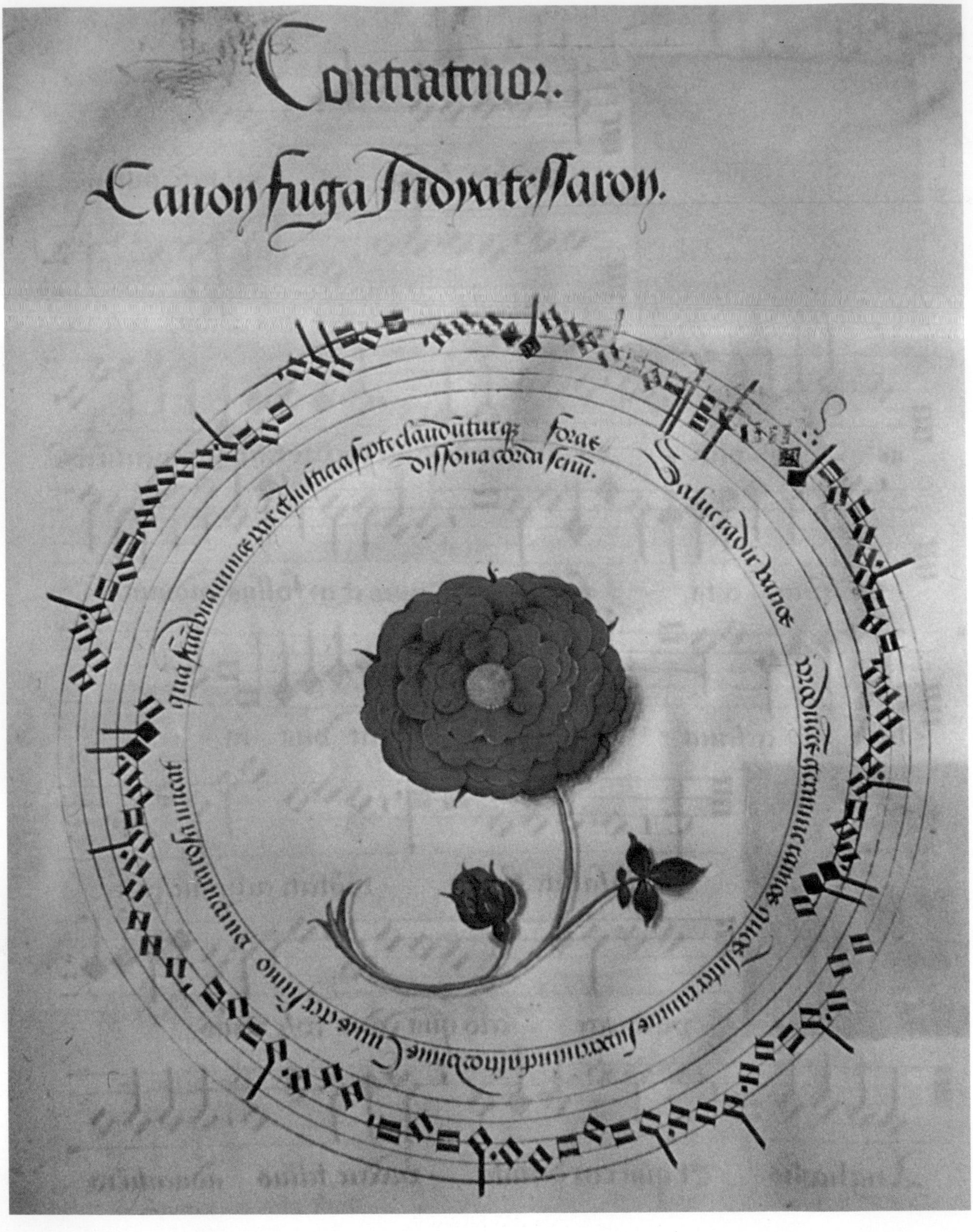
Contratenor.
Canon fuga In dyatessaron.

The Music of Man

YEHUDI MENUHIN AND CURTIS W. DAVIS

A METHUEN PAPERBACK

Every reasonable effort has been made to ensure that all required permissions have been granted for this publication. Apology is made for any inadvertent errors or omissions.

Material quoted on page 107: Reprinted from African Music: A People's Art *by Francis Bebey, published by Lawrence Hill & Co., Westport, Conn., U.S.A.*

Photographic Research: Michael Sheldon Text Design: Brant Cowie/Artplus Ltd.

Printed and bound in Hong Kong

1 2 3 4 5 6 7 8 9 10

A Note to the Reader

The Music of Man is the expansion of an eight-part television series broadcast by the Canadian Broadcasting Corporation in 1979. It is written to increase your awareness and appreciation of the miracle of music and how it has influenced all humankind through the ages. It is not intended to serve as an exhaustive history book of music; for this purpose you may wish to consult the appended bibliography.

We would like to point out that the type rule along the left margin of the text indicates the interpretative statements by Mr. Yehudi Menuhin.

Table of Contents

4. The Age of the Composer   124

Vivaldi, Bach, Mozart, Haydn, Beethoven and Schubert establish music as an idiom commonly understood throughout the Western World. The production of the towering masterpieces is begun, works which continue to dominate our present-day concerts. Bach establishes the tempered scale and perfects the art of counterpoint; Mozart speaks of human passion with a last gesture of elegant restraint; Beethoven announces the composer as creator of his own personal idiom; Schubert addresses the inner man.

5. The Age of the Individual   160

The industrial age brings with it the modern grand piano, the huge symphony orchestra, the massive grand opera. Paganini, Chopin and Liszt become the embodiment of the romantic solo virtuoso. The cities grow, popular and folk music becomes urbanized, the national anthem emerges. Verdi is the cultural hero of an emerging Italian nation, and Wagner cuts Western music loose from its moorings. Nationalism takes musical shape in Tschaikovsky and other composers, and in popular forms such as the flamenco. Brahms retains his sense of contact with folk roots, and the waltzes of Strauss sweep Europe.

6. The Parting of the Ways   200

Immigrants, the willing from Europe and the unwilling from Africa, become the population of North America, where a new music begins to take shape. The songs of Stephen Foster, the rags of Scott Joplin, the marches of John Philip Sousa are part of an America coming of age. Edison's invention of the movies and the phonograph revolutionize the shaping of musical taste. In Europe, the old conventions break up under the impact of the impressionism of Debussy, the splendors of Strauss and Mahler. Charles Ives foreshadows the inevitable, and Igor Stravinsky brings on the revolution in music with The Rite of Spring.

7. The Known and the Unknown   232

The pace of life in the twentieth century accelerates, and music absorbs new elements with astonishing speed. Jazz breaks like a tidal wave and comes to the concert hall with George Gershwin. Arnold Schönberg formulates the twelve-tone system, Edgard Varèse creates an abstract music independent of conventions. Aaron Copland forges an American music comparable to that of other nations. The era of the big band is concurrent with Hollywood and Stokowski, radio and Toscanini. The music of Bali is rediscovered. Alban Berg sums up and lets go of the past in his final work, the Violin Concerto.

8. Sound or Unsound   270

Junk-heap or compost-heap, that is the question: whether music has lost its way, or whether it may flower anew. John Cage questions the validity of music itself, Steve Reich treats it as process, Muzak makes it into subliminal filler. Technology transforms both the making and mass marketing of music. Canadian pianist Glenn Gould argues that the recording has replaced the concert hall. Popular music is transformed from the sentimental ballads of Sinatra to the driving beat of Presley, the emotional intensity of the Beatles and the street roughness of the Rolling Stones. Young people begin to rediscover the music of the more distant past and of other cultures; and the role of sentiment returns to both classical and popular music. Béla Bartók is the epitome of the uncompromising artist, one who nonetheless does not lose touch with his roots in the soil and the people.

Foreword

"Where wast thou when I laid the foundations of the earth? declare, if thou hast understanding. Who hath laid the measures thereof, if thou knowest? or who hath stretched the line upon it? Whereupon are the foundations thereof fastened? or who laid the cornerstone thereof; When the morning stars sang together, and all the sons of God shouted for joy?"

38 JOB

How better to start *The Music of Man* than with a quotation from the Old Testament, throughout which runs a constant theme of music and its healing properties. Here in Job is the very Creation itself, joining heaven to mankind on earth in song.

That fools should venture where angels fear to tread is perhaps the ultimate justification for the existence of fools. Perhaps, again, that is why God permitted them in the first place. Sometimes it is the wisdom of the wise that is confounded and can occur simply by the stumbling into the unknown by the untaught. Be that as it may, I offer here the results of my wanderings, prompted by an insatiable curiosity into a world so rich, so complex, so full of the treasures of mankind, that I can only believe that music does, indeed, lie at the heart of all men.

The Music of Man is so vast a subject that to attempt to confine it to the time it takes to watch eight television programs or to read eight chapters of a book is indeed impossible. The performance of a single Wagner opera may take almost as long a span. Therefore, anybody who imagines that we have set out to explore every manifestation of music, every style, instrument, musician and composer or purpose, would certainly be as deluded as we would be conceited in proposing to attempt this giant task. The scope of the book had to be dictated by the same limitations.

Perhaps I can best explain our intention by suggesting a comparison in the visual and mechanical field. Today, with telescopes, satellites, balloons and planes, our means of looking outward proliferate; similarly, we have every type of internal scanner for looking into our bodies, inside our earth and into basic molecular structure. We are able to see space and matter, organic and inorganic, at every distance. It is the correlation of those various perspectives which offers us a global, balanced and profound comprehension of relative time and space, of life and death, mass and energy, of speed and directions, which are essential to our maturity as human beings and which should give a genuinely modern man his scope and his purpose and his potential freedom from prejudice.

In very much the same way, I hope this book will provide the equivalent of topographical maps showing the position of music throughout the ages, alternating general overall views which reveal long-term trends, cultural interactions and ways of life with close-ups of particular situations and periods. These maps, of course, can only be taken as samples, but I should like to think that *The Music of Man* will also provide a compass, a guide, to our aural environment. With this crude compass, you might be able to polarize the relative positions of various styles and types of music in the scheme of things, to find out where, perforce, much else has had to be omitted, and to discover for yourself where it might properly belong.

Music may happen to be expressive, communicative, moving and inspired, but it is rarely accidental, even when it recalls the everlasting sounds of the sea or the spontaneity of birdsong. The cry of the newborn child is as much the intrinsic sound of music as is the staccato hammering of the woodpecker, the crash of thunder, the rustle of wind through the wheat field, the cooing of the dove, the rattle of seed pods, the clank of metal, the soft tread of feet on underbrush. Is it not in these very natural sounds that is largely found the raw material for the creation of man's music? Out of these we have built, constructed, continue building and constructing, musical languages, whether the most subtle and sophisticated monodic (melodic) and rhythmic textures such as developed thousands of years ago in India, or the most complex harmonic textures which have developed only recently in Western Europe.

It has been my good fortune to spend my life doing the thing I love most, being a musician. To be in tune with oneself, with one's environment, with the music one plays and with those who listen, sounds almost pagan in its wholeness, in its total unity with nature. If that be pagan, then making music would seem to establish, paradoxically, a contact with the remotest human religious expression, for I am convinced that even sacred music must have its roots in the profane. Because I have rejoiced in the many masterpieces of Western musical literature, it is from this experience that I must continuously draw. Nor would I put music in a false and distant perspective, crowning it with awe-inspiring halos; the pagan element in each one of us is basic to creation, as the power of artistic expression is born of fertility. The Greeks knew this well and acknowledged man in his wholeness, giving due respect to his dual nature: one half the Apollonian, always striving for clarity and moderation; the other the Dionysian, driving toward the fantastic and orgiastic. We revel in our senses, as we revel in the powers of our mind and soul. Today these senses are at the mercy of commercial society to whom all tastes are but appetites to be used and abused for the sake of profit. Inexorably, since my boyhood in San Francisco, I have seen the dislocation of the natural and instinctive flair and taste for the genuine twisted to the acceptance of the odorless flavors, the plastic plants, the whole flattening of the aesthetic responses, even to the acceptance of the appalling distortion of pure sound when something termed music pours through various mechanical devices in one long adenoidal wail.

How does one distinguish the true from the false, the beautiful from the ugly in music, as in life? Is it not perhaps at that moment when we are cognizant of an ever-renewed awareness in the growing depth of our powers of mind, of heart, of compassion, of all our senses? When these correspond to our communion with ourselves, our fellow men and nature, when we can move freely between serenity and emotion, between thought and action without prejudice to others or ourselves, then it is that we know truth: the eternal truths of Beethoven, of Bartók, of Socrates, Buddha and Jesus. Then it is that we can begin to trust ourselves, as we trust, implicitly, Shakespeare, Michelangelo and Bach.

By contrast, science is about the study of the objective, measurable phenomena of our world; art is about the human, the living domain. In the hearing of Beethoven's *Eroica*, in the presence of a portrait by Rembrandt, in the rhythm and import of a sonnet of Shakespeare, we are in direct contact with the truth and spirit of the creators, as surely as we are in a different dimension through the perception of Einstein who, paradoxically, while bringing science closer to metaphysics than ever before, fixed the human situation as forever relative. We may thus surrender to truth, whether of science or of art. But at the same time, we must defend our flanks, fight the false, the presumptive, the pretentious, the commercial, the propaganda as we would the devil, the eternal tempter, ever ready to catch us unaware and somnolent.

Fortunately, civilization, like life itself, never proceeds along a straight line in the manner of a Roman road, but follows peripheral motions such as the swing of a pendulum, the circular path of a wheel or the elliptical orbit of a planet. Progress may seem deceptively small, but it *is* measurable. Civilization depends upon just such wide and free-swinging motions, which constantly threaten to break away from their moorings for regeneration. It is only by exploring the extremes that we learn to locate the center. A cycle of emotions is as vital to us as is a variety of foods: we are capable of revelling in extremes, we crave our opposites, we put ourselves to the test, feeding on risk, dependent upon our adversaries, as sweet needs sour and hot needs cold.

For my part, I should like to manage to be that most improbable and paradoxical of creatures: the "moderate fanatic." In other words, I would like to be the kind of man who can muster intensity and passion, commitment and the will to sacrifice in order to defend not some one-sided dogma bent on the destruction of whatever lies outside its precious cant, but rather the possibility of encouraging a constructive exchange between people representing all varieties and ranges of opinion and intent—helping only, perhaps, to exclude such extremes as lead to the loss of equilibrium. I believe that people and civilizations can survive and even need, like the effective drop of arsenic in the medicine, a modicum of poison in them. It is merely a question of dosage.

Governments exist partly to maintain the correct dosage of poison in society. Religion, of which government is the temporal reflection, also maintains the equilibrium of societies and souls. Man is, by definition, religious and, by the same token, artist, for he is constantly trying to transform a vision into reality, a mystery into common sense. He can never quite succeed and, to find his inner balance, he must accept his limitations. At the same time he must never lose faith, nor his sense of belonging to a greater purpose, to a wider reality than he can ever encompass. Faith, trust and love are kindred feelings, and the music we call religious is votive and therefore has much in common with love and dedication. It is the union of these feelings in music that is, really, one of its glories and one of its oldest functions.

In this attempt to explore the music of man, my modest intention has been to demonstrate that it is music that welds spiritual and sensual, that can convey ecstasy free of guilt, faith without dogma, love as homage and man himself at home with nature and the infinite.

To see a World in a Grain of Sand
And a Heaven in a Wild Flower,
Hold Infinity in the palm of your hand
And Eternity in an hour.
WILLIAM BLAKE, *AUGURIES OF INNOCENCE*

YEHUDI MENUHIN

Acknowledgments

When John Barnes, Head of Arts, Music and Science Television for the Canadian Broadcasting Corporation, asked me whether I would consider making a television series on the subject of "The Music of Man," I readily embraced a project which promised to be as inspiring as it would be fulfilling. I was particularly pleased, as an American, to feel that this great conception should originate in the New World. In John Barnes, I quickly recognized a man of imagination, discretion, determination, and, as was to be proven, of infinite patience. Who could have been more fortunate than I, embarking on such a journey with so much sympathy and trust to send me on my way?

I owe a debt of thanks, too, to my three producer-directors, of whom Curtis Davis, the first, undertook with diligence and extraordinary imagination the main body of the enormous amount of research necessary to such a subject. The other two, Richard Bocking and John Thomson, with whom I actually worked on the various locations, from the remotest villages of Senegal to the cloisters of Sylos, from the courtyards of the Alhambra, the amphitheatre of Delphi, to my own homes in London and Gstaad, I can never thank sufficiently. It is on the "set" of so abstract and elusive a medium as television that one relies upon just such guidance, such equable temperament and such ready cooperation as both of these gifted men showed me.

If the films manage to convey my conception, a great part of the credit is due to their loyal support, helpful suggestions and consummate skills. As for myself, I have had, over the many years during which I have organized my own festivals, given master classes, played music as varied and alien as the European classics, modern music of all kinds, Indian and jazz, the great, good fortune to find one or two very close collaborators who have rushed to my aid whenever I have needed that expert advice which I, as a plain and busy violinist and conductor, cannot summon at will. Therefore, to guide me in the recorded history of Western music, I enlisted my dear and trusted long-time friend, Professor Denis Stevens, now of Santa Barbara, California, who, witty and erudite, precise and elegant of mind, prevented me from making too many gross errors of fact.

As for the other friendly experts, Ravi Shankar, that incomparable exponent of a very great art, has long guided me in the Indian classical tradition, and John Blacking, whose years spent among African peoples have gained him the position of the senior and most distinguished anthropologist on the subject in Britain, clarified for me much of the complications of African chanting.

Another of my close supporters has been the distinguished poet and author, Christopher Hope, whose infallible sense for the exact word and the sound of a phrase has been invaluable in the working out of the dialogue for the scripts (as can be imagined, one of the most complicated parts of any such enterprise), for such words and ideas must stem from a collaboration. I am totally incapable of putting across one single sentence that has not contained at least the origin of my own idea or the conception of a fact as I conceive it. This stubbornness must have made me a maddening person with whom to work, and I am grateful to Curtis Davis, whose malleability and patience so well conceded that, if I could not feel that the idea were couched in my own terms or, conversely, that the dialogue did not represent my intention, I simply could not put it across until I had converted it myself.

All the way through the long and sometimes hectic journey of this production, I have felt closer and closer to the team, all of whom offered advice, proffered suggestions, cheered me as I tried to concentrate on my words under freezing rain in Rothenburg, icy blasts in the Alhambra, torpid heat in Senegal, and I defy anyone to find anywhere a more piercingly cold, damp interior than an ancient church, unheated for nigh on eight centuries, in a remote corner of Castile.

And yet, under all these circumstances, I was only conscious of loyalty, interest, concern and skill. What man could ever hope to be more fortunate who has embarked on such a voyage in seas mainly uncharted, and who therefore knew that his life depended upon the perspicacity and watchfulness, the sympathy and companionship of his crew? Among these, and of prime importance, was my dear, devoted secretary Eleanor Hope and my untiring assistant Philip Bailey, who worked throughout many nights, unceasingly retyping drafts to meet deadly deadlines and to whom I beg forgiveness for being such an exacting taskmaster.

Lastly, I come to those who helped guide me through the putting together of my part of this book; for again it was an arduous task of reduction, restraint and agonizing choice, made easier by a dedicated, imaginative team at Methuen. No author could ask for more sage, perceptive counsel.

But above all (and against all her resistance), I do want to say how lucky I feel to have had my wife, Diana, by my side during the whole project. Her literary talents and stage training were invaluable, and her whole heart was joined with mine in our desire to give all we had in return for John Barnes's faith in us.

Y.M.

One day in August of 1974, John Barnes, head of music programs for the English television network of the Canadian Broadcasting Corporation approached me with the invitation to develop the concept for a major series for his network, already given the project title, *The Music of Man*. For the exhilaration of five years of totally absorbing work, I am first indebted to John Barnes, for his unwavering confidence and his breadth of vision.

The encounter with music lasts a lifetime; it has been a central part of my life as far back as I can recall. Three early memories spring to mind: listening over and over to Chaliapin's recording of the prayer and death of Boris Godunov while my father brought the scene to life for me, for he had seen the great basso perform the role in Moscow at the Bolshoi; in the early forties, with my violin teacher attending a concert by Yehudi Menuhin at Carnegie Hall and knowing that I would never be a performer; taking part in a composition seminar with Edgard Varèse at Columbia University, while he grunted over my scores saying, "You cannot put everything in, or the sounds will kill each other. You must choose."

The most difficult aspect of *The Music of Man* has been the question of choice. Yehudi Menuhin has pointed out that neither our television series nor this book can hope to be encyclopaedic. The attempt has been to try to ask questions: What is music? Why did we invent it? What is it for? Though much has necessarily been omitted, I hope that our choices are stimulating, and representative of that immensely larger territory which a lifetime of exploration could not exhaust.

My thanks go next to my good friend and co-writer in the early phases of *The Music of Man*, Chuck Weir. It was his outline concept, presented with CBC producer Raymond McConnell to John Barnes early in 1974, which became the genesis of the project. Chuck Weir is a gifted writer with the largest fund of new jokes I know, and the many working sessions together were for me one of the venture's special joys. I also want to thank CBC producer Neil Sutherland, whose advice early in the project was both wise and illuminating.

What Yehudi Menuhin and I owe to CBC producers Richard Bocking and John Thomson cannot be adequately conveyed here, for *The Music of Man* could never have been achieved without their endless patience and great skill. I have not enjoyed a personal and professional relationship more than that with these two gifted men.

Dr. Paul Henry Lang, musicologist, editor, critic, and a former teacher of mine at Columbia, did me the great honor of reviewing the first draft manuscript of this book, making detailed observations throughout. He understood our aim immediately, responding to the personal reflections of Yehudi Menuhin arising from a half-century of musical activity, and his comments were as reassuring as they were scholarly in the best sense.

Christopher Hope, poet, novelist and playwright, was a guide through the labyrinth of editing what was inevitably a much longer first draft, pruning the forest thicket until we reached the end with a judicious calm for which I can only express admiration.

To Michael Sheldon, my resourceful, tireless picture researcher, I want to say that the visual treasures of this book are a reward in which he can take justifiable pride, for they are the ambience, companionship and wine which enhance any meal. The assistance of Lorraine Wright and Anne Penketh at the CBC's London office is acknowledged with gratitude.

Finally I am grateful to Yehudi Menuhin for his generous spirit and inspiring example. To work with him for three years is to learn what discipline, vision and genius can accomplish. When the CBC chose in the fall of 1975 to go ahead with my plan for *The Music of Man*, I was delighted, but the real test came when Yehudi Menuhin was asked to become its spokesman. His acceptance crowned my efforts, and those of John Barnes.

It is Yehudi Menuhin's particular good fortune to have as his companion Diana Menuhin, whose charm and perception are ever-refreshing, and whose many contributions to our work were astute, and helped to keep us on course. My own wife, Julie, displayed a patience and understanding without which I could never have gone the distance.

Yehudi Menuhin is one of the great figures in the history of music, a role he sustains with extraordinary grace and equanimity. To be his partner in conveying the message of music is a privilege for which I shall be forever thankful.

C.W.D.

The origins of music are examined from prehistoric times to the first great civilizations of Sumer, Egypt and China, and to the classical age of Ancient Greece. Man discovers how to create musical instruments from what he finds in nature—bones, horns, willow bark, animal gut—and from what he learns to create himself—the bow and arrow, iron, bronze. The evolution of the sense of hearing is described, and the resonating principle of overtones is applied.

1. The Quiver of Life

For Stern —
with the realisation
that, in this life, there
is nothing to be done
but to make the most
of what I cannot
help -- I love you.

MUSIC IS OUR OLDEST FORM OF EXPRESSION, older than language or art; it begins with the voice, and with our overwhelming need to reach out to others. In fact, music *is* man far more than words, for words are abstract symbols which convey factual meaning. Music touches our feelings more deeply than most words and makes us respond with our whole being. This book is about that unique human gift, both creative and recreative, which draws on our ability to synthesize discovery with memory. As long as the human race survives, music will be essential to us. We need music, I believe, as much as we need each other.

We have been making music for a very long time. Archaeological evidence suggests that primitive man was using bones, drums and flutes long before the last Ice Age. We do not know to what purpose such instruments were put three hundred centuries ago, though we can speculate on ceremonies and rituals, both sacred and profane. More exact knowledge begins later with China, which had developed sophisticated musical theories by 3000 BC. Western music is a far more recent accomplishment; with the exception of Greece, it had not developed at the time of the Christian era. Rome borrowed most of its music from conquered territories. After the fall of Rome, Western music languished, tainted by past associations.

All my life I have played the music of Johann Sebastian Bach, a music whose purity expresses our highest ethics, our strongest morality, our

Five thousand years ago, a noble Egyptian couple would be serenaded by a harpist and three singers clapping out the rhythm. These clay figures were buried as part of the household of the dead, helping them to travel to the next world (they are now in the Cairo Museum).

Two Gimi musicians invoke and become the lush forest in which they live. The Gimi are among the Papuan people of New Guinea, found some fifty miles south of the provincial capital of Goroka.

noblest sentiments. It frees us from our baser selves, speaks to us of man at peace with himself and God, and reflects the rhythm of a society which has established its faith and security. This is music standing on the pinnacle of human discovery and invention. In fact, I would propose that music is a mirror of the process of thought itself. The repeated rhythms and sequences of tones clearly helped to establish the principle of recognition and comparison, drawing on memory, and on trial and error. All the various symbolic methods we use to investigate the nature of the world and ourselves are to be found within music. The fugue, for instance, is the very exemplar of thought, working by proof and reformulation, analogy and the refinement of memory

I believe that is the lesson of all music. We seek knowledge in order to gain control over the unpredictable, for in all of us there is a psychological need for reassurance if we are to create order and sense out of events, to give them focus and direction. Any one cell may become ten million, giving its genes to its offspring, and thereby establishing the repetition of the genetic pattern. With man the process is conscious as well as physiological; we hand on the products of our minds and hearts, and among these is music. Just as the involuntary heartbeat produces life's first rhythm, so music gives back to us the pulse of life.

Music took a long time to flourish in the West, but this was not without its advantages. Time allowed us to take in all the developments of past ages and turn them to new purposes. The West domesticated the scale and developed harmony in a new way, building vertically as well as horizontally, creating an entirely fresh language, which had never been heard before. This process, nonetheless, took over a thousand years. Slowly, the West rediscovered that music is more than flesh and bone and heart, that we use these only as tools with which to create something intangible, something which puts us in touch with the vibrations of the universe. It is this impulse which shaped the growth of Western music during its many centuries of struggle to become what we now know, and to a large extent what we now take for granted.

The path to reach the exalted level attained by Bach has been a long one, and we are still struggling to keep to it, threatened as we are daily by violence and degradation, by a pendulum which may swing too far. There is more than feeling in Bach's music. However passionate it may become, there is always form, balance, a process of logic, of construction, wherein he reached a perfection which has never been surpassed. That is one of the lessons of Bach's music, and of all music.

The apparently solid world we take for granted began in the torrid heat of molten stone and swirling gases, transforming itself over eons into a cosmos cool enough to allow the first faint stirrings of life. On this planet, apparently unique (at least in our solar system), an extraordinary balance of natural forces has evolved. The pendulum swings from hot to cold, from height to depth, without exceeding the precise conditions needed for life. Yet that boiling unrest deep within the earth persists, sending us earthquakes and tidal waves to remind us from the moment of our birth of our powerlessness before nature.

In our technological age we have come to believe that safety lies in control, in mastery over man as well as nature. Admittedly, this has brought us certain advantages, but can we claim advances when, as our many wars in this century confirm, we still pillage and kill without purpose? We fail because man is neither at peace with himself, nor has he mastery over himself; therefore he seeks mastery over others.

Man is a land creature, and the air with which he fills his lungs is the carrier of animal sounds. Animals make noises which say "I am here," and "I am me." With these sounds they attract mates, terrify enemies, lead flocks and freeze prey in their tracks; they warn their fellows of danger and comfort each other in distress. The voice is one of the most basic tools of self-preservation. Not all creatures produce sound by passing air through the vocal cords, the narrow bands at the end of the windpipe—dolphins and whales use the flap covering their blow-holes, crickets use hind legs and the frog its pouch. But from the beginning, a particular sound is an indelible part of that creature's identity.

The baby's cry asserts his new independence, and perhaps a premonition of responsibility and hope. It is both a joyful greeting and a regretful farewell. His lungs acknowledge the new realm of air, but he carries a sharp memory of that warmth, comfort and safety he knew in the aquatic womb. The mother's heartbeat remains deep within long after we emerge into the light of day, imprinted on us like our identity. We feel its loss and must replace it with other sounds, especially that of our own voice, for sound and rhythm are communication. We could hear long before we could see.

Some hospitals have experimented with quieting newborn babies by playing them recordings of the human heartbeat, finding in some cases that the babies are comforted and lulled to the point where they forget to breathe. Living creatures communicate with one another through sounds as recognizable to their species as a baby's cry is to his mother. At the

Victoria aquarium, Paul Horn has demonstrated that the whale, the world's largest mammal, responds to the musical sounds he produces on a flute, answering him as though belonging to his tribe. The keenness of every creature's senses is part of its ability to survive, to mate, to feed. Thirty thousand years ago, living in caves, among trees or in the open, our senses were our best weapon. Hearing was as important as sight; every rustle had a message; we came to know the noise of every other creature.

For our ancestors, food gathering was vital work. The ecological movement today partly reflects a sense our forebears had, that the animal was his cousin, sharing the same world and its interlocking life cycles. The Australian aborigine or African Bushman thinks of his spear as a hunting tool, not as a weapon of war. There is a splendid African proverb which expresses this sense of kinship clearly: "Before you cross the river, never curse the crocodile's mother." Both animals and men hunt for berries and roots, melons and nuts, even as they may prey on each other.

The bow and arrow became part of the games of children, miming the actions of their hunting fathers. This South African Bushman boy has decorated his bow with colored stripes.

On the dry grasslands of the plains of the Kalahari in South Africa, where the Igwi people live out their harsh lives, music binds family and tribe together. There a musician may sing about the perpetual search for food and water, and about the endless distances which separate people. He also sings about the animals attracted to the new grass that springs up after a fire, about the kudu and porcupine on which he feeds, or of the sly

hyena who, by making himself small, creeps among people and devours their clothes.

In that translucent light and air of the plains, it is possible to hear for miles, to smell the coming of a storm, detect the movement of prowling beasts. The hunt became as much a part of survival as the harvest, and no instrument altered the balance of power more swiftly in man's favor than the discovery of the bow and arrow, which gives man control over the animal from a distance. For the hunter this was not yet a weapon of war, but a matching of forces; only the necessity of food made man and animal antagonists. From the ritual of the hunt sprang music; the bow could produce a mellifluous twang. A widely held view is that the bow and arrow are ancestor to the violin.

In food-gathering rituals we began by invoking the blessing of the gods for the success of the search. The North American Indian may don the bearskin in the conviction that he cannot hope to trap a bear unless he becomes one in spirit. The Eskimo sings with pride of the size of the huge fish or seal he has caught, in lieu of the snapshot of the fisherman standing beside his marlin or salmon.

Every ritual we share calls for its own music: birth, marriage, death, the planting and the harvest, the changing of the seasons, the coming of spring and fertility, the sufferings of illness and the recovery of health.

The Amahuaca Indians of Peru are among many people who have developed the mouth bow, but this one is bowed, not plucked, the mouth cavity serving as a resonating chamber.

Our first music was doubtless concerned with consecrating such events. As agriculture and the building of shelters developed, music became associated with work. And as our societies grew, music to honor leadership came into being—royal processions with musical instruments go back to Egypt and Sumer. Such uses of music are natural, for leadership helped to bring us out of caves and into civilization. Moreover, acknowledging our leaders is a trait we share with the entire animal world.

Human beings are not only musical creatures; we are noisy, we chatter, we shout, sometimes across great distances. For a long time music and speech were one continuum, both produced by the voice. Even after the first instruments appeared, music and speech were still overlapping entities. According to recent finds in the Near East, the first written word symbols began to appear some ten thousand years ago, mainly to facilitate trade. Writing helped to separate music from speech. Words on clay or papyrus could convey simple messages quickly, whereas music was tied to the expression of complex feelings. There are places in the world where ancient languages survive, such as China, Vietnam and parts of Africa, in which the inflection of speech and music remains inseparable, though not identical; where parts of melodies follow the same rise and fall as the language, and a change in the musical line may also alter the meaning of the word.

This Bushman's dance is found in the "Valley of Art" near Jamestown in the Cape Province of South Africa, one of hundreds of paintings made by generations of artists over the ages. Some paintings have been found in desert caves in areas which must once have been fertile green land.

There is anthropological evidence that music came before speech. Ligaments that attach muscles to bones leave traces on the skeletal frame which tell us much about how those muscles were used, and make possible reconstructions of prehistoric creatures from scanty evidence. Our vocal mechanism is complex: for chanting the lungs and vocal cords are enough; when we speak, the mouth and tongue are drawn into play. Early human skeletal remains reveal signs that the use of the voice to produce speech goes back some eighty thousand years, while also suggesting that chanting began perhaps half a million years earlier.

The combination of music and speech into the single expression of song has unique power, conveying feelings of great elation or almost unbearable poignancy. When we gather for common celebrations, music helps to raise the sharing of feelings to a level of intensity which words alone could not hope to attain. Music does not reproduce the world outside and around us, not even when we consciously imitate the sounds we hear; music is first and foremost about us, it is our identity.

This West African singer cups his hands to his ears in order to hear more clearly the resonance of his voice. It is a technique found among folk singers throughout the world.

Over the millennia, tasks which were once the role of entire communities brought forth specialists—the best fishermen, toolmakers or midwives. Those who possessed the gift of imaginative hearing and skill with sound were also recognized. In many societies everyone shared in the music, and the semi-professional musician was rare in such groups. Gradually, the musician came to be valued and was given increased responsibilities, for he could galvanize the people, speaking for them, as together, they spoke with him. With his help, music gave them the will and courage to make war, defend property, give voice to joy or mourn their losses.

Man invents almost nothing. For the most part he discovers, drawing on his experience of the world outside and within himself, whether it be the discovery of the principle of the wheel or the theory of relativity. Both were inspired deductions from immediate reality. Our whole development, in fact, is one of analysis, fitting together clues, observing and reflecting, and finally creating something new. Such discoveries seem to me related to the beaver's inborn ability to build a dam or the bees their hive. But I do not intend to demean that extraordinary human capacity for dreaming, and would rather define it through those two notable creations, music and language.

The creation of musical instruments is one of the great human miracles. I remember in Africa hearing the sound of two drums echoing back and forth between the hills. When I asked my guide what music was being made, he answered simply, "Oh, they are just good friends saying goodnight." It is a practice which goes back to the dawn of music and speech, and to an era when the stillness and quiet we have lost permitted the echoing drums to send their messages a long way through the calm evening.

The French philosopher Pascal said, "Man is but a reed, the weakest in nature, but he is a thinking reed." Man has an endless curiosity about the sounds things make; that is partly how he recognizes what they are. This natural experimentation led to the fashioning of a huge array of resonating, vibrating tools, the instruments of music. The oldest traces we now have of specific tools for the making of music have come from excavations in Siberia, and have been dated back some thirty-five thousand years. These include an ensemble of mammoth bones, the huge hip and shoulder joints, with markings showing the places where the best resonances could be secured. Found with them was a bone carved as a beater, and two small flutes also made of bone with four holes above and two below, suggesting that they were held by the thumb and two fingers

of both hands. This already implies a sophisticated fingering system, and thus, by extension, a musical scale—the existence of primitive melodies long before the last great Ice Age. This find may well be a fragment of our oldest known orchestra, as tantalizing and exciting to musicians as it is to anthropologists.

Other sites have yielded carved stone drum shells over which skins were most probably stretched. Stone itself does not vibrate, except for those lengths carved by men in early Asian civilizations into tuned scales. Materials that do vibrate sufficiently to produce music are usually perishable, such as wood, gut and reed. Even horn does not last as long as bone. So we may be sure that a great deal of evidence has vanished. We may not be able to reconstitute an accurate picture of the music of primitive man, but the known evidence confirms that this society was not as primitive as formerly supposed.

Old logs are often naturally hollow, giving off a deep resonant sound when struck, and in parts of Africa, the Far East and the Pacific the art of hollowing out a huge tree section, extracting almost all of the interior through a single narrow slit, was highly developed. It was a rite often shrouded in mystery, carried out beyond the prying eyes of the uninitiated. It was also found that by placing a wood beam across an open pit and striking it, a fine resonance was obtained. This was the first natural amplifier. The ground bow was an extension of the log over a pit. A bridge was added at the mid-point and a string drawn tightly over it, fastened at either end. The string might be of natural fiber or animal gut, and could either be plucked or struck. There are anthropologists who hold that the ground bow came before the hunting bow, theorizing that the bridge might have come loose and been propelled into the ground by the string. A natural consequence was to make the effect portable.

The shoulder blades and hip bones of a mastodon, uncovered in the Siberian ice, are part of a prehistoric musical ensemble; two bone flutes were found with them, and markings for resonance points are still visible after 35,000 years.

The talking drum is one of the oldest methods of long-distance communication in Africa. This pedestal from an Ifa bowl comes from the Yoruba area of northern Africa.

The tuning of stone slabs by careful chipping is also very old. Such tuned stones have been found in Vietnam and Cambodia, where the art of striking tuned lengths of wood, metal and stone remains the basis of a sophisticated musical art found in the gamelans of Cambodia, Java and Bali. There are Chinese sets of tuned stones which we know to be over three thousand years old. Similar xylophone-type instruments arose in Africa, where wood was used instead of stone. The contemporary version is the Senegalese *balafon*, among others. Metal came later, both to Africa and Asia, and is now the basis not only of the gamelan but of the *sansa*, or thumb piano, of Africa, which was already a perfected instrument by the time the first European travellers reached that continent.

It is of special interest that the large gamelan ensembles of Southeast Asia like to tune the same notes on different instruments slightly apart, setting up a "beat" between them, as when two piano wires are slightly mistuned. I am convinced that this has arisen from their familiarity with the use of the sound of bells, which are so commonplace in Thailand. Nothing is more elusive to define than the exact pitch of a bell, whose overall sound seems clear, yet tantalizingly contains all kinds of impure overtones.

It is significant to remember that the sound one people consider beautiful may not necessarily correspond to another's taste. In Africa, even neighboring peoples may have different conceptions of beautiful sound. It is imperious to imagine that the bright, clear tone of our modern Western xylophone should automatically please an African; he often prefers an instrument with a muffled sound or one with a buzz or rasp. The particular sound favored by a given people arises from their identity and is conditioned by their surroundings.

Another instrument of shaped stone or wood is the legendary bullroarer, still used today by Australian aborigines. It is an oblong piece with a cutting edge attached to a thong or rope, which makes a deep whistling sound when swung round the head, a roar that can be heard for miles. Some are made of bone, and such artifacts have been found in excavations of settlements going back tens of thousands of years. The bullroarer is as old as the drum, an instrument whose ancestry cannot be traced because it is so widespread.

The principle of the amplifying resonator was applied to many kinds of sound production. Gourds served as the foundation for early harps, as did the shells of living creatures, from the armadillo to the turtle and conch. Their ready availability may have accounted in part for the early development of the string instruments, through which we could also refine our sense of pitch because of the variable tuning of the strings. The *kora* in Senegal and the *berimbau* in Brazil are contemporary examples.

The discovery of the principle of the flute and horn is fascinating, for these make use of another resonating property altogether, that of an enclosed vibrating column of air. The earliest flutes and horns were made from hollowed bones, and probably also from branches and bark, though these have not survived. The willow flute is still made in Scandinavia and Rumania today by carefully stripping off the unbroken bark from a length of green branch. It yields the most liquid of sounds, yet lasts only two or three days until the bark begins to dry up. Naturally hollow substances like bamboo have served as flutes and stamping tubes for a long time, and as part of the ensemble of gamelans. Clay became a useful substance for making flutes, for it could be shaped and fired, a method first discovered in the early Stone Age. The ocarina, popular since the turn of the century, is a fired clay flute.

The willow flute is played without finger holes, by blowing through a mouthpiece fitted back into the bark, and using the finger to open and cover the other end. Varying the breath pressure does the rest. Such flutes are found throughout eastern Europe and the Near East, often blown directly across the open top end, like a bottle. Sometime in the late Stone Age, rows of single-tone pipes were linked to form a series or scale—we sometimes call these pan pipes. The Chinese have one called the *sheng*, its pipes arranged in a circle and fed from a central blow-hole. Perhaps China's reputation as the creator of the first organ stems from this instrument. In southern Africa there are societies which have created veritable pan-pipe orchestras. In Rumania, the pan pipe is called the *nai*, and its players have reached an extraordinary virtuosity. Flutes are also made in pairs for a single player, sometimes carved from the same piece of wood, and known as male and female. By the skillful interplay of hands, the player may offer duets in which each flute freely covers a span of well over an octave. These remain popular among the Arabs.

With animal horns, the air column is made to vibrate by the use of the lips. The horn had great carrying power, and was widely used as a signal. It took time and the refining of the shape of the horn opening before it could yield more than one or two overtones above the fundamental. The ram's horn, called the *shofar*, is used as part of the services celebrating the Jewish New Year. Finger holes were eventually added, as with the flute, to extend the horn's range. Long horns are used not only to make music, but as a form of telephone or signal, from the Swiss Alps to Tibet and New Guinea, the Amazon and Japan, a splendid form of communication, from hill to hill, valley to valley. These horns, sometimes two or three times the length of a man, yield a rich, deep sound rising to higher overtones of great sweetness.

The horn, manmade or animal, has been a musical instrument since prehistoric times. These five examples (reading clockwise) show two children in Sikkim playing horns six feet in length, a horn called the narsing used in Nepal to celebrate weddings, the Swiss alphorn which served as an early form of telephone, a monk in the foothills of Mount Everest selling prayers, and a musician in Gambia playing on the antler of an antelope.

The vibrating reed mouthpiece, almost as old as the flute and horn, replaces the lips or cutting edge and sets the air column vibrating. Reed instruments seem to have originated in the Near East, perhaps because of the change of climate at the end of the Paleolithic Age some eight or nine thousand years BC, which marked the end of the last great Ice Age. At its peak, the ice had reached down into central Europe and over the southern half of North America. As it receded, the water level rose, covering Near Eastern lowlands, and forming marshes where reeds multiplied. A piece of cane crushed flat by a hammer blow may be the oldest reed mouthpiece. Two flat pieces are bound together and gripped by the lips. Players found that cane reeds tended to rot with too frequent wetting, they covered them with a tube and a cup which prevented the lips from coming into direct contact—the solution found in the medieval shawm and bagpipe. Yet another answer was to take the entire reed inside the mouth, placing the lips against a cup retainer, as in the Greek *aulos* and many Near Eastern instruments.

Not long after the Paleolithic Age we can begin to use the word civilization to describe the activities of human communities clustered in the areas of Babylon, Sumer and Egypt. A new skill had been mastered, that of blending tin and copper to form bronze. Fire was still essential to survive rigorous winters, though by the time Egypt's civilization rose to its height several centuries later, the world climate may have been generally warmer than it is today. Fire was used in metal tool making, and the techniques used to produce bronze cups and bowls also served to create instruments derived from animal horn. The oldest we have is called the *lur*, a name based on the old Norwegian word for horn. The Celts knew it as the *carnyx*. Egypt fashioned instruments from silver and gold. Two silver trumpets dating from 1320 BC were found in the tomb of Tutankhamen in 1924, and one could still produce a decent tone.

True brass as we know it was not smelted until around AD 500. From brass came yet another type of noisemaker, the percussion instruments, cymbal and gong. With bells, they became part of religious life in the Near and Far East. Such sounds were already popular in Egypt with the *sistrum*, a hand-held frame on which many shaped metal discs were strung. It is still used in Latin America. The modern cymbal had to wait for the mastery of brass to give out its characteristic sizzle, for the natural vibration rate of brass is faster than bronze or iron. Brass is less susceptible to decay, though all three metals remain in wide use in the gamelans of Southeast Asia.

Putting instruments together into ensembles seems to have appealed to some cultures, while others preferred the pure sound of one family of instruments at a time, or even the solo instrument. With skill in

manufacturing came skill in performance. The mastering of a single instrument could become a lifetime occupation, for there are few more specialized tasks in the world. Despite the supposed devotion of a musician to his instrument, it is surprising how little we actually know about the evolution of the instruments in the West. The reason may lie in part in a difference of attitude which grew from the time of the Roman Empire onward, gradually tending to rob the instruments of their reputed magic properties. Music had been associated with sacred mysteries, each giving special status to the other. Some of the most ancient instruments have survived simply because they were buried along with other household goods in the tombs of dead rulers, where they could help clear the path to heaven.

China and Greece both equated music with morality; it stood as a symbol for the good in man. Confucius, writing around 500 BC, said, "Character is the backbone of our human culture. Music is the flowering of character." Instruments producing music under human guidance were considered to be a link to the divine and eternal. Naturally, musical objects would be preserved in a society where tradition and ancestor worship played a central role. Possessing a truly ancient instrument was like possessing a bit of a forebear's soul, and new fingers could follow where theirs had played. However, in the West musical instruments slowly came to be identified with the immediate and transitory, and took on new values.

In Nepal both the horns and the drum bodies are made of bronze, and the working of metal remains a refined art throughout Asia.

The violence of natural forces on this planet did not abate to conditions suitable for life for millennia. The oceans, rich in every chemical element, were an ideal medium for this miraculous event.

Since music consists of audible vibrations, I would like to consider our ears for a moment. What extraordinarily demanding instruments they are, and how indefatigable, asking constantly to be satisfied, never at rest. I find it symbolic that we have eyelids but no earlids, no means of shutting out or turning off the noises all around us. Our ears wake us out of the deepest sleep, and it is left to the deaf, whom I feel must be the loneliest of people, to conceive of a world of total silence. At best, our ears can detect sounds vibrating at less than thirty beats per second, continuing upward past fifteen thousand per second. But these sounds are only part of a much longer continuum of vibrations found throughout the universe, some of which we can hear as distinct beats—for instance the heartbeat, whose average is seventy-two per minute—and some of which we can only see, such as ocean waves, the cycle of day and night, the phases of the moon, the shift of the seasons.

Other vibrations lie beyond our conscious senses, though the eleven-year sunspot cycle affects us nonetheless, setting off earthquakes, breaking up icebergs, and even influencing, grimmest of all thoughts, the peak years for fine French wines. The universe offers much faster waves, too, flowing through matter and through ourselves as though nothing were there, and waves that move so infinitely slowly they take years to pass us by. Sound lies at the heart of the cycle of vibrations, beginning just where touch stops, and ending just before radio waves begin. I believe profoundly that music helps keep us in touch with the entire vibrating world, and thereby centers us in our own being. When the lowest notes are sounded on a great church organ, we feel the vibrations in our entire body, while the violin, producing sounds up to seven octaves higher, penetrates us just as surely.

At the dawn of life on this planet, when living creatures existed only in the sea, there was no hearing, only a sensitivity to light, touch and the presence of food. Plankton still rise and fall with the sunlight. Early vertebrates needed only to detect changes in water pressure, some broad and others more subtle which we would not recognize as sounds. For that purpose, the fish developed a line of sensitive points running down both sides of the body called the midline. These indicated the direction of movement, the presence of land or other creatures, even the depth of the water. The midline operated in partnership with the semi-circular canals that govern balance. Response to light had by now developed in the eye.

From these fish came the first amphibians, sturdier than their forebears, with fins capable of supporting them on land. It was a huge step, venturing into untested air, and it took eons. Perhaps there was no choice: when rivers dry up or a body of water cuts us off from the ocean by upheavals of the earth, life in that water must die or reach other water. The motive may also have been the search for a safe place to spawn, a pattern many species follow today, from the sea turtle to the grunion. The newly hatched young, without contact with the parent, instinctively head back to the sea as their primary home. It may also have been part of that instinct we all feel to reach upward toward the light. When they emerged some three hundred million years ago during the Devonian period, these amphibians found an earth already covered by vegetation, a new source of food.

Out in the open air, amphibians relied on sight and touch, until taste and smell could slowly adapt to the new medium. Gone was the contact with water through the midline. Through several cycles these creatures continued to alternate between water and land, all the while lacking a way of detecting changes in air pressure. Not far from the semi-circular canals lodged at the base of the skull were the first of the sensitive midline points. These moved forward by a process still not fully understood, became grafted onto the semi-circular canals, and developed gradually into the internal mechanism of the ear.

On the scale of evolution, hearing was the last of our senses to develop fully, after the arrival of a primitive brain. Cells and plankton live without a brain, but primitive amphibians did have this center of self-awareness. Photosensitivity, touch, taste and smell had evolved before the brain was hardly more than a large nerve ganglion, as in jellyfish. Only hearing entered after the arrival of simple awareness and emotions, and it proved to be a great teacher, uniquely linked to all our emotional states, to pain and pleasure, mating and hunting, exploration and escape.

Many animals can adjust the angle of their ears to collect sounds, just as the giant radio telescope at Jodrell Bank focusses on faint pulses from deep space. This brings me to another of my idiosyncratic theories: that all consciousness in space-time is simply a matter of degree. It is not something which comes suddenly to man at the moment of birth, but, rather, can be compared with different degrees of temperature, or the difference between a solid, a liquid or a gas. I believe, too, that consciousness is akin to sensitivities which can be measured in a rose or even in a stone. Long before there was life, the elements out of which our world is made responded to all kinds of vibrations, from chemical reactions to electromagnetic forces, the pull of gravity, the cycles of light and dark. Somewhere within ourselves, I believe we retain an organic sensitivity to those same waves. From the moment our most primitive animal consciousness appeared, it was already affected by these forces; the mainly unconscious sense that "I am" is more than animal instinct, as it is more than human intellect. Through it I feel that we are irrevocably linked to the universe, just as much as any rock or plant. I cannot fathom any other way to account for such widely documented experiences as telepathy and precognition.

Recent tests with fish and birds suggest that their ability to wheel and turn in schools or flocks is governed not by watching the moves of the group's leaders, but by a communal telepathic message received simultaneously by all members. The minute electrical energy of our nervous system is measurable, and as the brain consists entirely of nerve cells, the greatest part of human electrical energy is concentrated there. Our brains emit pulses of several kinds, from two or three cycles per second to as many as twenty-four or so, now referred to as delta, theta, alpha and beta rhythms. The most rapid waves seem concentrated in the frontal area of the brain where the most complex mental processes take place, and these diminish when we sleep.

Recently, a technique called Kirlian photography has begun to tell us something new about the energy field all living things carry with them. The Soviet scientist Semyon Kirlian found that, by generating a high-frequency field, he could obtain pictures of the electrical patterns generated by many kinds of living matter, from a leaf to a human body. Some refer to this field as the aura, others as the biological plasma body. It is not chaotic but a unified network, and measurable only in living matter. Moreover, the aura seems to want to continue unbroken, even when part of a leaf or a limb is cut away, as if the aura had a will of its own.

Kirlian photography shows that when a new person comes into a room, their aura and that of persons already in the room undergo a change, linked to the emotional states of the individuals. We respond to the others, "feeling their vibes," as we do to the sound of a friendly or a hostile voice. Deep within us is the never-silent sound of our own vibrations, which we may ignore, but which is the musical core in us all. We vibrate like the untouched violin string lying next to its neighbor, trembling in sympathy though unstroked by the bow.

The incredible sensitivity of the human ear contributes to the complex interplay between hearing and our emotions. We separate the intelligible from the random, the wanted from the unwanted, holding the thread of a conversation at a crowded party or on a noisy train. Our memory allows us to put sound and meaning together; and memory relies on repetition and recognition to create language. But there is a critical distinction between music and speech. By this I do not mean the obvious fact that the one has "melody" and the other "meaning." After many a concert I have been asked what the music I played "means" to me; we have had to develop an elaborate set of terms to describe what music "means." The key difference lies in the fact that words refer first and foremost to the real world outside of us, to things and actions for which they serve as useful, acceptable symbols. Music, on the other hand, has a special relationship to our inner being. Our feelings become entities in themselves apart from literal meaning, and music shapes and alters them.

What concerns me most is the tendency to substitute the synthetic for the natural, and as if by reaction, the accidental for the willed. We are finding it harder and harder to say where music stops and noise begins. A Canadian musician and writer, Murray Schafer, has given much thought to this question. His book *The Tuning of the World* is a virtual milestone in human progress or in the humanization of progress. Murray Schafer began by analyzing the noise content of many environments to determine how people decide what is acceptable and what is not. As a frame of reference, he has drawn up a list which gives us a measure of our sound environment, adapting his selection from the list created in the thirties by the British scientist, Sir James Jeans:

Threshold of hearing	0 decibels
Rustling of leaves	20 dB
Quiet whisper (3 feet)	30 dB
Quiet home	40 dB
Normal conversation	60 dB
Average car (15 feet)	70 dB
Loud singing (3 feet)	75 dB
Average truck (15 feet)	80 dB
Subway (inside)	94 dB
Kitchen gadgetry	100 dB
Power mower	107 dB
Pneumatic riveter	118 dB
Amplified rock and roll (6 feet)	120 dB
Jet plane (100 feet)	130 dB

Such a list reminds us forcefully of the noise which surrounds us today, and of the paradox that people exerting far less physical effort then ever before may still individually be accountable for much more noise.

Schafer has also made a list of a number of sounds favored by some people and disliked by others, for instance the sound of thunderstorms or of the night, which in so many parts of the world are considered threatening or ominous. Yet in New Zealand, where neither the risk of fire nor manmade warfare are such immediate dangers, these sounds have been found to be acceptable, even pleasant. We have different responses to industrial sounds, for the gentle chug of the steam engine is liked by most people, a sound almost vanished now, while that of the airplane generally is not. Schafer has shown that our response to sounds can be affected by removing their visual association. When he made close-up recordings of an ordinary coffee grinder, most people mistook it for an instrument of terror. Sophisticated contemporary modes of torture subject the prisoner to the sound of others groaning in agony. The imagination does the rest and the victim is often reduced to abject surrender within an hour or two.

I remember from my boyhood in San Francisco the low sound of ferry boats making their way across the bay in the fog. I also loved the mournful wail of the steam engine, as I adored the wonderful train announcers with their litany of place names chanted like beads, or the recitations of the Talmud or Koran. The diesel engine has no such appeal. The logger's chainsaw can produce a noise level which almost equals that of the loudest jet plane, a sound that exceeds all human proportion. The noise of a gnawing beaver is not unpleasant, and is natural.

Murray Schafer offers us a new appreciation of silence, and of sounds from unexpected sources. We had the opportunity to meet for nearly an entire day not long ago, and he had prepared a surprise for me in a beautiful old barn, part of his home out in the countryside north of Toronto. Murray Schafer is a composer, but he has also conceived a new science, a new art which he calls soundscapes. Some of these involve performers, others taped sounds, but the one he installed for me was entirely unexpected. It was part of our exploration together of the nature of sound and of physical and musical hearing. Although I had heard of Murray Schafer's soundscapes, I never imagined what fun they could be.

SCHAFER You were talking about the soundscape in the country, the beautiful sound the wind takes from different kinds of trees.

MENUHIN I love the sound of poplars because they have so many leaves. They are not stiff, and each one seems to rustle freely.

SCHAFER It's different with evergreens, they are much stiffer and make a kind of turbine motion. This is what I call a hi-fi soundscape, one in which the signal to noise ratio is quite favorable. There are few noises here; therefore every sound can be heard at a great distance. By contrast, the city is a low-fi soundscape. There are so many noises, it's hard to tell what the signals are.

MENUHIN The North American Indian knew all about this. He could probably interpret sounds better than any other race.

SCHAFER Do you know why? Because he lived in a dense forest like this one, where you must rely on your nose and ears for vital sensory information. Where you can't see through the environment more than six feet in any direction, the ears become terribly important.

MENUHIN I consider it a tragedy that those who settled in North America deprived themselves of that intuitive awareness, the sense of belonging to this country. If the settlers had intermarried instead of killing Indians, exchanged knowledge, we would have been a richer civilization. But they had diametrically opposed views of ownership. The Indian thought that the forest, meadows and streams were free, as we now think air and water are, belonging to humanity as a whole.

SCHAFER It is also a question of the difference between acoustic space and visual space. You can mark off property lines, but acoustic space is simply the area over which sound passes. You possess it momentarily but you can never own it.

Now I want to show you this stream, if there's any water left, for it is a most beautiful sound. If you change the rocks, you change the sound. An exercise I sometimes give students is to close their eyes and try to find out how many different places they can hear the water coming from at the

same time. We can hear it right here, but also from many other places further down. Sometimes you can hear it from four or five different point sources. I make them hunt for such places.

MENUHIN The description of it would naturally lead into poetry. You would have to find the words that catch the melody and rhythm. Mohammedans used water for the sound of a spring indoors, running through their rooms.

SCHAFER We could use water in many more interesting ways. The fountain in front of the city complex is unimaginative, trying to quiet or contradict the traffic.

MENUHIN We are proud of the power of water, as in Canberra, Australia, where there is an enormous fountain—or Lake Geneva. But the difference between these and a waterfall at Yosemite is night and day.

SCHAFER The Renaissance gardens used water, the Villa d'Este for instance, with all those tiny pools and marvelous little spouts, all striking different kinds of surfaces. It was done by hydraulic pressure, filling a space with water that would push the air out and into tubes up into these artificial birds in the trees.

MENUHIN We have great symphonies, wonderful music, but musicians tend to forget about their relationship to nature which has a sound of its own. Music must have begun out of natural sounds impinging on our ears, and those to which we listen with our inner ear in silence.

SCHAFER The emotion from inside and the harmony from outside. You notice when you come into this evergreen forest how the sound changes? You begin to hear not just a hush, but a soft roar, which gets quite ferocious in a heavy wind, quite different from a deciduous forest. The birds are all around, some far and some close by. In the city you wouldn't hear dogs barking as far away as we did a moment ago.

MENUHIN What bothers me when travelling is a sense of estrangement from what my eye and whole being would love to partake in. One sees mountains and streams, one drives through lovely countryside, but until one has sensed and tasted it, the sight remains divorced, hardly different from its appearance on a cinema screen.

SCHAFER Travelling across the Rocky Mountains by train not long ago, they were playing Muzak. I sat in the dome car looking at the splendid scenery, and with Muzak it was like a travelogue movie. Now if you'll step across this old board, and look down occasionally, you're tramping into the unknown. (They enter the barn.)

MENUHIN In London and Gstaad I run around every morning barefoot in the garden. I love the feel of grass underfoot. And I love the smell of this barn. I only miss the cow and donkey. There are still traces of former four-legged inhabitants here. Now whatever is this? It's heavenly, it's open to the sky. People don't realize what bliss it would be to live without walls.

SCHAFER These were originally chinked log walls. Then the chinks all came out. We've put them back in. Now let's start. Where is that sound coming from? Try to figure it out.

MENUHIN There it is.

SCHAFER No, that's not the one you're hearing. It's here.

MENUHIN Oh, of course.

SCHAFER You can hear the light sound when the nail hits, then the heavy one. And these too, a bit less because they are all moving.

MENUHIN The extraordinary thing is they are activated only by a little tug on these ties.

SCHAFER Only by the pendulum. But there is a more complicated part. You see this teeter-totter? Don't get on it for a moment but just move it up and down and see what happens.

MENUHIN Oh look at it! I love the objects themselves, they're wonderful. This is the apotheosis of our civilization. This is where the rims of motor car wheels and old rusty metal belong—fulfilling their highest aesthetic function.

SCHAFER It's using them for a purpose one never dreamt possible.

MENUHIN A far better purpose, I think. Now that's a musical saw, isn't it? When you bend it you get a watery liquid sound.

SCHAFER Look at these huge sawblades. Watch your head. When this strikes, that moves. It all works with the teeter-totter. Three wires move up on top, and when that strikes this, you get a great gong-like effect.

MENUHIN I've always adored gongs.

SCHAFER Then a nail scrapes it slightly for an after-effect. It is a revitalization.

MENUHIN The complexity of rhythm is extraordinary.

SCHAFER That was the problem when we started, to fix one sound and add a second in counterpoint to the first. There's no point in having everything go at once. One object is cantilevered so it triggers something else, which gently starts to move, and something else will start from that.

MENUHIN There are certain things I can't wait to hear. I don't believe I've heard the piano as yet.

SCHAFER Well, these things on the wires do a dance over the top of the piano strings, at random. Sometimes it works.

MENUHIN (laughing) It's the best use I've ever seen a piano put to.

SCHAFER Well, it was an old piano.

MENUHIN And it will last forever, much longer than those that need to be tuned all the time.

SCHAFER The musical saw here works the same as the other one, it scrapes against this, moving up and down. Strange how an old piece of metal like that can give so many sounds. And then these little bells, very strongly pitched. Do you know the secret to discovering these properties? If you were to go to a rubbish heap and simply pick up things like this, striking them together, you would get no sound. You have to find the right node in the vibrating column. If you hold it at the end, for instance, and tap yours against mine, you'll notice the difference. The middle is dead. There's a loop with nodes, and if you attach wires to the nodes, they resonate.

MENUHIN This is far from random, each is fixed at the precise place. It's a work of art.

SCHAFER We worked very hard to find those right places.

MENUHIN Isn't it wonderful to lead a life that allows you the time to do something like this.

SCHAFER It's a restoration of the original sound properties in old junk.

MENUHIN No one would have suspected there is an inherent life in every object. That's why I love the African and Druid attitude, believing that every object was inhabited, and we cannot make contact with the object unless we listen to it. Everything has a vibration, and unless we can be in contact, we don't fulfill ourselves.

SCHAFER It's a nice antidote to all the electronic wizardry.

MENUHIN I loved Japanese wind chimes as a boy in San Francisco. The shops used to have little glass panes hanging in the doorway and they made a beautiful sound in the breeze.

SCHAFER These here rotate gently, cantilevered from way up top so they just touch.

MENUHIN I was once to my horror in a rope factory. I nearly went deaf. I don't know how people stand it.

SCHAFER This gong is one of the most violent sounds in the whole thing, very aggressive. But with a nail that just scrapes, there is an after-effect. You can get two different sounds out of one surface. Like the piano.

MENUHIN As a violinist I have a malevolent pleasure in seeing the piano reduced to that idealized sound which doesn't drown me out and which is perfectly in tune with the violin—not the awful tempered scale which kills it.

SCHAFER There are places in Bulgaria where you hear singing in major and minor seconds among the peasants. A Bulgarian musicologist once told me this, too, is a result of listening to cow bells and sheep bells. The beat is what they love; they get it into their ears and it comes out in their vocal music. Now lay this tube on your two fingers so we can find the nodal point.

MENUHIN What if the wind goes through it? Can you blow it?

SCHAFER I used to play the trumpet. Now do you want to try?

MENUHIN I can't get any other overtones.

SCHAFER But you feel it in your whole head.

MENUHIN Even with the violin, if one plays delicately, one gets the sense of the vibrations in one's bones, and you know where it should be placed.

SCHAFER Don't you think that's the difference between making music yourself and listening to it? When you make it, you are a vibrating mechanism. When you're listening, you're not.

MENUHIN Now what happens if one sits on the seesaw?

SCHAFER Oh, everything goes at once. Come on over and we'll sit on it, start the prime mover. Watch your head. You get on first. Now push a bit.

MENUHIN This is the most beautiful part in a way, because you hear the individual sounds stopping when we stop.

SCHAFER Let's listen to find out what the last one is that we hear.

MENUHIN It's a lesson in listening, something every child should have.

SCHAFER Actually, what children should do is build one, because then they'd discover all the properties of sound inherent in objects.

MENUHIN It teaches them to refine their hearing, to try to understand. It is a lesson in tolerance and compassion. When did you put this up?

SCHAFER Just the other day, in preparation for you. We were going to do an interview, so I decided to make a teeter-totter. Look at the violence over at that end.

MENUHIN I love the contrast of the little tree.

SCHAFER I haven't heard it yet. Let's listen just for the tree. Subtle, isn't it. We should figure another way of putting that tree up so that it could ring afterwards. Sometimes we get some birds up here, swallows that get into the barn. Perhaps they are attracted by the high frequencies. They listen and they make sounds right along with the sculpture. It's pretty.

MENUHIN Would you train children that way?

SCHAFER We were talking earlier about the necessity of teaching people to clear the sludge out of their ears. "Clairaudience" is what I call it, or clean hearing, literally meaning "having special hearing powers." This can be arrived at through exercises. People can be taught to listen discriminatingly, starting by making judgments about simple sounds: for instance, how many sounds you hear at a given moment. It's an exercise I give children lots of times.

MENUHIN You also take them around what you call "soundscapes" in town.

SCHAFER I take them on listening walks where a group will go as a gang, and of course everyone will talk. So I tell them, "I want everyone to walk one behind the other just out of earshot of the footstep of the person ahead of you." Kids love to do that, listen for the footsteps; it puts them in a private cocoon.

MENUHIN It's an Indian walk, single file. And do they report on it at the end? Do you ask for the highest, lowest, loudest, nicest, most objectionable sounds?

SCHAFER Yes, and also questions such as, "Can you think of three sounds you took with you on the walk?" In other words, some sounds in space move around you and others you move in space yourself. Some sounds move and some are stationary. I may ask, "Can you think of a sound that originated from a second-story window above you?" Questions of that sort cause a person to think carefully about what he or she has heard. That's the beginning. Perhaps it is not exactly music education, but sensory education.

MENUHIN The subtlety of it is so extraordinary. Here you have metallic objects which would make a brutal sound if hit frontally, but the way they are hung, the more they can turn freely, scrape and delicately touch each other, the subtler the distinctions become. I imagine each time you build something like this it must take wing and go out of your hands, for each time it will have another character.

SCHAFER It is like any work of art. You have one free gesture. You can start with anything you want. But once you have hung one piece and struck it, everything that follows comes from that choice. You have committed yourself and things grow by themselves from that.

MENUHIN Visually the heavy pieces are at the center, the gong which is loudest and the rock which starts everything moving. The finer sounds gather around in a curious way. When you think what these rusty bits of metal were originally, shiny parts of internal combustion engines or God knows what, I don't think anyone would object to arms sales and supersonic fighter planes if they knew they would reach this disembodied stage. Future generations will have the advantage; they will listen to fighter planes in old barns.

SCHAFER I can imagine cannons, great big metal objects that would ring and make beautiful sounds. There's been a long history of the bronze used in church bells being recast in the form of cannons in times of war, and then back to church bells in times of peace. So we're just doing our part, finding the alternative to destruction.

MENUHIN I've just had an awful thought, Murray. Do you think that Hitler's or Stalin's bones might have yielded an interesting sound?

SCHAFER A human skull! I wonder.

MENUHIN This is a most constructive contribution to music education. Africans had this approach to any object. They don't judge by the visual aspect. They will knock it until they hear what it is, whether it is a tree, a metal object, or whatever. They would have adored this barn.

SCHAFER Africans live in an aural society. They mistrust the visual. Perhaps we're getting back to the same kind of thing.

MENUHIN We've been too long in the materialistic visual aspect, where we only judge a thing by its appearance and cut ourselves completely off from its emanations. That's a much more pagan way of thinking, of course, but I think the pagan is returning, sometimes in rather a brutal form, but at its best in this very organic way.

In the sound environment which Murray Schafer had created in his barn, its apparently random tinklings stirred to life by the action of strikers and scrapers, objects of the junk heap re-animated as if by some magician, interlinked by a web of strings running back to the seesaw, I thought again of the relationship between natural and manmade sounds, which in the pagan world were so intertwined. It struck me that the modern pagan must also accommodate the urban dweller, and that since we wander among skyscrapers, a work for solo violin and traffic noise might be a plausible sound sculpture today, a new form of concerto. After all, at the turn of this century immigrant fiddlers in the cities of the New World were in a similar position. The sound of a violin scraping away down the street was once familiar. Conversely, I recall rehearsals when the accidental whine of a siren or fire bell penetrated the hall, seeming at times to enter the music at just the right moment, even the correct pitch, becoming one with it, thereby creating an unholy alliance between the deliberate and the random or accidental. The adventure with Murray Schafer made me sharply aware that our ears are constantly on the alert. For me it is only hearing which restores the wholeness of our being, and somehow for a musician conveys with it aesthetic and moral purpose.

Language does this also, but in a different way, for it is not registered or generated in the same part of the brain as music. Speech lies in the left half of the brain, together with the power of logic. Music arises first in the right half, the seat of the emotions. Both music and speech depend on hearing, and both involve an interplay between feeling and analysis. But through the mysterious vibrations of music, we are instantly able to share our own feelings and those of others. The music simply becomes part of who we are. Music has the power to combine feeling and thought without words. A recent study, devoted to what the late humanist psychologist Abraham Maslow called "the human peak experience," may well prove this point. After completing investigations on five continents, he reported that the two most universally acknowledged peaks were music and sex. Of course, musical hearing involves judgment, linking our feelings to our aesthetic sense, which has also greatly evolved over the ages.

Music, like language, has developed its own structures, grammars and vocabularies. It had to move in a way that corresponded with human ways of thinking and acting. To me the structure of music is part of the structure of nature, of the very vibrations themselves, the system of overtones. Every voice and instrument produces tones which vibrate at a basic rate, but their characteristic color is obtained from the overtones generated at the same time.

The overtone principle is like that of the skipping rope we all turned as children. We discovered quickly that by turning the rope faster, it could be made to divide into two or three loop segments, perhaps even five or six if the rope was long and was wielded with a strong wrist. These extra loops appeared because the rope had to follow the laws of tension and inertia, like molecules of vibrating air. When the loop segments multiplied, they turned in opposed waves, forming a continuous peak and trough. Ripples on a lake and sound waves in the air follow the same laws of the balance of opposing forces.

A string player constantly uses the overtone phenomenon, for he can produce the same effect on his vibrating string as the multiple loops in the jump rope. By touching the string at exactly its midpoint, he makes it vibrate in two opposed halves, producing a sound exactly an octave above the note to which the string is tuned. Touching the string lightly at one-third its length makes it vibrate in three equal parts, producing a sound a fifth higher still. At the quarter length, the string vibrates in four parts, giving a note two octaves above the fundamental. Those are the first three overtones. But touch the string at one-fifth its length and a critical new note appears, a major third above the fundamental, though two octaves higher up. This note completes the components of a major chord, the foundation of Western harmony. It is also nature's great secret, hidden for so long because that fourth overtone is so far above its parent. The overtone series continues upward in smaller steps, maintaining an unvarying sequence of mathematically pure ratios.

Although we can derive the entire scale, the twelve semitones of the octave from the overtone series, scales probably originated as social conventions, and there are many scales in the world that do not maintain pure intervals. Some scales may have arisen from a desire to produce evenly spaced holes on a flute or frets on a string instrument. The resultant scales sound quite unnatural to Western ears.

Such words as "octave" and "fifth" are themselves only convenient Western labels that have come into common usage because of our widely adopted seven-note major and minor scales. In this system, the note vibrating at twice the speed of another is always to be found eight notes up the scale (octave comes from the Latin for eight). The fifth is another matter, for the Western scale is built of whole and half steps, again handy labels, and the distance between any five steps in the scale is not always a perfect fifth. Our scale system was probably derived from the circle of fifths, rather than from the overtones, and that circle is a closed one—almost.

So far as we know the Chinese were the first to examine the relationship between fifths. Surviving documents, predating 3000 BC, show the importance to them of these relationships. They found that a series of fifths in a row will produce twelve separate notes before the notes begin repeating. Those twelve notes put in a series include all the semitones of our Western scale. Starting at the bottom on the piano, the circle can be played (the keyboard is just wide enough). You will find the thirteenth note at the top, seven octaves higher, is the same as the one on which you started.

The discovery of the circle of fifths was a great one to the Chinese, for they honor the number five as sacred, dividing the basic elements into

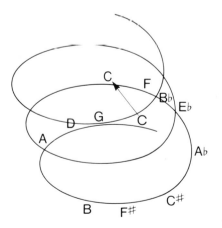

The smelting of bronze was well developed in China 3,500 years ago when this temple bell was cast. It is now in the British Museum.

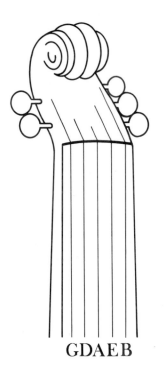

GDAEB

five, namely earth, fire, water, wood and metal, as they also recognize five basic human relationships and five basic kinds of grain. The Chinese used the circle of fifths to establish the five-tone pentatonic scale. Extending this series by two more intervals produced the notes needed to complete a major scale as we know it in the West. Music based on this seven-note scale did become popular in China, and later Chinese music used a scale with all twelve of the semitones we know. The Chinese also evolved a form of musical notation. Yet the five-note scale remained sacred, and was maintained for music expressing the highest moral, ethical or spiritual ideals, while the seven-note scale was designated to serve the music of the court or street.

For the Chinese, music was a tool to govern the hearts of the people. It is said in China that when there is music in the home, there is affection between father and son, and when music is played in public there is harmony among the people. Their standardized scale was one they could duplicate on many kinds of instruments, for instance the zither-like *ch'in*, ancestor to the Japanese *koto*, both still in current use. By the seventh century BC, the Chinese poet Le Ly Kim could write, "Virtue is our favorite flower. Music is the perfume of that flower."

The violin demonstrates part of a circle of fifths, for it is tuned to a series of such intervals, G D A E, from lowest string to highest. If there were an extra string above it would be tuned to B. The viola, deeper than the violin, tunes its lowest string to C, a fifth below G. Any five such related tones can be rearranged in a series within one octave, for instance G A B D E, where they form the familiar Chinese pentatonic scale. But the circle of fifths is a human deduction, not a natural phenomenon. Nature always has its loose ends, elements that appear to our minds as mistakes, as if they simply should not happen. In our arrogance we feel that we should offer nature a correction, squaring the circle. The beauty of nature is that there is always an element that allows for mystery, for development or evolution. So it is with the circle of fifths, for when you come back to the note with which you started, providing the fifths have all been perfectly tuned, you find that this note has gone a little sharp. It is one of the mysteries of nature, as the Chinese knew by observation. We had to wait for Pythagoras to establish the precise mathematics of the difference, and it is now known as the Pythagorean Comma. Its existence is an important aspect of the difference between Western music and that of much of the rest of the world—our music has always been based on pure or natural intervals (at least until this century). As we shall see, the rise of the keyboard instruments—the organ, harpsichord and piano—brought on a crisis in tuning precipitated by the conflict between pure intervals in one

key and those in another. As with so much else in Western life, we adjusted the tuning to an uncomfortable compromise, a homage to the keyboard with which the voice and the string player are never totally comfortable.

There are parts of the world, of course, where impure intervals are the rule, at least to our ear, as is the case in Java and Bali. On the other hand, no musicians spend more time tuning up than do the Indians. The flowering of Western harmony is one of our unique, glorious and imperishable contributions to music, while at the same time, our ability to compromise and experiment has led to the abstractions of electronic music, chance music, and to the twelve-tone system. Those whose musical practice is based on the purity of intervals must finally reject ours, because when our harmony is applied to their music, it produces only hybrid monsters. The West's creation of the "tempered" scale, to which Bach contributed so much, is one of those instances where man's artistic will is manifest, adjusting nature to meet aesthetic and practical needs.

For music to speak to us, it needs more than the structure of a scale, of intervals, or even of our emotions. It needs a recognizable form corresponding to something in our own being. I have often thought that the earliest musical form must have been a simple repetition, a double image rather like the right and left halves of a leaf when folded upon each other. We recognize the repetition of two roughly equal halves in a rhythm or melody, and this gives us a sense of security and completion, and with that musical memory we begin to build. Once we hear a sound we can repeat it, creating a simple rhythm at first. When we put a few sounds together in groups or phrases of related tones, we have the

Two dancing girls and a singer are accompanied by eleven seated musicians in this collection from Burma, demonstrating the fondness of many cultures for the sound of several instruments blended together.

beginnings of melody, a blend of feeling with logic. We can also turn these phrases or rhythms upside down or backwards, for one of the basic tools of conceptual thinking is to consider a situation in its reverse. How does the world look when we stand on our heads? What does it feel like to walk backwards? Children love to experiment with tricking their senses in this way all the time.

The wonder of music is that it organizes our feelings into a logical order. My colleague Manfred Clynes refers to such organizations as a "sentic cycle." He has written a fascinating book about his experiments in measuring that cycle, both within music and within ourselves (Manfred Clynes, *Sentics*). For Dr. Clynes, the classic emotional cycle begins with anger and proceeds through hate, love, sex and joy, until at last it reaches reverence. Music may draw on any of these emotions, any of these passions. But it is when music carries us through an entire cycle, Clynes asserts, that it is at its most satisfying. That sense of tension and relaxation is in fact built directly into Western harmony, in the alternation between the major and minor. The major chord is the first and only pure one we encounter in natural overtones, and the major is generally regarded as happy, the minor as sad. I think this has to do with the fact that the minor has dropped the natural interval of the middle note in the chord by an artificial semitone. In C major the natural middle note is E, and in C minor that note becomes E-flat, where it conflicts with the implied E. The conflict is not so strong as to upset the strength of the basic three-note chord, but it is disturbing to the natural overtone series beyond. And what is sadness? It is a division, a sense that things are not right, that you want what you cannot have or lament what you have not done. You bewail the loss of something, you are not at one with yourself or the world. In that minor chord, that loss is the purity of the middle note, which wants to rise, to become major, to unite again with its natural series.

But it is not wise for us to ascribe everything about the discovery of harmony, overtones and scales to man alone. Not long ago I had an extraordinary experience on the island of Mykonos, in the Aegean Sea south of mainland Greece. Outside the harbor of Mykonos, there is a tiny island, uninhabited except for many, many bees. There is one small sloping beach, and at the topmost point of the isle, a little stone chapel for the rare visitor. The terrain is rather rugged, with a steep cliff rising sharply where the beach ends. One day in April when I was walking on the flowering cliff top, listening to the buzzing of the bees on their honey-making rounds, I distinctly heard one sound, which I will call the fundamental, and another sound exactly a fifth above. When I came closer, it seemed to my eye and ear that a larger bee was producing the

lower sound and a small bee the upper one. It struck me as quite extraordinary that such an adjustment of sounds should be achieved by two bees. Then they were joined by another, making a sound that fell exactly in between the other two, which was in fact a third above the fundamental, establishing a full major chord. I was so surprised I had to go back in the afternoon to make sure; and there it was still, that same sound.

The Talmud says there is a temple in heaven that is opened only through song. Another ancient practice was to tell stories with the help of music. Music helps lower the barriers of the word, and its meaning comes across enhanced. The great epic legends, from the Icelandic sagas to the German *Nibelungenlied* and Spanish *romancero*, were all passed on from generation to generation by word of mouth, thanks in part to music. Chanting helped the singers remember the story more easily. Thousands of verses were committed to memory by the many poets whose work we now ascribe to Homer, each one singing his version of the tales of Ulysses, keeping alive the memory of a civilization. We can imagine the Greek troubadour seated in the great hall chanting for a gathering of nobles, while the open hearth fire sends its smoke curling up to the roof.

Sikkim lamas play the sacred reed in a culture whose origins go back to prehistoric times.

Largest and oldest of Japanese bronze lanterns is this one from the Golden Hall of Todai-ji Temple in Nara, inaugurated in AD 752, and probably cast by the lost wax process. A Bodhisattva plays the flute. There are four such panels. A single lantern of bronze or stone customarily hung in front of the main hall of early Buddhist temples in Japan.

In Kuwait, the folklore group Al Arda sings and dances to commemorate the past glories of its people, together with the vitality of the present culture.

Preserving the past is a function of all folk ballads. In Finland they still sing tales of the great hero Lemminkainen from the national epic, the *Kalevala*. Thanks to such singers, the Finnish language itself survived, for it was not until the mid-nineteenth century that it was standardized in written form.

The late astronomer Harlow Shapley once said, "On a lesser planet, circling a second-rate sun in a small solar system out on the less populated fringes of our galaxy, far from the densely active areas of the universe, it seems to me unlikely that we could possibly be at the center of anything." But humans are a shamefully self-centered lot, and we think of our histories as so important that we appoint specialists to keep track of them—genealogists and historians. In parts of Africa, these people are the musicians called *griots*, chanting complete family lines and stories in minute detail, a task for which they are often well paid. Close behind the storytellers come the priests, and music is used in worship almost everywhere, even in places where worship is communal.

Quite recently a Syrian musician in Paris named Abed Azrie attempted to reconstruct the music of ancient Sumer, as old or older than that of Egypt. Whether his interpretation of lost traditions is accurate seems less important than the fact that Azrié made the effort. He composed an entire setting for the ancient Eastern epic *Gilgamesh*, probably the oldest of all surviving epic poems. He did so after extensive research into the many versions of the poem in several archaic languages, and into contemporary documents describing the practice of music in those times. He also studied the sculpture and other visual evidence of music making in

Sumer. Azrié was further guided by familiarity with the oldest living musical traditions of the Middle East, some of which still preserve stories similar to those of King Gilgamesh, who was regarded as a demigod, and his pagan friend, Enkidu. It is heartening that there is so much interest today, more than any previous time in history, in the music of the near and distant past.

We are living in an age in which we are beginning to understand that everything is connected by degrees. Primitive man may have thought that ice, water and steam were separate things, just as we once thought that music had nothing to do with noise. Today we realize that even noise and

Royal processions accompanied by instruments go back to Egypt and Sumer. In Nigeria, the guards of Erair at Kano announce the arrival of a dignitary with a splendid noise.

light have a common denominator—vibrations of different speeds. Primitive man found music in noise, of that I have no doubt. As a child I remember being struck by the noise of work, watching laborers breaking up paving stones on the street. It was marvelous to see how one would raise his hammer, while the other brought his down in natural syncopation, and I realized that by listening to the rhythms they avoided hitting each other. There is universal validity in this kind of rhythm: it is like our own bloodstream; the sweep of the boatmen at their oars; or the women pounding wheat in a huge mortar as they wield two or three long pestles. It is the rhythm of those wonderful Greeks who danced upon the circle of stones, called the *aloni*, to thresh the wheat.

The painting of these musicians is among the finest known from ancient Egypt. It was among the many paintings found in the 18th dynasty tomb of Zeser-ka-Sonbe in Thebes. In this full-scale copy in tempera of the original, the instruments are the arched harp, lute, double oboe and lyre. A child snaps her fingers for rhythm.

The vitality of music in the daily life of these early civilizations is reflected constantly in the frequency with which it serves as a subject for the decoration of household utensils. Some of the most beautiful are found on Greek vases and urns, and on tomb carvings, even from the time of Homer. We owe to the Greeks some of the first and most critical theoretical discoveries about music. The mathematician Pythagoras, whose work gave a scientific basis for later musical theory in the West, established the connection between music and mathematics. His work was rediscovered and celebrated in the Middle Ages.

No civilization held music in as high esteem as classical Greece; it dominated religious, aesthetic, moral and scientific life. The very word for an educated, distinguished man meant "a musical man," and to be called unmusical was to be labelled brutish. Music and poetry were one; recited poems were chanted, and sometimes joined to the dance. Unfortunately, little of the music of ancient Greece remains. We have the plays, sculpture, architecture and statecraft, the science, philosophy and ethics, but not the music. The reason seems to be twofold. First, the music was traditional, often improvised, and passed on largely by ear. There was a system of letter notation, but it was clumsy compared to the one we have now, and not used except for special tunes of great importance. We do have some dozen fragments of written Greek music, dating from a more recent time than that of Pythagoras. We may gain some idea of an old Greek melody or phrase by deriving the rhythm partly from the words, but the performing tradition is lost. The second reason has to do with the fact that their music was built on a practice which endured only so long as the culture lived. Greek music today is partly the product of centuries of Turkish and other Near Eastern influences, and is of limited help except in isolated instances in establishing the nature of music in the Golden Age.

The Greeks believed absolutely that the beautiful and the good are indivisible. They had a single word for both: *kalokagathia* (*kalos*, meaning beautiful and *agathos*, meaning good). Moral precepts paid tribute to aesthetic principles. The effort to cultivate a high Apollonian moral purpose was tempered by that other equally potent aspect of man represented by the Dionysian rites. The Greeks abandoned themselves to ecstatic, intoxicating urges, for, like all of us, they had two souls: the one striving for clarity, temperance and moderation, the other for the ecstatic and the orgiastic. The pagan fabric was torn apart later, when mono-theism grew powerful, when commandments replaced traditions and authority was derived from the written word instead of the oral, when Moses wrested the Ten Commandments from a single God. The good became the right and only truth; the beautiful became a muse forever banished. In Greece around 500 BC, we find the flowering of the whole man, with all his inbuilt contradictions and paradoxes, his tragedy and comedy, his logic and passion, his science and art. It was a civilization where man could strive to be a god, ensuring a two-way traffic between heaven and earth, a flow which monotheism made a one-way street.

There is surely no more impressive site in the world than the Temple of Apollo at Delphi on Mount Parnassus; of all the glorious holy places, this

The ancient Sumerian harp is preserved in this clay bas-relief now at the Louvre in Paris; the form of the instrument, with its hollow resonating box, is not unlike the kora *of Senegal.*

The lute was known to many civilizations, as this T'ang dynasty figure from China demonstrates.

site of the Oracle of Delphi established the link between music and mystery. Rulers and merchants, pilgrims and peasants made their way up this sacred hill to ask their questions of the oracle and to worship Apollo. For the Greeks, music was intertwined with the idea of the nine Muses, sources of inspiration for all the arts, who made their home together with the other gods on Mount Parnassus. Apollo, son of Zeus, was the leader of the Muses, a master athlete and warrior as well as a master musician. Mount Parnassus came to be thought of as the home of music. The *Hymn to Apollo* is one of the few fragments of early Greek music that has survived, its importance underscored because it was written down, carved onto a stone at Delphi.

Music ran in Apollo's family; his half-brother Amphion was reputed to have secured the fortifications of all of Thebes by forming blocks of raw

stone into sturdy walls at the mere sound of his lyre. It was the infant Hermes, brother to Apollo, who killed a turtle, fastened gut strings onto its shell from the entrails of an ox stolen from his brother, and then offered the new instrument to Apollo to appease his anger. Apollo and his lyre became the faith and drama of the citizen state.

The perfection of the city state went hand in hand with a supervised musical education, and was considered essential for a disciplined people. The primary role of music in Greece was to build character and health. It was at Apollo's temple that the devotion to music reached its height, for in its amphitheater the first known musical contests took place. These games began in 586 BC, at the same time as the Pan-Hellenic athletic games started. Plato declared that music should precede and dominate gymnastics, for the soul should form the body, not vice versa. The word

Music in Greece was well developed in Homeric times, as finds among the Aegean Islands of the Cyclades show. Here a player holds the samvike, a four-string harp. The figure dates to about 2300 BC and is one of the few male figures found in island graves.

The Greeks introduced the hydraulic organ into Western music, though how it got there from its probable origin in China is unclear.

In the Golden Age of Greece, music was a revered accompaniment even in death. In these two tomb sculptures from the fifth century BC, a youth plays the lyre and a girl plays the double-reed aulos (the originals are in Boston and Rome).

music itself comes from the Greek word *musiki*, meaning all the arts of the nine Muses. The word *nomos* also means music, as it means logic, representing the moral, social and political laws of the state. The Delphic stone was the center of the world, and it was here that Herodotus of Megara won the Olympic prize ten times over playing on the lyre and the *aulos*, the latter a double-reed which probably came from the Orient.

We also know that dance played an important role in Greek festivals and rituals. This is true of all cultures, for when the rhythms become insistent one cannot refrain from swaying and clapping. The chorus in Greek drama was danced and mimed, forming as important an aspect of stage spectacles as worship and festivities. It was not written down and therefore its exact usage in those days is also lost to us, though imaginative attempts at recreation are being staged now, drawing on written description, illustrations on urns and vases, and a few surviving folk dances.

The world dances to a wonderful variety of names, and ancient Greece is no exception. Among the dances that would have been known to Socrates and Aristotle are the Piglet, the Itch, the Snort, Scattering the Barley, Setting the World on Fire, Stealing the Meat. We think of our civilization as more advanced, but take pride in being able to hand on to posterity the Bump, Hustle and Jerk, along with the Waltz, Samba and Fox Trot.

In many villages in Greece, the threshing floor, the *aloni*, is the only large, flat place suitable for communal dancing. The round dances that are still characteristic of Greece can be traced to it, and many villages along the Peloponnesus or scattered among the Aegean Islands have kept their original stone floors, possibly two thousand years old or more, on which some seventy generations have threshed and danced. One such dance is the *zervos* from the island of Karpathos, and because it moves to the left it is thought of as a dance to honor the forces of the lower world.

The Romans adapted the music of conquered people, borrowing the cornu *from the Celts and the hydraulic organ from the Greeks.*

Another is the *serra*, a war dance from Pontos, one of the communities along the southern coast of the Black Sea which preserved the old traditions faithfully, and where a dialect was spoken which still preserves within it many phrases of ancient Greek. In the Greek theater, the *aloni* became the nearly circular orchestra, the place in front of and lower than the main stage where the chorus would sing and dance. In modern urban Greece the function of the old *aloni* has been transferred to the taverna.

When Rome defeated Greece, it borrowed its music, along with its architecture and sculpture. But the importance of music diminished greatly, for Rome was oriented to the word, the law and the sword. After the fall of the Roman civilization, another force slowly began to prevail in Western culture: and that force was the Christian church. The church was able to produce its great art emanating from centers in Rome and Byzantium because it had absorbed the prevailing pagan beliefs, transferring adoration of Greek and Roman gods to the Christian saints. But the influence of the church on music was a slower process; in fact, nearly a thousand years were to pass before the music we know began to take shape.

Rabindranath Tagore has written: "In the very beginning the first utterings of creation sounded in the language of waters, in the voice of the wind." (Tagore, *Lipika*, London: Peter Owen.) However it may change, music remains man's invention. We have only experienced a small section of the huge scale of vibrations, turning it to our expressive purpose, finding within it the quiver of life. I feel that tolerance, love and social harmony can and should be the by-products of an artist's way of life and creation. I would like to believe that beauty and truth, two great disciplines, when combined as they are in music, where order is based on self-restraint and a better understanding of repose, will lead to greater maturity, awareness and equilibrium in our civilization. Words may conceal truth, but this is hardly possible in the case of music. Even when it is used corruptly, we should be able to detect the unwholesomeness within if we listen with care. In any event, I feel it is the musician's role to maintain our trust in the world and the world's trust in us, to help us express genuine emotions. When music takes on that responsibility, it draws upon the best kind of human effort and is deeply therapeutic, harmonizing the physical and the spiritual, the intellectual and emotional, joining body and soul.

At the Temple of Apollo, Delphi, Yehudi Menuhin joins with musicians from the island of Karpathos whose music contains traditional dances of great antiquity.

The growth of music in Western culture is traced from the early Christian chant, known as plainsong, to the abundant outpouring of the Renaissance. Moors and Christians struggle for possession of Spain, and the Crusades are launched, bringing with them a clash of cultures. Music becomes a blending of many voices, the principles of harmony are codified, orchestration begins, and the notation of music evolves from the approximation of neumes to the present staff and note system. India perfects the art of the single, decorated musical line.

2. The Flowering of Harmony

A jester's dance (c.1340).

CIVILIZATION, LIKE LIFE, depends on its capacity for regeneration. A cycle of emotions is as vital to us all as a variety of foods; we may sometimes feed on risk, good or bad, as a way of testing ourselves. Governments exist partly to prevent society from going to extremes, and religion has been another guide—though faith itself is not exempt from excess, and God has not always been a vision of benevolence. In recent centuries Western music has grown with astounding speed into one of man's greatest arts, and the genesis of this music cannot be grasped unless we look at the role of faith in unifying Western society. Faith provided music with a codified written form and widely accepted rules of harmony.

Of course, the connection between music and faith is hardly unique to the West. The North American Indian, alone on the plains invoking divine aid with his chant, is not far removed from the Moslem muezzin alone in his tower, praising Allah and calling the faithful to prayer. The Tibetan or Mongolian singer generating many overtones above a deeply chanted fundamental tone all in the single voice, is experiencing the impulse to worship quite directly, for the purity and unity of the two resonances are a link between man and the Divine. The sound of plain-song heard in Christian monasteries and churches in our own day is a link to the origins of our Western music, and such kinships are reminders that music begins within us and finds its most natural expression in the voice.

We give emphasis to the voice here because the voice is central to the Western music we know best. Since Christianity arose in the Near East,

Opposite:
The Adoration of the Lamb *is part of a Spanish copy (c.950) of the famous* Commentary on the Apocalypse *by Beatus which contains one of the oldest Christian world maps. Here the elders flank half-figures of four winged beasts, while the Lamb of God stands on Mount Zion surrounded by saints playing citharas.*

the birthplace of Judaism and later of Islam, the early Christian chants drew on the highly decorated vocal tradition of the Jewish and Arab peoples.

In the Jewish tradition, in which I was raised, chanting is an expression of faith. As circumstances would have it, I never went through the Bar Mitzvah ceremony; on my thirteenth birthday I was in Paris studying with Georges Enesco and preparing for more concerts. In a way I rather regret not having been officially declared an adult; perhaps that is why I never grew up. Be that as it may, I never sang at a Jewish service, although the sound of my father's touching and plaintive voice has continued to ring in my ears—a memory from childhood when we drove through the beautiful California countryside, his singing every bit as fervent as it might have been inside a synagogue.

Nothing is more moving than the chanting of the cantor in the synagogue. Here music is no mere ornament. When the cantor pours out the joys and woes of faith, it is the very essence of worship, of praise of God. His singing, magnifying the meaning of the word, is a passionate expression of faith. Jehovah did not forgive. He was quite capable of punishing us, and one bore in mind that He always had His thunderbolts at the ready. Fortunately for me, thanks to my mother, who was not a Christian by religion, Jesus was from my earliest years always part of that pantheon of Biblical prophets, and I feel this appreciation gave me a broader sense and an added awareness of the conviction in the cantor's singing. His song must go straight to God's heart; but because words are deflected through the mind first, he must ever strive to avoid this detour.

The traces of these early chants are difficult to find, since so few written documents are extant from biblical times, and the early Christian prohibition against pictorial representation precluded one of the most reliable sources, iconography. The Bible provides our only meagre reference. What is heard in synagogues today is Western nineteenth century music, and even most Eastern orthodox music does not rely on traditions much older than the seventeenth century, except in some parts of central Europe, Greece and the Near East. What is certain is that vocal and instrumental music was already flourishing when Christ was born. His followers must have sung in a tradition with which they were familiar, adapting it to new sentiments. The songs of the Jewish cantors had a direct influence on early Christian song. Ornamented cantorial melodies were absorbed almost without change into the Christian ritual. Many early Christians continued to take part in Jewish services, comforted by the older tradition, and it was common for a cantor to serve a synagogue on Friday evening and then place his skills at the disposal of the Christians on Sunday.

In AD 326 the Emperor Constantine declared that Rome would adopt Christianity as the state religion. Constantine took another crucial step: he built a second capital city at Byzantium on the Bosphorus, at the mouth of the Black Sea. Later, the city was renamed Constantinople; today it is known as Istanbul. The style we call Byzantine had its origins there. By dividing the seat of government, Constantine effectively paved the way for the split between the Eastern and Western Christian church which came seven hundred years later. Nonetheless, he gave to Christianity the legitimacy it had so long sought. The pantheon of Roman gods was deposed. In AD 475 Rome itself fell. The Byzantine culture is no relic, however; it remains alive in the language, rites and music of Slavonia and the Near East.

Even though the ornate cantorial style is designed for the solo voice, the heart of Christian worship is the slower-moving unison singing of many voices. This form of chant, called plainsong, dominated Christian worship for a thousand years, and is still heard in Orthodox, Catholic and Anglican churches today. Plainsong is a free melodic chanting of sacred texts, intense yet devotional and serene, drawing on the natural stress of language for its rhythm and on the length of a human breath for its phrasing.

Plainsong is also known as Gregorian chant, but that name is not entirely correct, suggesting as it does that Pope Gregory I somehow created it single-handedly (many later medieval illustrations would have us believe he did). In fact, around AD 600 he did reform the liturgy, establishing the Schola Cantorum and instituting the new concept of missionary activity. Graduates of the Schola were sent as far as Britain to teach the Roman chant. Gregory also wanted to develop a reliable system of notation, but this took much longer. The process of standardizing plainsong took several hundred years.

In Gregory's time instrumental music played no part in the life of the Christian church. Instruments had too many associations with the debauched life of Rome, and had lost their mystery and magic. Only the voice had the purity and nobility worthy of God's ear. Above all, the organ was rejected because it was associated with Roman combat and entertainments held in outdoor arenas. The organ did not return to favor in the West until the eighth century, and was then a clumsy instrument which no one would connect with earlier barbarous events. Some Eastern Orthodox churches still forbid instruments as part of worship.

Plainsong was still new in the West when another threat to Christianity appeared. In AD 622 the Prophet Mohammed proclaimed Allah as the only true God and launched his campaign to conquer the world in His name. Islam's warriors penetrated as far north as central France, and conquered all but the northwestern corner of Spain. The tide turned under Charlemagne, who on Christmas day in 800 accepted the crown as Emperor of Rome from the hands of Pope Leo III himself. It is a period difficult to chronicle; writing was a restricted activity, and few records survived the fierce strife. The absence of reliable musical notation is a further problem, a lack which doubtless exists because music, like language, is essentially aural.

The feudal system which marked Europe for a thousand years opened the gates to music in a fresh way. As various courts gained power, music became an increasingly important part of secular life. Jugglers and tumblers, dances and revels, songfests and love ballads, all were doubtless enjoyed. Musicians travelled as part of the households of princes and nobles, and many a bawdy lyric was traded among cooks and stableboys. The difficulty we face is that so little of this Western popular music survived in any form until after 1200: there was no adequate written means for recording it; by its very nature it was considered perishable. We owe some surviving fragments to those patient monks, so well trained by the church, whose ear was not merely open to plainsong, and whose skill in writing preserved a few songs.

It is important to remember the aura of mystery which surrounded the arrival of the first Christian millennium, for it was widely thought AD 1000 was to be the year of the Apocalypse, the Second Coming of Christ. For the Western world the prospect of consignment to eternal flames was eminently real. In a spirit of awe and fear people waited, as terrified as we are of atomic annihilation. The year came and went, nothing was changed, and the Christian world emerged with renewed faith. Within the century the devastating Crusades were launched.

The expression of faith is after all a deep human impulse, and by this very token it has never been exempt from man's tendency to push things too far. Faith, however, does help to give us order, purpose and patience, and to this end music clarifies the meaning of the word. Such music belongs to all people, not just to a chosen few. It would seem to us now that all music preserved from ancient times was based on established, rigid rules. However, I cannot help believing that long before music was codified, it must have sprung spontaneously to tempt our ears with forbidden or "pagan" progressions.

Human beings universally assign values and symbols to their beliefs or codes of behavior. In Christian architecture, the Byzantine dome is a shelter, whereas the Gothic spire reaches up to God. We think we all

Charlemagne, Emperor of the Holy Roman Empire, could scarcely read and write. This monogram signature Karolus *dates from AD 783.*

know what we mean by beauty, but all men do not define the beautiful in the same terms. What is difficult for us to accept is that other people should recognize symbols for things which differ so totally from our own.

While the Crusades raged in Europe and the Near East, music had already reached a peak in another part of the world, India. Although Islam was also penetrating this territory, its rule was peaceful enough. The arts flourished and instrumental and vocal music rose to heights which have probably never been surpassed. I have admired and studied the music of India for many years, and in the process have had the special pleasure of sharing in the making of it with the great sitar player, Ravi Shankar. This one man has probably done more than any other in our time to bring the message of his music to the West, and such is his musical integrity that he has been heeded by the devoted scholar as much as by the Beatles. The name Shankar has a long distinguished history in the music of India, not unlike the family name of Bach in Germany.

I want to introduce the music of India at this point because we have reached a crossroads in European musical history, a period where the individual decorated voice was largely abandoned in favor of the

The Hindu god Siva is the lord of letters, music and dance, part of the trinity including Brahma and Vishnu. In this carving from one of Madura's many temples in southern India, he plays an early version of the sitar, and something of his character as the destroyer god is also apparent.

harmony of many voices. It is this, together with notation, which most clearly makes the difference between the traditions of Eastern and Western music. Even in places like Java and Bali, where multiple instruments sound together in ensembles, there is a strong sense of the solo voice, although the actual system is different. Performers play their parts in unison, no matter how complex the rhythm or changes of instrumental color. In India, the solo voice reaches its peak in the *Karnatic* singing style of the south, in many and complex stringed instruments, the *veena, saranghi,* and above all the sound of the instrument which Ravi Shankar has made a household world, the sitar, which is a Moslem importation by way of Persia.

In music the difference between East and West begins even before actual performance, for the Indian method of tuning instruments is not at all like ours. Their sense of the meaning of a particular scale varies from ours. The Thai people can tolerate octaves that seem out of tune to us. An Indian listening to a Western orchestra for the first time might well consider the tuning-up to be the most promising and interesting part of the performance, for Indian musicians spend half an hour or more tuning up. Their accuracy of pitch is in fact inseparable from their inspiration. The audience enjoys the preparation just as much, feeling that it is

Ravi Shankar has made Indian music known and popular throughout the world for more than two decades. He is accompanied by the brilliant tabla player Alla Rakha.

already sharing in the process of what is to follow, and in its turn the music emerges imperceptibly out of the process of tuning. The perfect fifth supports the sympathetic strings tuned to the particular scale or note sequence called a raga.

The Indian raga lies somewhere between a scale and a melody. There are hundreds of ragas, each designed for a particular time of day and night, thus uniting performer and listener to nature and time in a unique way. Once purely votive, the raga has now had to adapt itself for Western tastes, shrinking the long span of improvisation and development; but in the hands of a genius like Ravi Shankar it has not been ravaged, only condensed.

To me, Indian music is like a river, ever·fluid and subtly changing, whereas European music is like a building, carefully structured upon constant principles. The Indian experiences his music as part of his sense of the eternal continuity of life. We see ours as distinctively man-made, a separate artifact. For the Indian, the individual note, with all its inflections and colors, equates with the idea of personal salvation, of resignation and acceptance. India once entertained the idea of counter-point, but while they could have developed it, their philosophy was alien to it. Their music does not favor sharp contrasts of mood as ours does; it can remain in one mode for an hour or more. It is meant to create a state of being, not put the listener through an emotional wringer. I think sometimes that we should establish such exotic interludes in our own concerts. It would encourage people to become aware of what is not their own, while strengthening their sense of what *is* theirs. I am not suggesting we blur or lose our musical identity, for although we may well admire another culture, we can never penetrate to its very heart, no matter how much we love it. There is something at its core which is so particular, so unique, as to make it indecipherable to those born outside it. The music of such a culture remains forever beyond our ken.

Comparisons between the music of different cultures offer illuminating perspectives; what happened to Western music at the time of the Crusades was fundamental. It was no less than the creation of polyphony, music for more than one part or voice which was to lead inexorably to the creation of harmony and intensify the need for a reliable system of notation. Perhaps this evolution had something to do with the need to be heard as individuals rather than as a mass, or the discovery that the stone interiors of churches amplified the voice and gave it wider resonance. The change began imperceptibly, at first with voices in unison at the octave, accommodating differing ranges of bass and tenor, alto and soprano. Then a third voice was added, singing at the interval of a fifth above the

The Four Winds and the Nine Muses surround the figure of Christ in this thirteenth century manuscript, in which the instruments take a prominent part.

lower voice. Surely this was more than mere convenience. The simple open harmony had an austere, penetrating clarity, like the resonating overtones of Tibetan monks. It was not so great a leap from this simple harmony to the idea of starting in unison, moving apart to the fourth or fifth, and coming together again. Yet even that process took some two hundred years.

The practice was referred to as organum, a term borrowed from the Latin meaning the entire body of music-making resources, instruments and voices. It seems likely that some of these ideas were borrowed from popular music, but since we have no written proof, we can only guess. Organum was at first an improvised practice, and plainsong was still taught as a single line. It was at precisely this time that the church itself split in two: the Eastern Orthodox, based in Constantinople and the Roman Catholic church in Rome. The tendency to divide had long been apparent, and when the split actually came in 1054, the Eastern Orthodox church stuck to the practice of unison plainsong.

A fascinating place in which to follow the changing sound of Western music is Spain. Here the Moors were supreme for several hundred years, except in the northwest corner whose center was the town of Santiago de Compostela. Christian tradition held that the bones of the Apostle James were buried here (Santiago means Saint James). The Moors displayed a powerful relic of their own, the mummified right arm of Mohammed, to remind Spanish Christians of Islam's might. The discovery in the ninth century of the tomb of Saint James seemed a revelation sent by God; though proof was moot, the site immediately became a point of pilgrimage. Charlemagne himself visited it. The faithful came by the hundreds of thousands. Their progress, from France, England, the Low Countries, Scandinavia, Germany, was helped by hostels set up by the monks of the Monastery of Cluny in east-central France. Some say this godly kingdom of Cluny extended to two thousand sites, but the number is likely to be under 350, still a considerable realm for the Europe of that day, and the pilgrimage route to Santiago was its backbone. Christians came to believe that a visit to three sites—Jerusalem, Rome and Santiago de Compostela—assured a stay in eternity. One of the purposes of the Crusades, launched in AD 1096, was the taking of Jerusalem. Its capture three years later sent a shiver of joy throughout the West, especially among pilgrims to Santiago, which became a site of inspiration in the wars between Christians and the Moslems. Along this road an immense variety of music was heard, as people from every part of Christendom exchanged songs, chants, dances. The cathedral at Santiago was erected, destroyed, erected once again.

The cathedral we see today has a late seventeenth century façade, hiding the old twelfth century main entrance with its noble arches. Here we find one of the best examples of the vital role music played in the life of the people and the church. In the central arch, known as the Portico de la Gloria, is carved an entire medieval instrumentarium. At the apex of the arch there is an early portable keyboard instrument for two players; one turned the handle, the other played. Elsewhere we find viol players and plucked strings, some performers seemingly transfixed by their own sounds. Notably, there are no winds or brasses (the prohibition against

instruments was still enforced from time to time). Such music must have had a splendid resonance in this fine cathedral, one of the earliest of the Gothic era, and it was surely enriched by the famous school of composition which was established here at the same time.

It was also in Spain that the three principal monotheistic religions, all originating at Mount Sinai, came together again, a blend which has much to do with the unique sound of Spanish music. The Moors remained tolerant toward all the people they found on the Iberian peninsula, for there were not enough Moors to colonize the whole area. Jews and Christians who did not wish to convert to Islam were permitted to continue undisturbed, though the Moors neatly exacted from them a special tax in return for their tolerance. Unconverted Christians came to be known as Mozarabs, which can be translated as mock Arab or would-be Arab. Under Moorish influence their ancient form of plainsong became more ornate, and long after the Moors were gone, the Mozarabs clung to their tradition, resisting every attempt to make them conform to the practices of Rome. Their center was the city of Toledo. The Mozarab rite is still observed there today by a few surviving families, at a chapel of the Church of Santa Maria la Blanca. They link us to that time over a

The Portico de la Gloria *at the Cathedral in Santiago de Compostela in Spain is one of the treasures of medieval art and music, showing that by the late 1100s the stringed instruments at least were no longer considered pagan.*

thousand years ago when Moor and Christian learned to live side by side.

The Crusades were more than a clash of swords—they were a clash of cultures, arts and sciences. When the Crusaders penetrated North Africa and the Near East, they came in contact with different peoples who followed their own musical tradition, and the Christians were struck by the force of this music. The double-reed instrument called the shawm, which has since developed into the oboe and bassoon, flourished there in a profusion of sizes and pitches. Some had the volume and intensity of a trumpet, and an Islamic military band of dozens of these could make a deafening and terrifying sound. The Moslems were a diverse people, unified by Islam as Christianity had unified Europe. Moroccan Moors, for instance, considered themselves quite separate from those of Spain, and by AD 800 there was already a Spanish quarter in the old Moroccan capital city of Fez, occupied by repatriated Moors.

We cannot recapture the spirit which animated the Crusades, any more than we can the sense of splendor which music must have had for the armies returning home, in the great French Gothic cathedrals rising in Saint Denis, Laon and Chartres, and later by those in Spain at Burgos, Leon and Toledo.

Notre Dame in Paris became a center for Western music, as France itself became the focus of medieval European cultural life. The music of the School of Notre Dame is not easy to approach. Our reconstructions of it are still partly based on conjecture; but this music has the unmistakable stamp of Europe, especially in the works by the first two composers whose names have come down to us, Léonin and Pérotin, active as Masters of Music at Notre Dame between 1150 and 1236. Their practice of organum produced harmonies which may sound strange to our ears; the concept of harmony as we know it had not yet emerged. But they are nonetheless a revelation, like the rays of the sun filtering through the extraordinary red and blue stained glass windows of the cathedral. For the first time three and four separate voices could be combined in parts which were not improvised, but the product of a single creative artist. The harmonies were controlled by his sense of the compatibility of intervals and voice leading. In this music the only regularly tolerated intervals were the octave, fifth and fourth. Thirds and seconds were admitted as momentary disturbances brought about by the independent movement of the voices. In organum for three or four voices, each part seems to have been added separately above a *cantus firmus* or set chant usually taken from plainsong. It was more important that the added voices agreed fully with the *cantus firmus* than with one another.

The number of separate voices used in organum seems to have been related to the importance of the occasion in the church calendar, for

Overleaf:
While many medieval manuscripts preserve sacred music and texts, the illustration of tales of chivalry and adventure provide one of our richest sources of information on the nature of popular music of the time.

The Tickhill Psalter *is an English volume (c.1310) which displays the exceptional gifts in manuscript illumination developed in Britain. Within the letter S stands King David, playing both the harp and the vielle.*

instance Pérotin's beautifully elaborate and lengthy work in four voices beginning with the words *Sederunt Principes*. In such music a single syllable of the *cantus firmus* may be held for a minute or more as a buttress, while the other voices embroider it.

The written copies we have of the music of Léonin and Pérotin owe their survival to the fame of the music, for it travelled far beyond Paris. Scotland, Italy and Germany have been our best sources. But the work of

Guido d'Arezzo (c.995–1050) developed the teaching of music by giving names to the notes: the syllables ut, re, mi, fa, sol, la were placed on the joints of the fingers, along with certain sharps and flats. His system remained in use throughout the Middle Ages. This version comes from the music treatise written in 1274 by Elias Salomon.

copying may also have been done by Irish monks, who were among the most able musical transcribers, recruited as far back as Charlemagne's day for the chapter schools on the continent.

Notre Dame then was no ancient treasure, but the newest, tallest structure in Paris, its twin towers visible to all. Inside the cathedral there were no orderly rows of kneelers, but the straw and dung of ambling beasts brought in from the cold in winter by their owners. In poor weather, the marketplace on the plaza in front of the church would empty as buyer and seller sought the shelter of its roof, the warmth of many bodies.

The rules for music established at Notre Dame may have banished all but the purest intervals, yet at that same time, far from the splendors of Paris, another sound was being heard, that of voices moving in parallel thirds. To the strict French ecclesiastical mind, such harmonies were barbarous, a sure path to the devil—they may have originated with popular songs and were thus associated with the carnal and sensual. In the Orkney Islands north of the Scottish mainland, one of the oldest evidences of the use of parallel thirds was discovered, the *Hymn to Saint Magnus*, a patron saint of the area. It is one of many clues suggesting that the practice came from Iceland and Scandinavia, where parallel thirds were not prohibited.

The Vikings may have liked tunes sung in parallel thirds, but we cannot say for certain; their music is lost. But already in the Iron Age their metal horn, the *lur*, was in widespread use. The Etruscans probably brought the art of working copper to the area, and metal horns in pairs and groups were known here by early Roman times. Such instruments sound well when they play at the interval of a third. Perhaps this may have influenced the musical practice in song, particularly after the eleventh century conquest of England where duets of all kinds were popular, including those for instruments intended for dancing. English music teachers were the first to claim officially that the interval of a third was acceptable.

Out of this period comes one example which remains justly famous and is still sung today, the celebrated canon "Sumer Is Icumen In." Although the manuscript containing it was written about 1260, and the canon added two or three decades later, the music is a good deal older and was already widely known. The medieval instructions ask that the work be sung by four voices, each entering at a fixed distance, accompanied by two lower voices and probably reinforced by instruments. Most rounds or canons could be readily passed on by ear, but this one was too hard, the melodic variations too subtle—it was easy to lose the thread. "Sumer" had to be written down to ensure that the singers would render it correctly

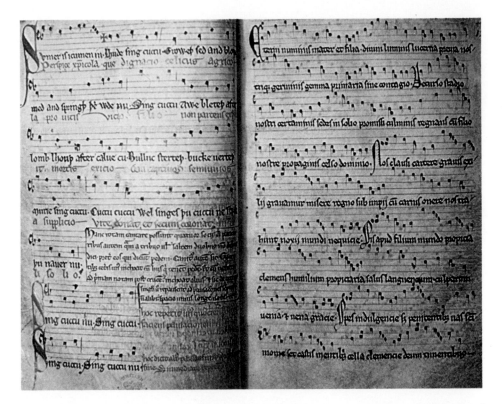

and thus make it easier to teach. It survives as a masterpiece of technical ingenuity and immediate appeal, and because its difficulty presents a challenge. Something crucial about this song must be noted: when all its voices sound together, they blend into two alternating chords which contain the seed of something extraordinary, the most powerful effect we know in Western harmony, the tension set up between the home key and the chord which serves as the gate leading to it. How wonderfully ironic it is that one of the earliest evidences we have of this musical breakthrough comes to us in the manuscript of a popular song. In many areas of cultural evolution the fact precedes the record; notation itself may even have held back harmonic progress because for such a long time it was unequal to the challenge of transcribing what the ear readily accepted.

The difficulty in describing the music of this time is made even greater because we still know so little of its popular side. The few dances and songs of the people we have exist partly by accident, for the paper on which they were written was used later as scrap to help strengthen the binding of a book. Undoubtedly one of the most fascinating collections of popular music of the time is *Carmina Burana*, written down around 1300, and containing lyrics and music of the previous two centuries. These include love songs, drinking songs, game songs, an Easter and a Christmas play—a veritable anthology of favorites. The notation is

On the manuscript for "Sumer Is Icumen In" the point at which each succeeding voice is to enter with its opening phrase is marked with a cross. The song was given both a sacred and a secular text.

volo studere pie mgr
volo studere me mgr

The whip was often used in medieval times as an encouragement to the learning of lessons in music and other subjects, as this early thirteenth century illustration reveals.

obscure, and only in recent years has it been possible to reconstruct them with reasonable accuracy by careful comparison with later copies of a few of the same songs. *Carmina Burana* preserves for us an irreplaceable heritage of the early troubadours. We can imagine these irreverent, bawdy ballads being exchanged among the wandering scholar-singers known as Goliards. As the business of the church was to minister to the needs of the people, it is hardly by accident that *Carmina Burana* survived in a monastery, the Benediktbeuren Abbey in Bavaria.

Fortunately, we do have knowledge of one aspect of the music of the Middle Ages: the evolution of the instruments. Single and double reeds had accompanied the Crusaders home; the Arab *rebab* had become the *rebec, vielle* and *fidula*. The harp, making its way into the Celtic north from its apparent source in Syria, became so popular that Ireland made it a national symbol. With strings of different lengths, it was easier to tune than the lyre inherited from Greece. The lute was Persian, deriving its name and shape from the Arabic word *Al'ud*, meaning wood. The psaltery, a plucked zither, which could be also struck with mallets, is Persian, though its name derives from the Greek. The juggler-jester, able since Roman times to play both flute and drum at the same time, was a crowd pleaser. The herdsman's bagpipe is so ancient an instrument that its parentage is untraceable. Associated with animal husbandry, it began to appear often in Christmas pageants.

In the Middle Ages, the music of Western Europe reached a relative uniformity, consistent particularly with the culture of the educated class. National boundaries were not yet firmly set, though cultural boundaries were clear. One religion dominated, the Roman Catholic, and one official language, Latin. The first great universities were coming into existence at Bologna, Paris, Oxford and Cambridge. The changes which were about to overtake the West are reflected in the work of its artists: individual names were emerging from the collective body of artisans. One of the most remarkable instances is found in the architecture of the cathedral at Autun in central France, in its entirety the work of one man, Ghislebert. So grateful was the church that it permitted him the unheard-of luxury of signing his work. Across the stone entrance is carved in Latin, *Gilbertus Hoc Fecit*, literally, "Ghislebert made this." The artist was becoming a vital source of energy driving the engine of Western civilization.

Under the influence of learning and the arts, the rigid social cement of the Middle Ages was crumbling. Dance is a good example of this; it has always been one of the ways we express change. In the thirteenth century one of the latest dances was the *estampie* (known in England as the *stantipes* and in Italy and Spain as the *estampida*). This dance travelled to all parts of the Western world as social dancing became a barometer of social taste. Of the *estampie* one medieval scholar said, "The complex nature of its uneven phrase lengths directs the dancers' minds away from depraved thoughts." This critic was obviously aware of the hazard involved in letting men and women dance together.

Troubadours such as Bernard de Ventadour introduced songs of earthy and passionate love, such as the popular "Kalenda Maia," which spread across Europe. It even became a part of many settings of the Holy Mass as

From the Book of Music of the Cantigas of Alfonso X The Wise *(c.1275), kept at the monastery of the Escorial, the Spanish royal palace, comes this image of troubadours playing the lute and viol, instruments already beautifully developed by this time.*

Overleaf:

Among the most beautiful images of the age of chivalry and knighthood which have come down to us are in the copy dated 1316 of the Roman de Fauvel, *a satirical allegory, whose hero was half-man, half-horse. Made for Chaillon de Pestain, this volume contains motets by Philippe de Vitry, settings of portions of the text of the parody.*

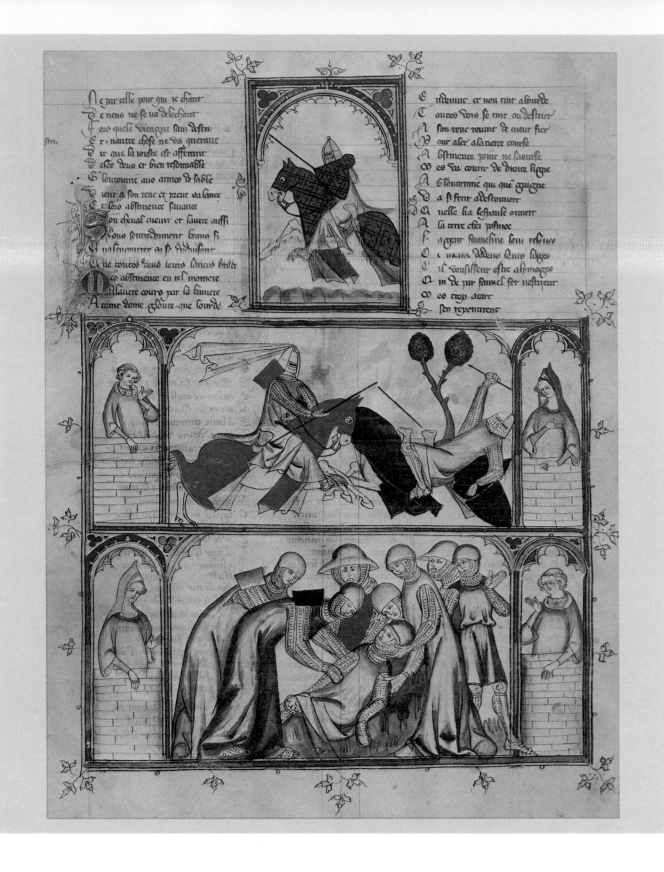

a secular *cantus firmus*. As women rose in status, under the emerging code of chivalry, the love duet was established. It was possible now for the voices of a man and woman to join in singing the praises of the pangs and rewards of love. Love songs were usually addressed by a knight to his "lady" (usually not his wife). The knight was bound by the code of chivalry to a marriage arranged for reasons of property, family ties or by royal decree. He might consummate his earthly love with one woman while dedicating his idea of pure love to another.

One of the most prolific composers of such love ballads was Jacopo da Bologna, active in the mid-1300s. His love duet *Non al suo amante* was composed to a poem by Petrarch, whom he may well have known personally. Petrarch addressed his love poems to his lady, the divine Laura, and they have been taken to heart by lovers ever since. Petrarch's importance for a musician lies in his exquisitely tuned ear for the cadences of language, which Jacopo understood. He could take the balanced twists and turns of Petrarch's verses and make them into music as clear and radiant as the Italian skies. At the library in Faenza a version of Jacopo's duet exists elaborated for instruments, the upper voice festooned with ornaments. It is music of the dawn of the Renaissance.

The medieval plague, the Black Death, hit Europe with a fresh calamity. The first epidemic struck in 1348 and raged for three years, sweeping through Eastern lands as well. The loss of life was unprecedented. Petrarch lost his beloved Laura. In some towns nearly everyone was killed. The fury of the plague seemed to be visited by God upon man without reason. It shook the faith of all Christians, and recurred with dismaying frequency for three hundred years. One major outbreak was in London in 1665. That pestilence gave us a familiar song, "Ring Around the Rosies." The first line mocks the sick with their open sores. "Pocketful of posies" recalls the perfume of flowers used to ward off the stench of death. "Attishoo, attishoo" (rendered in America as "Ashes, ashes") is for the rapid, gasping sounds of the dying. "All fall down" is death itself, which now became as common a subject for art and music as love had been. Europe was at war but the enemy would not be laid low by a Crusade.

For Europe, with its great churches and intimidating fortresses, its growing cities declaring the genius of man, such a reduction to helplessness was intolerable. There were frequent hysterical reactions, a paradoxical gaiety and debauchery. People escaped contamination by leaving town, for the plague was chiefly spread by rats clustering in city sewers. There may be a connection between this retreat to safe hiding and the practice among composers in the late 1300s of driving music to ever greater complexity, to rhythmic contortions and melodic twists so

The woodcuts by Hans Holbein for his famous The Dance of Death *were carved between 1522 and 1526. The skeletons play the xylophone, tabor, krummhorn, busine and kettledrum.*

Multituds flying from London by water in boats & barges

Flying by land

Burying the dead with a bell before them.   Searchers.

Carts full of dead to bury.

A contemporary print of the Great London Plague of 1665 shows the flight past old Saint Paul's, a coffin preceded by a bell near Covent Garden, the dead buried in trenches by the cartload. Some seventy thousand died (about fifteen percent of London's population).

difficult that only the most skilled could perform it. The new music was dubbed *Ars Nova* by Philippe de Vitry, himself a leading composer and theorist; but the best-known name from that time is undoubtedly that of Guillaume de Machaut (c. 1300–1377), considered by many to be the West's first great composer. One of the finest poets and musicians of any century, he brought rhythmic and harmonic daring into Western music, and the acceptance, at last, of the interval of a third. He was ingenious in managing the intertwining of independent voices, but he avoided complexity for its own sake. Machaut's *La Messe de Notre Dame* (*Votive Mass for the Blessed Virgin*) is the oldest complete setting of the Mass text we have. However it was in his songs that Machaut endeared himself to his age, earning the title of the last of the great troubadours.

Machaut shows us as well that worship of a lady need not be an honor reserved solely to knights in armor. He was well past sixty when he chose

as his lady a girl of nineteen, Peronnelle. She admired his songs and had written him a poem of praise, and though they met only once or twice, Machaut fell hopelessly in love with the image of Peronnelle. Her infatuation doubtless passed more quickly. Many of Machaut's letters to Peronnelle still exist, and in one of them he declares:

> I swear to you and promise that I shall serve you loyally and diligently to the best of my power, and all to your honor as Lancelot and Tristan never served their ladies; and have your likeness as my earthly deity and as the most precious and glorious relic that ever I did see in any place. Henceforth it shall be my heart, my castle, my treasure, and my comfort against all ills.

The legend of Tristan and Isolde probably originated with a poem by a twelfth century Anglo-Norman poet named Thomas. The story almost immediately became a favorite of troubadours and artists. In this thirteenth century miniature, the lovers display the spirit of chivalry by sharing an informal picnic.

Guillaume de Machaut was one of the first artists to put all of his collected works in order, and he also left us an autobiography and much other documentation. Posterity obviously meant much to him, and he reasoned rightly that his works would survive best if he assured their safety himself.

A miniature by the Master of Bocqueteaux, one of two in the volume of collected works by Guillaume de Machaut, showing the master composer receiving the honors of royalty and clergy. It is the first known portrait of a Western composer.

"Sweet are the uses of adversity." Indeed. During the plague, the continual conflict between Christians and Moors abated. It was in 1348, the year of the first European plague, that a most beautiful work of Islamic architecture, the Alhambra, summer and winter palace of the Sultans, was completed. Situated in the hills overlooking Granada in southeastern Spain, with the Sierra Nevada as a backdrop, the Moors had chosen the ideal setting for their fairy-tale dwelling. Mathematics and science flourished alongside music, and echoing through the grace and

lightness of these filigreed arches, competing with the sounds of flowing water from fountains and canal, rose the voices of the musical instruments, completing an exquisite scene. The languid, sinuous, poised beauty of Moorish music, which was to leave its stamp on all of Spain, rang forth not only in the blossoming gardens watered by sibilant fountains, but indoors in the harem, and especially in the baths. Here musicians performed from the upper gallery for the delight of those dallying below. As the baths were one of the most popular places of assignation, these unfortunate players were first blinded and then emasculated to remove them from temptation.

Moorish music is essentially improvised, its players as adept at decorating sound as Moorish architects were with stone and plaster. This principle affected a huge territory, not only in Europe, but through north and central Africa, as Islam spread. In Spain the practice of spontaneous invention is found in the flamenco, where the brilliance and verve of the performer are encouraged by the shouts and handclaps of colleagues. This music developed among the gypsies who came to Spain in the Renaissance after the Moors departed, and took the form we know by the nineteenth century.

Music was part of the Islamic storytelling in the Middle Ages; here the hero Abu Zaid tells tales called Maqàma, built around a witty rogue who puts rivals to shame with his eloquence; the accompaniment is by a ten-string lute, whose music was reputed to move the hearts of beautiful maids, and cause the mountains themselves to dance (from the Maqàma of Hariri, a copy dated 1334, probably from Egypt).

After AD 1400, the Renaissance was in its glory, and the days of the Moor in Europe were almost over. The final battles between Christians and Moslems had much to do with the rise of the Inquisition. On January 2, 1492, the last Moorish ruler in Europe, Boabdil, was forced to surrender Granada to King Ferdinand and Queen Isabella. The victory united Spain and later that year, confident in their new-found power, the monarchs financed the expedition of Columbus. Within half a century, Cartier navigated the St. Lawrence river, Balboa and Pizarro took Panama and Peru, and Magellan's crew sailed around the world.

Two Renaissance musicians brought stability to composed music in the West. John Dunstable (c. 1400–1453) in England and Guillaume Dufay (c. 1400–1474) in France achieved order and logic in the writing of music for multiple voices. They felt that accidental clashes between independent lines, still found in Machaut, should not be tolerated. They formulated rules of harmony, not for scholarly reasons, but out of sheer necessity, avoiding dissonances except where they might lend greater force of expression. There is great poise in works such as Dunstable's motet *Veni Sancti Spiritus* and Dufay's *Lamentation for Constantinople* (the city had fallen to the Turks in 1453), a new stability and control which impressed their contemporaries. The sound we now recognize as Western music was finally taking shape. The extent of this musical reform is made clear by these words written in 1474, the year of Dufay's death, by the composer and theorist Tinctoris: "There is no music not written within the past forty years that is considered by the learned as worthy of hearing." But the overriding reason why flexibility was giving way to order was not the growing Western sensitivity to harmony, but something which constitutes the major difference between Western music and that of most of the rest of the world: musical writing.

By the time of Dufay and Dunstable, the system of putting notes on paper had finally become dependable. Its evolution cannot be traced without a short step back to Charlemagne's day and the curious squiggles which comprise the earliest Western musical notation, called neumes. Neumes began to be attached to sacred texts around the ninth century. One, in the Bodleian Library at Oxford, is a melody to a Latin "Song to the Muses" whose words date from the fifth century, one of the oldest notated examples of secular music in existence. These neumes were developed mainly in the monasteries.

In the history of human thought, I feel that the cloister was even more important than the church with its sacred rites. In these quadrangles, with measured paces between measured arches, disciplined thought had the time, solitude and peace to pursue its meditation. It was here that the

The interior of the Alhambra displays grace and balance, and a mood of mystery which still casts a spell today, as in this corner of the Tower of the Infantas.

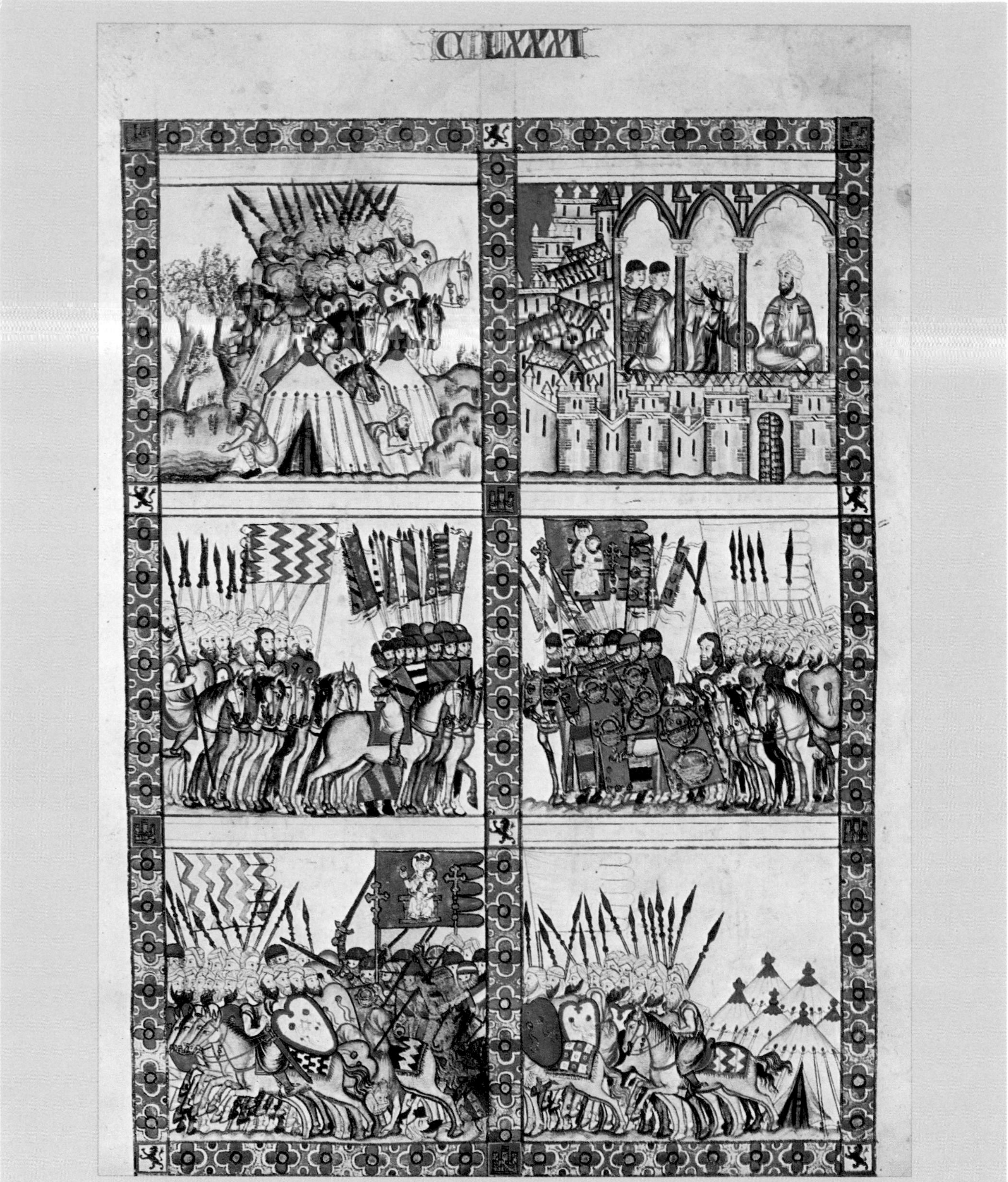
CCLXXXI

melody amplifying the word first came to be written down. The very first efforts indicate what had been a long oral tradition, and which simply prolonged the last syllables of words with a few symbols above the line indicating the oscillations of the voice.

Neumes were little more than shorthand reminders, of use mainly for those who already knew the basic chants, and stood both for the melodic line and for the hand signals of the *precentor*, or leader of the choir. In fact, at first, they were usually only seen by him, translated into gestures for the singers. In this early notation there was no reference line, no staff to help indicate where home base might be. Hucbald, a French musical theoretician writing around AD 900, said this about neumes: "The first note seems higher, you can sing it wherever you like. The second you can see is lower, but when you join it to the first one, you cannot decide whether the interval is one, two or three tones. Unless you hear it sung you cannot tell what the composer wants."

A reference point was obviously needed, and it came first in the form of a single, straight, horizontal line representing *doh* or *ut*, the first tone of the mode in which the chant was to be sung. This *doh* was movable up or down, according to the most comfortable vocal range for the singers. Neumes rose above and dipped below this line, gradually coming to represent more and more the notes themselves rather than the leader's hand signals. There was still much margin for error; so another horizontal line was added above, sometimes of another color, representing the interval of a fifth. Then another was added below, also a fifth away. These lines made it easier to judge the exact intervals between notes. This was still not precise enough, so lines were added between these three, at the intervals of a third above and below *doh*. In this way each line and space was reserved for a single specific note. The number of staff lines even reached six at one point; the five-line staff we know was recognized in the end as more stable, easier to read.

As the separate voices gained greater freedom, more accurate means had to be found to indicate the way these voices were expected to blend. This was becoming more than polyphony: it was the beginning of counterpoint. The first steps may have been tiny, but the leap in imagination was huge, and the addition of instruments undoubtedly contributed its share. Gradually singers became used to the idea that musical phrases need not be governed solely by human breath or diction, pace or speed.

Large volumes of notated liturgy, exquisitely written and illuminated, were placed on stands so that they might be used by many at once. Small stands served one singer at a time and were taken from place to place. As improved methods of notation took over, older manuscripts were used

At the medieval Spanish monastery at Sylos, where some of the most exquisite and valuable musical manuscripts are preserved, Yehudi Menuhin contemplates the quadrangle of the cloister.

Opposite:

The Cantigas de Santa Maria of Alfonso X The Wise *give us a detailed account, in some three hundred illustrated pages of the greatest variety, of the history of encounters in Iberia between Moors and Spaniards over the centuries of battle (c.1275).*

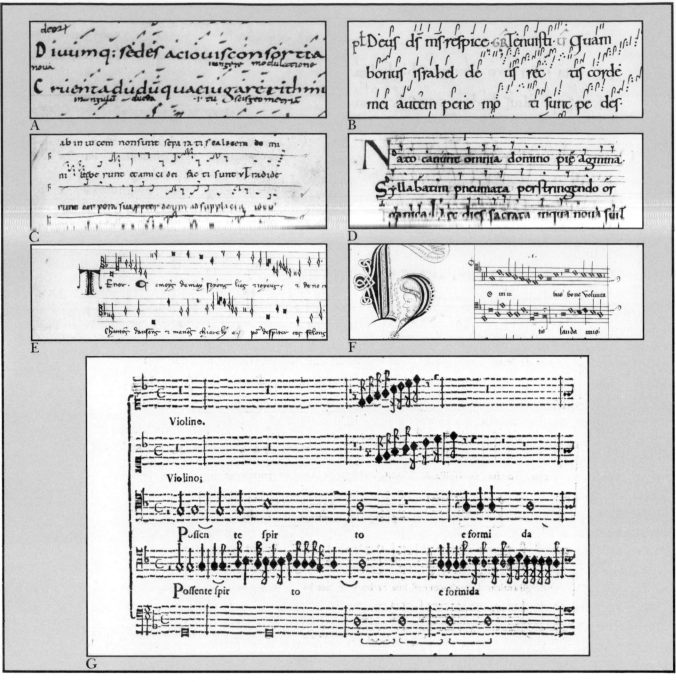

Tracing the development of western notation carries us from the tiny ninth century neumes of a Latin Song of the Muses (a), the mid-eleventh century neumes of the famed Winchester Troper(b), an Italian mid-twelfth century breviary (c) where the single doh-*line appears, the Winchester Troper again (d) with five-line staves added in the mid-twelfth century, a* chanson *by Guillaume Dufay (e)*

from a manuscript written within his lifetime, probably about 1450 in Venice, and finally a mass by John Taverner (f) written about 1530 in separate part books. At the bottom is the first printed score, Monteverdi's Orfeo *of 1607 (g) showing the tenor vocal line in two versions, the more elaborate giving the composer's suggestions for ornamentation.*

like scrap paper, sometimes glued inside a volume to strengthen it, sometimes as a flyleaf. The idea of a score, with the parts stacked above each other on one page, had not yet come into use. Parts were written on facing pages, or on upper and lower halves, and the performers had to count with care to keep themselves in line. There were no bar lines, a refinement which was not used consistently until the seventeenth century. Accents fell according to language stresses, often making for a wonderful ricochet of rhythms. Singers today would have to train strenuously to master this technique.

At the outset of Western harmony, composers were not unlike medieval alchemists; they liked to keep their secrets to themselves, locked away from competitors. Until recently, we assumed that musicians composed music first in their heads, and then wrote it out in separate parts, never seeing the whole on one page. Yet as the rules of harmony and counterpoint began to take over, the process of writing each part became more difficult. Music historians long suspected that composers from Dufay onward must have had some kind of scoring tool, a sketch pad where they could write out a work in score, and then transfer these to part books, erasing the sketch and re-using the paper. The heavy parchment on which they sketched was called a *cartella*. Confirmation of this process came to light some years ago with the discovery of a manuscript in Milan, a blank page found among works by Cipriano de Rore. On it was written, "This *cartella* was given to me by my master. On it I saw him compose his *Gloria*." The note is by de Rore's pupil Luzzaschi, and for musicologists, it was the missing link.

Printing was the final step, making possible duplicate copies of every kind of music, assuring its wide availability, passing from a treasury to an open market. In fact, not long after de Rore's death in 1565, his madrigals were printed in a pocket score edition. For a time, writing music by hand remained cheaper than printing, but by the end of the sixteenth century printed music was making it possible for amateurs and professionals to learn and perform a much larger repertory of works from many countries. Printing affected the history of music in much the same way as the printing of the Gutenberg Bible advanced literacy in one great bound.

With this notation of scores, the division between composer and performer widened. It is a distinction which, in our day, has narrowed again in the field of pop and rock groups, who mostly play only their own songs. Jazz musicians, like the folk performer of old whose music was passed on by ear, prefer to invent as they play or sing. Notation came partly from the need of many people to work together, and music naturally reflected this social fact. Indian music too can be notated, but

Monks and nuns who carefully safeguarded a treasured library gave us much of our knowledge of the first dozen centuries of Western Christian music. These monks standing within a letter C *(an illumination which begins with the words* Cantate Domino, *or Sing unto the Lord) share a single volume on a stand.*

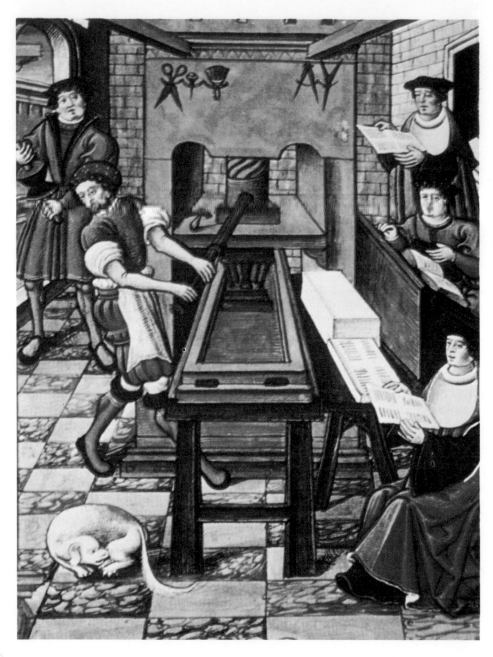

Printing was a technological breakthrough which changed our access to learning as perhaps nothing else had since the invention of writing itself. By the mid-sixteenth century establishments such as these existed all over Europe.

Opposite:
The Glorification of the Virgin *by Geertjen tot Sint Jans (c. 1465–1493), who worked at the monastery of St. John in Haarlem, Holland, displays an instrumental richness far beyond that acceptable to the church just a few centuries before.*

Indians are so trained in creative improvisation that they only write music down in those special cases when they require a reminder of a particular sequence. Their notation is cumbersome and used solely as reference, as is the case with medieval neumes. Our present Western notation is a flexible shorthand system, much quicker to read, but with certain limitations. It has now become so much a part of our musical lives we cannot imagine music without it. This same notation has helped to

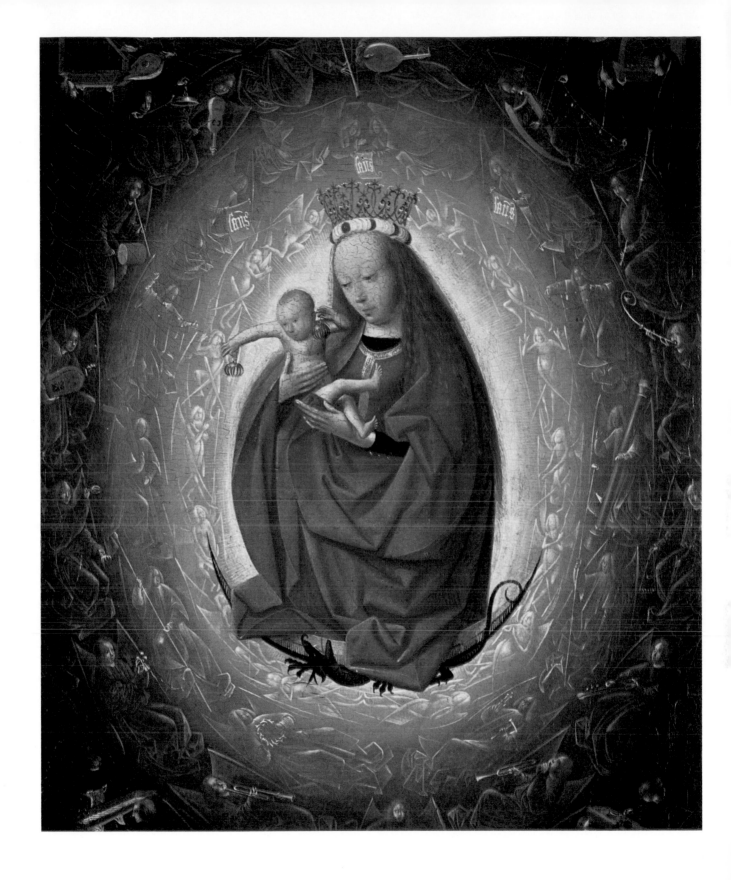

preserve for us the lasting masterpieces which stand apart from the everyday disposable and renewable world, and our musical culture is as dependent on it as printed books are to literature. But I am equally aware as an interpreter how much we must continually compensate for our servitude, how essential it is to have a lively imagination, an intuitive and sensitive intelligence. Otherwise, the notes entrusted to paper take on a greater importance than the very music they are intended to convey.

During the Renaissance, music became far less incidental, and more a part of the display of learning, power and wealth. Court choirs and instrumental groups became the rule, and composers were taken into residence to write for them, as painters were to adorn the palaces of nobility. Older music was quickly swept aside, and the musician was no longer considered an artisan like the builders of Gothic churches: he was an honored artist. Skills in instrumental manufacture took great leaps forward alongside those of performance, as noble patrons demanded higher quality.

What this means for the Western musician is the forging of the music we know and love out of the extraordinary stress of the period. To most, the Renaissance means painting, sculpture, drama, literature, architecture, and finally music. This cultural explosion was hardly noticed by the majority of people, who could hardly afford such products. But printed music could travel as the minstrels once had done, becoming part of even the humblest home.

Up to now, formalized attitudes toward the nature of the world had been largely the responsibility of the church, which continued to insist that the world was flat, and the sun circled the earth. Mariners taking part in long ocean voyages launched by Vasco da Gama and Magellan began to think otherwise, and so did the scientists. Music now made another vital contribution to our process of thought. When man first transformed sound into music, advances were made by the method of trial and error, a process which science now adopted. Science may not have been within the reach of all, but music sharpened the analytical sense in imperceptible ways. Singing to improvised accompaniments at home was a great achievement for Western man; he was becoming a tester and measurer of his own artistic capacities.

The open challenge to the status quo arose first not from science or exploration, but within the ranks of the church itself. In 1517 Martin Luther nailed his Ninety-Five Theses on the door of his church at Wittenberg, accusing the Roman Catholic church of corruption. The Reformation was born. Luther, himself a fine musician, threw out much old church music and wrote new hymns of which "A Mighty Fortress Is

Our God" is the best known among dozens. Luther was a sort of Master Singer, and was even called that, inventing melodies which were then framed in the learned art of polyphony thanks to his adviser and collaborator Johann Walter. These four-part settings were not as complex as the part writing developed by Dufay and others, for Luther intended these hymns to be sung by the people, the entire congregation, giving fresh voice to their growing sense of power, of individual rights, while at one and the same time they could learn to master the elements of harmony previously reserved for the specialists.

Artists are often the first to anticipate social change. The cultural fact that marks the Renaissance more than any other was the rediscovery of the classical Greek conception of the ideal human form. The works of Leonardo and Michelangelo reflect this, and Europe gained a fresh sense of continuity with its own distant past. The heroic quality in the Greek spirit accorded perfectly with a time when man would be seen as "the measure of all things." The violin is a symbol for man the measurer, and by the mid-1500s it had evolved into the instrument we know. Before the Renaissance the design and use of instruments was haphazard, parts would be taken by any players at hand, and the voice was still supreme. The violin is a natural leader, the ultimate musical match for man himself, and craftsmen whose skills were a match for the ideals of beauty of ancient Greece made it the king of instruments. All the instruments were improving and multiplying in a dizzying variety, shawms and sackbuts, bombards and rauschpfeife, krummhorns, lutes, bandoras and virginals. We can date only a few to a time prior to 1500, but hundreds after that. Musicians may have taken less care in the Middle Ages, or worn

University education took root in the Middle Ages, and by the Renaissance it was a flourishing enterprise.

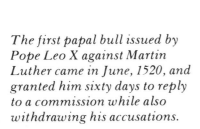

The first papal bull issued by Pope Leo X against Martin Luther came in June, 1520, and granted him sixty days to reply to a commission while also withdrawing his accusations.

Above right:
Far from recanting, on December 10, 1520, Martin Luther consigned the bull and other papal documents to flames. On January 3, 1521, he was formally excommunicated by Leo X.

Opposite:
Matthias Grünewald's celebrated altarpiece painted in 1515 at Isenheim in Alsace is in three panels, of which this one is named The Angelic Concert. *Grünewald (c.1475–1528) and his altarpiece later inspired the opera and symphony* Mathis der Maler *composed by Paul Hindemith in 1934.*

out the ones they had through hard use. Workmanship now assured quality with quantity, and princes collected instruments as the basis of house ensembles; they did not, in fact, belong to the musicians who played them.

During the Renaissance, the greatest of all keyboard instruments, the church organ, was brought to perfection. The primitive organ which re-entered the church and court life after the eighth century was either a small portable or a huge monster operated by heavy levers struck with the fist. Now it was growing into the elaborate console type of which we still find traces in Europe, for instance at Covarrubias in Spain, where there is a true Renaissance instrument, still in working order, producing the kind of sound which might have been heard by Antonio de Cabezon, one of the finest great organ composers. Born in 1510 and blind since early infancy, Cabezon nevertheless mastered both the instrument and the art of composition, becoming organist to Charles V, then to Philip II. Cabezon travelled around the world with Philip II and wherever he went he left printed editions of his music and his keyboard techniques influenced other musicians. Cabezon was an inventor of the form called theme and variations, which he named *differencía*. He also developed the *tientos*, called *ricercare* in Italy, meaning to search—a precursor of the fugue.

The characteristic mark of the music of Cabezon is, to me, similar to that which distinguishes the three major religions which met in Spain: Moslem, Jewish and Christian. That mark is the subjection of the human

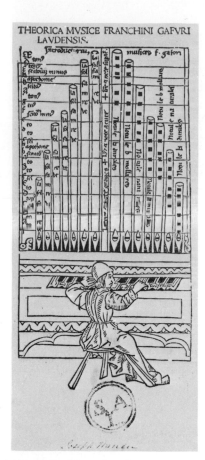

act to the written word. The emotional disembodiment of the Gregorian chant or plainsong, neither happy nor sad, has evolved here to a wonderfully expressive and elaborate consequence. This music is not subject to the pulses, rhythms, and the sensual emotions of the body. It is deeply spiritual, and its cadences follow the demand of the word. The old *cantus firmus* is now the theme, remembered in the mind. Decoration after decoration in multiple voices may follow, with unison at the octave at the end of every section. It is truly music of the spirit, not yet held within so strict a harmonic or rhythmic framework as we find later in Bach, but, nonetheless, standing on the bridge between the single voice and its later elaboration in the counterpoint of the Baroque. Hearing such music played on the organ at Covarrubias, its peculiar horizontal pipes giving out trumpet-like sounds, its tuning closer to natural temperament than the modern organ, is to give ear, however briefly, to the sound of music as it actually was in sixteenth century Europe.

The human voice had not yet lost its place as the driving force behind Western music, still dominating the principles of phrasing, even the range of any single line. Singing was now staked out as a battleground in the war between the Reformation and the Catholic church. Martin Luther died in 1544. By 1590, the great cathedral of Saint Peter in Rome was on its way to completion. Turkish forces under Sultan Suleiman had already come up the Danube valley, reaching the gates of Vienna. England had rejected the authority of the Pope. The Catholic church wished to shore up its position of leadership, and it knew that music could help. The Vatican called to it one of the greatest composers of any

*The Angelic Concert by the
noted Bavarian Renaissance
sculptor Tilman
Riemenschneider, a bas-relief
in wood now at the Deutsches
Museum in Berlin.*

age, Giovanni Pierluigi da Palestrina (1524-1594), giving him the task of reforming the music of the church. He made a start, but never carried this work to completion. It was his setting of the sacred texts and the Mass which made the greatest impression.

Almost all of Palestrina's music is intended to be sung by unaccompanied voices. On paper it may not look like much ("Too many white notes," Berlioz said), but when the music is heard echoing around huge spaces, like those of St. Peter's, we recognize how keen the Italian ear is to the unadorned singing voice. Palestrina is admired and performed still in churches of every denomination.

Under the influence of the Reformation, artistic and political power was moving northward. At the crossroads stood the city of Venice. This was an independent state ruled by the Doges, and, for a long time, Venice

An engraving by deBry shows the Spaniards revelling among the natives of Brazil, during the Second Indian Voyage led by Pedro Cabral in 1500.

continued to trade with all sides, providing larger armies and navies for hire than most kingdoms could muster. Venice was wealthy and powerful, uniquely situated on alluvial lands at the mouth of the Adriatic, and celebrated for her beauty long before the Crusades. By the late Renaissance, Venice was home to such artists as Titian, Giorgione, Tintoretto, Veronese and the architect Palladio.

The best musicians also came to Venice, the finest virtuosos and composers brought the newest ideas, and music here had the same importance it was to have in Vienna two hundred years later. The blend of people made possible a particularly happy coexistence of voices and instruments. We can even say that the idea of orchestration began here, the idea of designating specific instruments for every part. This emerged from the desire to gain control over the exact blend of tonal colors that would make the greatest effect. The printing of music also began in Venice in 1501; technical problems were solved, metal type introduced; Venice became a distribution center for the music of the entire West. Musicians and patrons who came here could take the latest treasures away with them not just in their ears but in their luggage.

Toward the late 1500s, the music of Venice was ruled by two remarkable men, Andrea Gabrieli and his nephew Giovanni. They evolved a balance of huge choruses with groups of winds, strings and brasses, placing them in opposing choir lofts in St. Mark's Basilica, a noble, venerable structure completed in 1067. These performers would throw musical answers back and forth to each other, and to the two organ keyboards which served as a base of support for the rich harmonies. It was a fitting climax for the music of Renaissance Italy, and a turning point into the Baroque, whose chief Venetian exponent a century later was Antonio Vivaldi. As the fame of Venice's music spread around the world, the Gabrielis were its absolute leaders. In 1583 the Doges played host to a delegation of princes from far-off Japan, and for these distinguished guests they unfolded all of their most elaborate musical wares. When Andrea Gabrieli died in 1586, Giovanni became Venice's musical ruler, just as the reign of the human voice in Western music began to wane.

This is the moment in Western music which marks the real beginning of independent instrumental music, even though vocal forms were still important. Giovanni Gabrieli already used the technique called thorough-bass, in which the bottom line in the written score is fitted out with numerical signs indicating the harmonies to be filled in above on the key-board. His concept of instrumental writing was precise, and had its effect on Monteverdi and his successors. Modulation from key to key was suited to the nature of this instrumental writing, and it is in this music that we find a feature which was to be of vital importance to the history of

The Concert *by Lorenzo Costa (1460–1535), active in Bologna and Mantua. The instruments shown are the viol and lute.*

The members of the Accademia Monteverdiana under the direction of Denis Stevens are assembled in Canterbury Cathedral for the performance of Giovanni Gabrieli's In Eclesiis Domino.

Western music for the next three hundred years: the new-found power of the suspended dissonance.

The deliberately planned dissonance, revolving around a note whose Italian name is *appoggiatura*, that penetrating dissonance in the flow of harmonies, calls to it all our attention and demands to be resolved. When that resolution occurs, it heightens our emotional response, while opening up fresh harmonic possibilities. With the help of these suspensions, the composer can change home keys within the same piece, moving from minor to major, up a fifth or down a third. It is, in fact, the beginning of modulation, the free movement from one key to any other, which became so prominent a feature of music in the Romantic period. The idea emerged from vocal writing, and the dissonance is often used by composers of madrigals, motets and cantatas to lay stress on such dramatic words as "I *die* of love" or "his *piteous* wounds."

The power of the suspended dissonant note was long known, being present in the ballads of Machaut and the chansons of Dufay. *Appoggiatura* means to lean upon or to support, and it is a graphic way of expressing the feeling in words given by a suspension, the sense of the home key and the gate leading to it hinted at so long ago in "Sumer Is Icumen In," but now made inexorable. The dissonance leans on the phrase until the pressure must be resolved by lifting the note up or dropping it down to the next. It is one of the West's most idiomatic contributions to the art of music. Wagner made it into a way of life. The vocal music of the Renaissance may have introduced it, but its fulfilment was not to remain tied to the voice. The instruments were about to become the chief source of energy for the masterpieces of Western music for the next three hundred years.

The Venice of Giovanni Gabrieli's day looked quite different from the city we know today. Wood was a far more common building material, as this painting by Carpaccio (c. 1515) demonstrates.

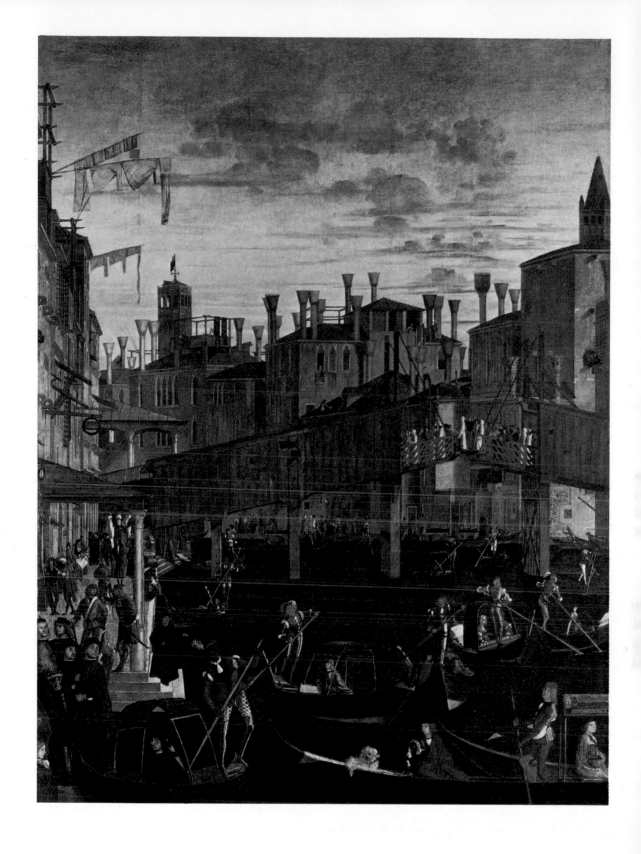

Monteverdi creates the opera, Corelli creates the sonata and concerto, and the city of Venice becomes a musical capital as the Renaissance turns toward the Baroque Age. Colonization of Africa and the New World is launched. Violin-making reaches perfection in Cremona, in the hands of Stradivari and Guarneri. As power moves northward, Lully becomes master of music for Louis XIV, and Henry Purcell is the last in a line of English Renaissance masters, his influence replaced by the German, Handel.

3. New Voices for Man

AS WE REACH THE SEVENTEENTH CENTURY, the great cities and courts of Italy are still the symbol of that astonishing burst of human creativity, the Renaissance—as they are of the temporal power of bankers, traders and politics, of families such as the Medici in Florence and the Gonzagas in Mantua. In the affairs of men, art had achieved still greater power to conquer human hearts, and the gradual closing of the gap between art and the lives of ordinary men and women is one of the most exciting facts of the century. No longer was heard the calm, balanced harmony of Palestrina or the Tudor composers, but a full-blooded expression of passion as in the music of Carlo Gesualdo, in which the rules of harmony are stretched to the limit of the day. Once more the artist personifies the human sensibility most alert to social change, helping us to become aware of the importance of each individual life.

What Western man now sought was a secure framework, a point of sure reference on earth. It was a time of fascination with numbers and measurement. The most precise and simplest instrument relying on a numerical mechanical system was the clock, which began to dominate the measuring of life far more than the sun and the stars. Similarly, in music a rhythmic and harmonic legislation was being formulated, a system whereby the voices of instruments and of man could be sounded individually and in large numbers without creating cacophony or intolerable dissonance. That achievement is what we refer to as Western harmony and counterpoint.

In the seventeenth century, France began to dominate the culture of Europe; Tsar Peter the Great sought to emulate Louis XIV, and French became the required language of the court. Offenders speaking Russian in the Tsar's presence had their beards cut off.

Opposite:

House Music *by Godert de Wedige portrays the Wintzler family in Antwerp in the year 1616. On the music stand of the exquisite virginal is a work by an unknown Italian composer, a completely legible work in five voices. The writing out in full of keyboard music was then still quite new.*

We also have seen that a planned dissonance was not only accepted, but actively sought. There is no such thing as an intolerable dissonance, provided it is resolved. At least that is how it has been in Western music until just recently. Just as life was thought to resolve itself in death, and an afterlife conceived in terms of heaven or bliss, so dissonance in music resolved itself, first to unison or the octave, later to the open fifth and fourth, and finally to the major or minor home chord. Courts of law exist to help resolve the dissonances of society, and, for many, faith can do the same for questions of the spirit. Music has the power to embody this ideal and to give it voice; it is one of music's noblest tasks. Music cannot offer literal realistic solutions, but what it does give can feel more real than any material satisfaction. Music embodies and expresses feelings and ideas which have been the heritage of humanity: the relationship of man to nature and to himself.

By 1600, after a century of exploration, new sea trade routes had been opened up to East and West. The Mediterranean, which had served Italy so well for so long, was no longer what its Latin name signifies, "the middle of the world." England had grown powerful under the Tudors and was now brilliant in Queen Elizabeth's last years. The complex, intertwined, intermarried Hapsburg family ruled many Germanic states, and their power extended westward to Flanders and south to Spain.

Even as the power of the Italian states began to fade, their music continued to influence the entire West, especially through the creation of a new form of entertainment which continues to attract huge audiences today: opera. Italy never dropped its love affair with the human voice, and opera arouses passions among Italians comparable only to those produced in other countries by soccer or boxing matches.

Why is it that this land, this Italian people, should have given the human voice its most melodic expression in song and in speech? Is it perhaps the warm climate, the volatile temperament which requires frequent emotional outlets? Or could it be the sense that life is but a play, and human beings set characters in inescapable roles? Whatever the reason, we recognize that the bright Mediterranean of clear skies and unpredictable seas, together with the experience of an ancient civilization, does not encourage illusions of perfection nor a fanatical determination to create an ideal society, come what may. Clear-headed and clear-spoken, the Latin peoples of Italy have always known there will be the rulers and the ruled, the sinning and the absolving, the builders and the dwellers, and that from time to time roles may alternate or be exchanged. Such an

attitude may not encourage a sense of duty, but it does produce great charitable initiatives.

Seized by the spirit of the theater, possessed by music, gifted beyond measure in all the arts and sciences, it was these people who made Grand Opera possible. The Catholic Mass itself is, in fact, a dramatic theatrical performance, and the leap between this and opera was not all that wide. Add to the blend the people's music—the madrigals, troubadour songs, popular pantomimes and mystery plays, along with the rapidly evolving techniques of counterpoint—and it is inevitable that a great man, one who breathes and feels the emotions of his fellow men, should give them voice in this new genre, the opera. That man was Claudio Monteverdi.

Born in Cremona in 1567, in that town where the first true violins had been made only two dozen years earlier by the Amatis, Monteverdi received thorough vocal training as a choirboy, learned the organ and many other instruments as well as the skills of composition. He published his first work, the *Sacrae Canticulae*, when he was only fifteen. Soon after, he entered the service of Vincenzo Gonzaga, Fourth Duke of Mantua, with whom he remained until 1612, the year of the Duke's death. It was here that Monteverdi came of age musically, creating masterworks which are still part of an active repertory. Almost singlehandedly he created a rage for opera beginning with *Orfeo* in 1607.

Monteverdi was forty when *Orfeo* was performed, and with that work he immediately came to the front rank of Western music. The Gonzaga family were proud of showing off the accomplishments of one of the most brilliant courts of Renaissance Italy, where fine artists and musicians flocked for recognition. *Orfeo* took Mantua by storm, becoming so famous throughout the land that the entire score was published immediately, the first time a work of art of this size was so honored. It was a major feat of the printer's art, still so new. Undoubtedly, a great many copies of the score were produced, but only a very few have survived. If so few copies remain of a work of this magnitude, it is little wonder that so

The courts and principalities of Europe vied with one another in the magnificence of their opulent parades, known as défilades, *which provided backstage employment for hundreds. Italy was at first the leader, but the form soon spread to all of Europe, as here in Holland. The practice survives in our own time at Mardi Gras and on days marking national independence.*

Monteverdi served the Gonzaga family for more than a decade. This portrait by Andrea Mantegna is of Duke Ludovico, grandfather to Vincenzo, for whom Monteverdi composed Orfeo.

much music of this age, extant only in the composer's original manuscript, has vanished. This is true also of several of Monteverdi's own later important stage works. But *Orfeo* paved the way for the development of opera and is the oldest work still included in the repertoire of major companies.

Orfeo triumphed because of the classic immediacy of its story, written by Alessandro Striggio the younger, whose father was a famed madrigalist, and because its text was set by a musical imagination acutely sensitive to the drama of sung words. Monteverdi was asked by the Duke to produce a second opera, and he set to work on *Arianna*. He had not finished it when his wife died after a long illness; Monteverdi was inconsolable, and the poignancy of his feeling is nowhere more evident than in the "Lament of Arianna." This declaimed song is in fact one of the few fragments of the opera to survive; its success was immense with the crowd of several thousand distinguished guests assembled by the Duke to hear the work in 1608. The "Lament" was soon sung all over Italy, the first truly popular operatic aria in history. Monteverdi had to make special arrangements of it to satisfy the demand.

Within a few years of the presentation of Monteverdi's *Orfeo*, opera houses were rising all over Italy in much the same manner as the cinemas of the West in the twenties and thirties. Nowhere were they more numerous than in Venice, where each year dozens of new works were performed, the more recent eclipsing the previous ones in splendor and popular acclaim. The prosperity of this city and these theaters made opera available to a paying public drawn from all classes. No longer were performances restricted to princely and ducal palaces; for the first time they became a popular entertainment held indoors. Opera remains one of the most popular entertainments in Italy; audiences are extremely exacting, particularly in the top gallery, demanding brilliance and intensity from their performers. Many a singer, not quite able to accomplish the musical acrobatics required, has suffered the shouts and whistles of a disappointed audience.

In 1613 Monteverdi moved to Venice, succeeding Gabrieli as director of music at St. Mark's. His fame was such that many masters from other countries travelled to Venice to meet him, notably Heinrich Schütz in 1628, who complimented Monteverdi by reworking some of his compositions and adding German texts. Monteverdi also evolved a theory of music which he called "A Second Musical Practice." Its impact can be traced all the way to England and Scandinavia. Monteverdi was equally inventive in his use of the orchestra. Already familiar with the work of the Gabrielis before he came to Venice, especially their brilliant use of wind and brass choirs, he introduced novel effects of special interest to string players. In his *Combattimento di Tancredi e Clorinda* he instructed the strings at certain points to put down the bow and pluck the string like a lute. This is now the familiar pizzicato, but for bowed strings it was such a new idea that Monteverdi had to write out his instructions in full. After *Orfeo*, Monteverdi used only bowed strings for his stage works, sometimes asking his musicians to play rapidly repeated notes, which we now call the tremolo, though in his music it has a hammered effect, intended to add excitement—sharper and more incisive.

Monteverdi's music is almost entirely vocal, as suited the taste of the day. Instruments were used to accompany voices, and sometimes for a dance or pantomime scene. The number and kinds of instruments would vary from work to work and even between performances, relying on the players available. Monteverdi's operas swept Europe over the next decades. In 1637 the first opera house in Venice opened its doors, the Teatro San Cassiano; Monteverdi was seventy, and lived for six more years. For this theater he wrote *Adone*, now lost, and his earlier works were revived with great success. Within the next sixty years, sixteen more

The canals of Venice retain their charm and still convey a sense of that age of musical glory of the seventeenth century, in a city where the sound of water, footsteps and voices replaces that of traffic.

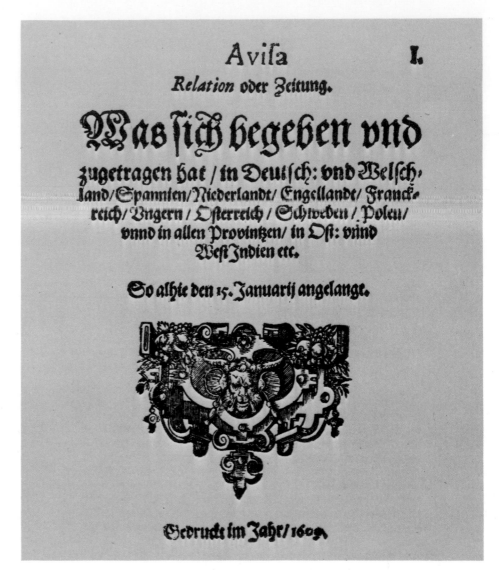

Aviſa I.

Relation oder Zeitung.

Was ſich begeben vnd

zugetragen hat / in Deutſch: vnd Welſch
land/Spannien/Niederlandt/Engellande/Franck
reich/Vngern / Oſterreich / Schweden / Polen/
vnnd in allen Provintzen/ in Oſt: vrind
Weſt Indien etc.

So alhie den 15. Januarij angelange.

Gedruckt im Jahr/ 1609.

News tearsheets were beginning to circulate, first in German-speaking lands, then in France and England, as literacy rose. This 1609 publication says "News: What is happening and unfolding in Germany, Spain, Netherlands, England, France, Hungary, Austria, Sweden, Poland, and in all the Provinces, the East, and West Indies, etc., today January 15."

opera houses opened in Venice, all dependent on public support and all successful. Opera was still presented in the homes of the wealthy, notably the palace of the Mocenigo family, and these private performances continued long after opera could be heard by a much wider audience.

Unfortunately, the high musical standards set by Monteverdi could not resist the pressure of popular taste. Spectacle became everything, for this was the heyday of the costume and scenic designers battling with the stage director and the prima donna for center stage. The prima donnas were always beloved by the public, and a soprano could order an opera written specifically to suit her taste and abilities. Even Monteverdi designed his deceptively simple melodic lines so that they could be ornamented according to the fancy and skill of each singer. We have a few indications in Monteverdi's works to show how this was done. In the great aria in which Orpheus charms the boatman, Charon, into letting him cross the River Styx, Monteverdi gives us the melody in two versions, the first unadorned, the other with the most elaborate twists and turns, repeated notes, catches of breath. These show clearly how far the purists were from the truth when insisting that old music be played plainly (though others today overdecorate fine melodies with absurd curlicues). Vocal decorations soon became more important than the melody.

Opera was from the beginning a social spectacle as well as a musical drama. The members of the court and the wealthier merchants were as intent on display as were the singers. The musical power of opera was irresistible, for nothing so potent had yet been seen or heard in the West. Opera is sometimes called the perfect combination of all the arts, but that is an open question for many, if for no other reason than that opera is so difficult to do well. Even devoted enthusiasts speak of those few miraculous nights in a lifetime when all the elements came together flawlessly. It is impossible to imagine the effect those first operas had on their public, or to recreate their style of performance.

Opera became possible in part because of the new security and wealth available to the small Italian city state, enabling the mounting of productions which would have been beyond the resources available to an isolated fortified castle. The opera public adored earthquakes, floods and fires on stage. The entire court of Neptune swimming suspended under water was not too much to ask. Composers vied with one another now to create vehicles for such effects.

These scenic effects were not restricted to the opera stage, for that matter. The people could on occasion catch glimpses of splendidly costumed open-air *défilades*, processions in allegorical costume, often on horseback, put on by the courts to impress their neighbors (and paid for by the people's taxes).

Opera was the bridge between the past and the future, helping to usher in the age we call Baroque in music, a style marked by strict forms and elaborate ornamentation. Musicians at first simply invented formulas and followed them but, like most entertainments, these operas were creations of the moment, serving their purpose and quickly forgotten. But they awakened a taste for novelty, for effect and drama, which spilled over into instrumental music, and here too Italy played a key role. It was in the opera house instrumental ensemble that the modern orchestra was molded, along with the classic quartet of strings: first and second violins, violas and cellos, with one or two double-basses for extra support. This ensemble began to be used for other purposes, to make music not as an accompaniment, but solely for its own sake.

In 1675 the Teatro San Germanico sul Reno in Venice possessed technical resources lavish beyond measure for the presentation of opera. Hordes of angels, gods and gladiators could be displayed amidst clouds of steam.

We sometimes use the phrase "pure music," and its implication of sanctity has not always been taken as a compliment. But the practice of pure music, not merely as a support for drama, dance or song, is extraordinarily recent. Of course, there had been solos for lute, portable organ or dulcimer. These usually took the form of short dance-like pieces, fast or slow, relying for their form on simple repetition, with variations introduced by the performer at his pleasure. From Italy once again, at

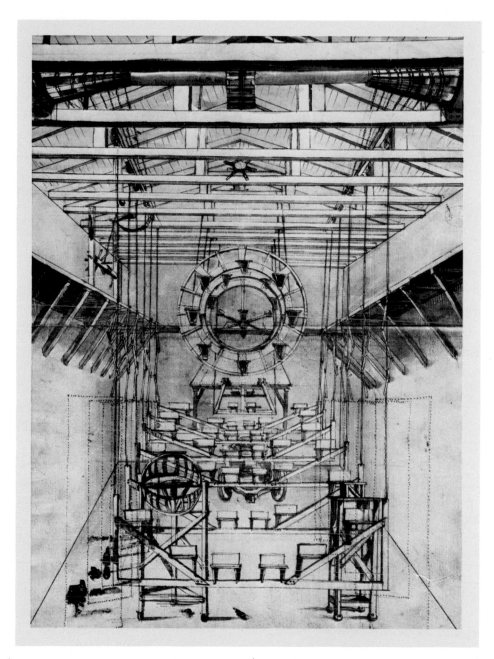

almost the same moment as the birth of opera, came two new instrumental forms of pure music: the sonata and the concerto. The word sonata means roughly "something played," and concerto means "something played by a group." What is significant to me is that neither word has any literal, dramatic or visual association. They are purely musical terms.

Both the sonata and the concerto were based on the position taken by the violin as the leader of the instrumental ensemble. Since Italy

The detailed stage construction sketch (anonymous) reveals how this impressive and expensive effect was achieved. It is the more surprising when one realizes that such works were intended to be seen for only a single season.

remained in love with the human voice, it is understandable that the violin should hold such an important place in the growth of Italian pure music. The violin was both louder and more flexible than most of the other instruments. Only the trumpet, and perhaps the horn, could drown it out, but these had no valves as yet, and were limited to the natural overtone series. There were models or crooks in all the common keys. Only the lighter *clarino*, a high soprano Baroque trumpet, could hope to keep up with the violin, with all the slides and ornaments which are its stock in trade, or match the violin's purity of tone, if not its vibrating warmth.

The early concerts of pure music took place not in public halls but mainly either in private salons or in church. Different forms of music grew for each, yielding the terms *sonata da camera* (chamber sonata) and *sonata da chiesa* (church sonata). It is worth remembering that for a long time the act of listening to music was a privilege conferred on rare occasions, and endowed with spiritual overtones. The first music societies were private groups with admission limited to initiates, accompanied by ceremonies of a religious character. There might also be competitions for the best new work or the outstanding performer. Members received medals which were their permanent ticket of admission. These medals were awarded only for merit, not for gold; they were cherished privileges. Thus there was a continuity of feeling between concerts given in private and those given in church.

For a time the two kinds of music took separate paths. The *sonata da camera* was basically a suite of dances, considered too frivolous for church—a form still in use in Bach's day. The *sonata da chiesa* was more dignified, contrasting stately movements with faster sections, displaying every resource of counterpoint. Both forms were parents to our present sonata, symphony, quartet and concerto. Sonatas began to pour out of Italy as abundantly as operas. We have the names of dozens of composers, of which a number have survived, thanks to their skill in writing for the violin. Arcangelo Corelli made the most vital, innovative contributions of the day. It was he who established the four movement convention for the sonata, and introduced the *concerto grosso*, in which a small group of soloists is contrasted with a larger ensemble. Born in Italy in 1653, he travelled to Germany and Paris, and was a friend of Farinelli, the celebrated castrato soprano. He settled in Rome in 1683, living at the palace of Cardinal Pietro Ottoboni, until his death in 1713, leaving an estate of great value and an immense collection of paintings.

The concerto pitting soloist against orchestra is really Corelli's invention, though works in that form by his successor Vivaldi are

closer in form to those of later times. It is in Corelli's music that the continuity of spirit between opera and sonata, between the vocal and instrumental, and finally between the world of the madrigal and of the symphony, is most apparent. There is a fluidity of decoration in his slow movements which calls on the performer to become an active partner in the creation of the work. Perhaps because he was a violinist, in all his vast output Arcangelo Corelli never wrote any music for the human voice.

The seventeenth century was also one of rapid scientific development, and we cannot leave music isolated from such happenings. In science as in music, new methods of investigation were taking over. It had been assumed that the universe revolved around the earth, and elaborate models were built to prove the theory. Men like Galileo Galilei (1564–1642) were evolving new concepts for the map of the heavens, chart-

Jan Steen's The Family Concert, *probably painted in the 1660s, expresses the joy of performing music at home.*

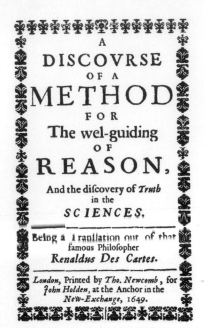

*The French philosopher René
Descartes had been living in
Holland for some time when
he wrote the* Discourse on
Reason *at Leyden in 1637. This
title page is from the first
English edition.*

*Adriaen van Ostaade's engrav-
ing of a singer, her violin
accompanist and a cheerful
companion dates from 1650.*

ing new movements for the planets. He proved that the earth was a planet,
that all the planets circled the sun. By 1610 he had perfected his telescope,
and word of this wonderful device spread quickly. The passion for
measurement became irresistible. Galileo was a danger to the church,
which eventually forced him to recant, but it was too late.

At institutions such as the University of Padua, students from all over
the Western world came to benefit from the latest in learning and
philosophy, leaving traces of their presence in the family insignia
painted on walls and ceilings. It was here, too, that the first full-fledged

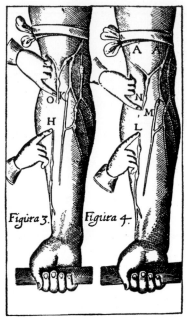

The circulation of the blood from William Harvey's classic study Exertatio Anatomica de Motu Cordis et Sanguinis *(1628), showing his experiment to demonstrate the valves in the veins of the arm.*

surgical teaching theater was built, extending the knowledge of the human body.

Amid the profusion of European language, culture and human traffic, French civilization and language were becoming acknowledged as the most scholarly, refined and courtly in the world. French began to replace Latin as the medium of international diplomacy and in all of Europe, from England to the Russia of Peter the Great, one was not considered educated unless one spoke French.

Fiddler-composers from Mantua, Venice, Cremona and other city-states travelled all over the West, bringing their music and their improved violins with them. One of them was Giovanni Battista Lully (in Italy, spelled Lulli). In 1642, then only a boy of ten, he followed bands of strolling players in Paris at carnival time, where he attracted the attention of a member of the King's court. Lully was first made a kitchen-boy to Anne Marie de Montpensier, the King's cousin. She admired his musical talent and put him in charge of her small band of violins.

The surgical operating and teaching theater at the University of Padua in Italy is one of the most perfectly preserved of all Renaissance scientific centers.

The Sun King, Louis XIV, was painted by Henri Testelin in 1667 when he was just twenty-nine. The occasion was the founding of the Academy of Sciences (detail).

In 1646 the king, Louis XIV, was only eight years old. He had inherited the crown on the death of his father three years earlier. By the time the king was a teenager, he was already creating what was to become the most celebrated court of Europe. He was so taken with Lully's playing that he recruited him as a member of *Les Vingt-quatre Violons du Roi*, the private royal ensemble. Lully was just six years older than the king. He

took the French name by which we know him, Jean Baptiste Lully, and
within a few years he had entirely reorganized *Les Vingt-quatre Violons*,
improving their skills, and making them internationally famous—all the
more remarkable since Lully was self-taught in composition and in the
violin.

After his marriage to his cousin, the Infanta Maria Theresa of Spain in
1660, Louis XIV set out to make his court the showplace of the Western
world. Having come to the throne so young, he had seven decades in
which to fulfill his dream. He called himself *Le Roi Soleil*, the Sun King,
around whom the rulers of other courts were to revolve like planets. Louis
XIV was inordinately fond of ballet, and took part in many himself. Lully
became ballet master and director, writing much of the music for these
spectacles, and began to consolidate his power while Paris was again
becoming the brilliant center of culture. Descartes had already produced
his treatises on geometry and reason, and coined the phrase, "I think,
therefore I am." Racine and Corneille were the King's leading dramatists—
the latter's *Le Cid* was probably the most influential play of the century
after those of Shakespeare.

*A performance of Lully's
Alceste, an opera-ballet, took
place in the courtyard of the
palace at Versailles in 1674. It
features a divided orchestra and
quantities of torches for illumination. The King, Queen
and Dauphin occupy the three
front-center seats of honor.*

Lully provided his operas and ballets at Versailles, outdoors when the weather allowed, to the accompaniment of gossip, intrigue and social chitchat. The tradition of the composer-performer in the permanent employ of a noble patron was already well established, but Lully eventually obtained from the King a monopoly on all of French opera and ballet. No theater in the nation could employ more than two singers and six violins without Lully's express permission. Lully could thus see to it that his own works predominated. He even carried the struggle for power to a confrontation with his chief rival for royal favor, France's master of comedy, Molière, for whose plays Lully had earlier written much incidental music. Lully and his musicians played for the King's private receptions, frequently in the Mars drawing room at Versailles, where the performers' gallery is now unfortunately walled off. Much of Lully's music has a stately quality, with a characteristic dotted rhythm, which Louis so admired and which soon became popular all over Europe as the French manner.

Around this time the West began its colonization of other lands in earnest. Spanish and Portuguese colonies in the New World and Africa were already well established, and a triangle for purposes of the slave trade was functioning efficiently. Ships would be outfitted in Spain or Portugal, sail down the west coast of Africa to pick up human cargo, cross the southern Atlantic to Brazil, and move from there to Central America and the West Indies. After her naval defeat by Britain in 1588 and the loss of the Armada, Spain was never again to be so potent. Later France and England vied with one another for control of many African territories, a struggle which continued into our own century. In 1626 France had established the Compagnie Normande in what is now Senegal, just above Guinea where the Portuguese had settled one hundred years earlier. The first important French colony was called Saint Louis, after the father of Louis XIV. Along with these western European forces came the missionaries, bringing with them not only the Bible, but the music which the church had so carefully nurtured.

Today it is odd to hear the Gregorian chant sung at the monastery of K'eur Moussa, not far from Saint Louis. In recent years the good Fathers have introduced the most popular local instruments, the *kora* and *balafon*, to accompany the Catholic service, which is sung in the main language, Wolof. Plainsong, born of the breath, gives resonance to sacred words, but studiously avoids the rhythms of the body. The melodies of the chant, fortunately for Christianity, fit easily with the chants and words of almost the whole world. At K'eur Moussa Father Dominic Cossa has succeeded in domesticating the rhythms and languages of various Senegalese cultures, the Wolof, Serer, Mandingo. He has achieved their integration into the Gregorian modal melodies and the sacred texts by avoiding the use of the harmonium, that ubiquitous portable organ which accompanied the missionaries everywhere. Instead, he has incorporated the sound and tuning of local instruments, the players improvising according to their custom, though fitting into the chant pattern. It may be a hybrid compromise, but it does not seek to impose Western harmony totally on the local musical sensibility. Generally, our chorded (harmonic) accompaniment, in whose absence the Westerner feels naked, insecure and unsupported, has been indiscriminately applied to much native music, in the same way that the European king or queen became the one temporal authority.

Senegal is a valid microcosm of what happened in many parts of the northern half of Africa at this time of colonization. The area was populated initially by Serer, Wolof and Peul tribes. By the eleventh century Islam was firmly established in the area. To the east the Mandingo kingdom flourished, and its capital city, Timbuktoo, became celebrated for its learning and wealth. The Moorish explorer, Ibn Batuta, came there from Granada in 1353. The Mandingos pushed west and took Senegal by force, completing the imposition of the Koran on the population. In turn, the Mandingos lost their huge kingdom to Morocco in 1591.

In the meantime the Portuguese had settled at the western end of the Casamance River, an area of fine land and lush forests. The French sought to drive them out, but the Dutch and English were also in the area, at Point Gorée and the mouth of the Senegal River. The situation was not resolved in favor of the French until the late eighteenth century, when they in turn pushed east, finally taking the decaying city of Timbuktoo in 1894. The independent Republic of Senegal was established in 1958, and Léopold Sédar Senghor became its president the next year. Senghor is acknowledged as one of Africa's outstanding poets and cultural leaders, a moving force behind the concept of negritude.

There is no music that can be called Senegalese. There are far too many tribes in the area for that, each with its own traditions. The *kora* and *balafon* belong more to the Wolof and Serer, whereas the Peul make much of a simple bowed string instrument called the *riti*. What is interesting is that Islam should have had so little influence on the music of these people, even though it has been the dominant religion for nearly a thousand years. Over eighty percent of Senegalese today are Moslem. The Catholic minority is centered mainly along the southern border, the Casamance district. Yet the influence of Western music throughout all of Senegal has been immense. We find it in the way instruments are tuned, in the turns of phrase used, even at times in the rhythm. Perhaps the explanation lies in the fact that for the Moslem, music is separated from worship. Music has no place in the mosque. The call of the muezzin and the chanting of the Koran are not defined by Moslems as music. The answer surely lies in the nature of Western harmony, whose power spread so quickly.

I believe that the rhythm of African music can never deteriorate under Western influences. Before the arrival of Western colonists, Africans had already developed a harmonic system in some ways similar to the European model; but the African approach to rhythm is unique. The complexities of beat grow out of the patterns established by many individuals, each keeping rigorously to his own particular subdivision of a given, usually long, measure. One may play a beat of seven, another of eleven, another of three or twenty, all meeting from time to time at a nodal point. The accented beats will vary, and each person must surrender his will to the one thing he must do.

The title page to a Venetian astronomy treatise (1537) shows the growing impact of navigation on measurement, long before the discoveries of Galileo.

In Indian music a sitar and tabla player may have the complete rhythm entirely in mind, but set up difficult counter-rhythms to one another, in which they may not come back together until the 49th beat or the 113th. Indian music is an intellectual mathematical process of the most extraordinary complexity. Players train from childhood to learn how to give natural expression to these difficult disciplines. By contrast, African rhythm demands of a player only that he keep to his own time and not be put off by the total effect. The principle migrated to Latin America, where the percussion of maracas, slip-stick and claves may all have a different rhythm in a samba or tango. At its strongest, this African music can build with overpowering force. Both players and listeners are mesmerized by its geometric proportion and multiplication.

The vigor of native dancing in Senegal is as infectious today as it has ever been; such sights greeted the arriving colonists who came in ever greater numbers in the 1600s from France, England and Spain.

Senegal is a land of many rivers stretching deep into the interior, excellent for transportation. It was a rich prize, well populated by skilled farmers, cattle traders and fishermen. They were much in demand as slaves. Moslems had been the first to export men from this area to the East, preying on some tribes with the help of others. Once Europeans arrived, the trade in slaves shifted to the New World.

Wherever they were sent, the slaves took their music with them. It may be that in parts of Brazil, Haiti or Venezuela, the traces of African music are closer to the time of the slave trade than anything heard in Senegal today. (The French spoken in Quebec is said to approximate the French of Huguenot times.) Moreover, in the New World slaves who had been rounded up from all over Africa tended to band together, reinforcing one another's traditions as they exchanged stories and songs. European immigrants to the New World were later to do the same. Music has always been one of the keys to memory.

The African musician is versatile and expected to be able to provide music for a wide diversity of occasions. The Dogons from the Niger say:

> When a musician sings or plays an instrument, he loses some of his vital forces which, through the sound, go to enrich the personality of the listener. In times of mourning especially, the funeral music is intended not only to ensure the reincarnation of the dead person's spiritual elements, but also to comfort the living in their sorrow. It is at the expense of the musician that this exchange takes place. That is why they are paid. They should also receive presents of food and drink accompanied by blessings and words of praise. These words and gifts replace the water that has been lost and moisten the dried up fats.

One of the most interesting of African traditions is that of the *griot*, a term which in many parts of West and Central Africa is considered equivalent in meaning to the word musician. But the role of the *griot* is more than that of an entertainer. His job is to renew the memories and emotions of past generations. In Senegal the *griot*'s chant is accompanied by the plucking of the *kora*, an instrument which has been known in Senegal for some three hundred years. The whole village assembles to hear its history told by the *griot*, and the bard historian doubtless adds an idea or two of his own from time to time, improving the history if he is well rewarded.

The *griot* also has some elements of the wandering medieval minstrel or king's jester, a man of learning and common sense paid to tell the truth, but always with wit. He must know everything that is going on, in private or public; truth is his weapon. Some may consider him a servant, a hired mouthpiece, a publicity agent, but the *griot* knows he is indispensable. In some parts of Africa the role of *griot* is reserved exclusively for women. The finest *griots* have become celebrated far beyond their immediate area. In the presence of such music, generations living and dead rub shoulders.

The role of *griot* is often a family way of life, the task passed from generation to generation. Or it may be passed on through the spirit of one

who has died, who now inhabits and inspires a new artist. At the funeral of a *griot*, an elder may cause the lifeless hand to bring forth sound from the precious instrument, inviting the newcomer to do the same. For an African musician, the idea of being inspired in this way is an unquestionable fact; the connection between music, magic and eternity is maintained, for through music we communicate with the spirit world. African musicians are often not even buried in the customary way; to plant such a body in the earth would render the earth barren. One of the common alternatives is to place the *griot*'s body inside the hollow trunk of a giant baobab tree. In Senegal, not long ago, such a tree-cemetery was found, filled to overflowing with bones.

The *kora* is a gentle instrument. It is played rather like the harp, but turned around, with the shortest strings furthest from the player. The straps circling the neck which hold the strings taut must be made very tight, thus making it difficult to tune. The manufacturer of a *kora* lavishes attention to the selection of the right gourd or calabash which he cuts in half. We might expect such care from a fiddle-maker from Cremona. There are twenty-one strings placed in two series, so that the

The kora *may also be played while being carried. Along with the xylophone-like* balafon, *it is virtually the national instrument of Senegal.*

strings may be played by right and left hand separately. Like all African musical instruments, the *kora* has been credited with magical powers, and there was a time when only an apprentice could watch how it was made. Even the musician who would play it was excluded from this holy process for fear of breaking the spell, and to protect the instrument maker's secrets. Yet to West Africans, the *kora* is also considered suitable to lead men into battle.

The Africans are right, music is magic; it puts us in touch with the spirits of the past, and also of the future. We create in our own image, and music is most genuine when it truly reflects who we are and how we feel. Music may be an individual act—the shepherd playing for himself and to his flock. It may be a small group—the village establishing a dance ceremony or communal song that distinguishes it from all other villages. It may be hordes of people—the civil rights marches in Washington, singing out their determination and solidarity, or the Jews facing extermination in concentration camps. Music is meditation; it is also action, a personal and a collective expression.

I am a violinist, or rather a musician who happens to have played the violin all his life. While in Senegal I had the occasion to try to play the *riti*, the bowed string of the Peul people. Yet I could not draw a proper tune from it at all, try as I might. It was quite extraordinary, for I understood the technique perfectly well. It is the same as with our four-string violin, except that the player can also use the thumb of the left hand on the string because the neck is so thin. I do not think the difference lies in the fact that both the strings and the bow are made from horsehair, whereas we use animal gut or metal for strings. The meaning of the music of the *riti* to a Peul musician belongs to him, not to me. The rhythm is exuberant and penetrating, and one tune in seven beats particularly caught my fancy. It was wonderful to see a violin reduced to its simplest components, a sound box with a movable bridge to adjust the pitch, the string simply tied down with a rope, the bow shaped like a medieval Western bow with a high curve. There was in the *riti*, in the sounds the musicians drew from it, a capacity for contentment with basic means, as opposed to the pride of control and domination. We have paid a high price for our pursuit of the maximum effects.

The bowed string is one of man's unique discoveries. It may have come to us from Persia and China more than a thousand years ago, but, like the drum, it became so widespread that its origin is lost. Stringed instruments are versatile. They are portable and come in a variety of sizes and shapes. We have already followed the *rebec* from the East to Spain, France and England; it is not the only parent to the violin in Europe. The Welsh

crwth may be descended from the Gothic *fidula*, which possibly came from Africa. Both the Hardanger fiddle from Norway and the Peking two-string instrument from China had their influence. The violin has set feet to dance and hearts to stir all over Europe, from China to Africa, to the blue mountains of America. These are all tough, durable instruments, for all their varied shapes. They survive sun and rain, good players and bad. They serve village dances as readily as they do court ceremonies.

The way to happiness, I feel, is to strive for the reconciliation of human achievement with the healing forces of nature. There is just such an achieved reconciliation in a well-made violin.

In the Middle Ages the alchemist's dream was to find a way of turning lead into gold. For musicians, the ideal for a very long time was to create an instrument that could sing like the human voice. The bowed string was the solution. Now at last the strings would be stroked, not plucked. But even after the medieval consort of viols had come into being, the search went on, for the tone of these early bowed instruments was gentle, hoarse and a little dull. Something was needed with more power and brilliance to cut through the noise of talk, the clatter of eating and the dancers' active feet. The answer came in the mid-1500s in Cremona and Brescia, towns lying some thirty miles apart in the province of Lombardy. There Andrea Amati and Gasparo dà Salo began turning out a new model of instrument far superior in power and purity of tone to the other bowed instruments of the day. It is pointless to ask which of the two men invented the violin. They simply applied all their craft to the handling of

Yehudi Menuhin encounters members of the Peul people of Senegal, whose most popular musical instrument is the riti, *a single-string bowed with a curved bow not unlike those used with medieval European viols.*

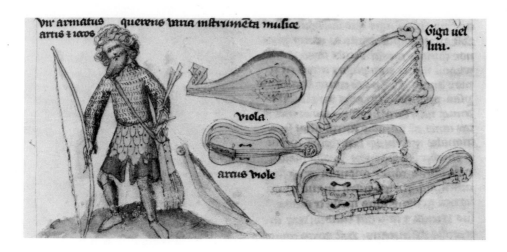

wood and varnish in the search for a better model because their customers demanded it. And they both discovered much the same answer at about the same time.

Andrea Amati produced sons and grandsons to carry on his work, as did his brother Nicolo, whose grandson of the same name became the teacher of Stradivari. Thus there are many outstanding instruments all bearing the name of Amati, but only a few by dà Salo. So celebrated were the Amati violins that to the end of the eighteenth century they remained the most desired of all, along with those by a celebrated Tyrolean maker, Jacobus Stainer. Johann Sebastian Bach performed on a Stainer violin, though Stradivari was making his unmatched instruments during Bach's lifetime. It appears that the Amatis were preferred for use in orchestras and chamber groups, whereas the Stainers made fine soloists shine the brighter. Two virtuosos turned the tide of opinion. At the end of the eighteenth century, Jean Baptiste Viotti in Paris and London championed the Stradivarius; Nicolò Paganini in the 1830s played an instrument by Guarneri del Gesù, so powerful in his hands it was known as "The Cannon."

The voice of the violin is individual, complex. Like our vocal chords, its strings vibrate. The violin's sound box can be the cavities of the chest, head and nose. The curious carved openings on either side of the bridge, called the f-holes, are like the mouth, though some would compare these features when defining the personality of the violin to the eyes in a human face. If God is said to have made man in His image, then surely man may be assumed to have made the violin in his image, rather in *her* image—for the violin is a beautiful goddess.

Is it any wonder that the sound of a violin, like our beloved's voice, can send shivers up our spines and grip our hearts? My feeling is that only a

A medieval manuscript already shows the awareness of a connection between the hunting bow and the family of stringed instruments.

very few instrument makers have the genius and the patience to master the many skills which must be so carefully coordinated in the making of a great violin. It is a task that is of course defeated by mass production. Fortunately, there exist a few fine contemporary violin makers of the calibre of Marino Capicchioni, David Wiebe, Premysl Spidlen and the late Bert Smith.

Virtually all the pitched instruments existed in families, already given the names which relate to the voice: soprano, alto, tenor, bass. When the violin was young it mixed easily with viols, lutes, bandoras, citterns, shawms, recorders. Renaissance musicians called a single family, playing as a group, a consort, from which we get the modern word concert. Both words are derived from the Latin for "companionship." Mixed groups were called "broken consorts." The refinement and elegance of the violin, its perfection of form, are interesting to compare with others of its family. It needs no extra resonating "sympathetic" strings lying just below the bowed or plucked ones, because the sound box is such a perfect amplifier. It is even difficult to say whether the wonderful school of Italian violin music came into being because of the instrument, or the other way around. To me this most feminine of string instruments is an object to cradle and to caress. It responds to the player's slightest touch, and can become quite cross with him if he is not gentle and understanding. In this it is quite unlike the piano. They are opposite breeds, and it is incomprehensible to me that anyone could describe the piano as feminine, with its keyboard like a bared denture! The harpsichord is a delicate instrument—not to speak of the clavichord—but the piano is a three-legged monster.

Early Italian composers applied what they knew about writing for voices quite naturally to the bowed string. Certain performers developed the technique of playing these instruments in ways to stimulate a composer's imagination. Alessandro Striggio, father of Monteverdi's librettist, reputedly amazed his listeners in the late 1500s by being able to play full four-part harmony simultaneously on a single instrument. This kind of playing came into its own with the successors to Corelli, among them Pietro Locatelli and Giuseppe Tartini, and also Corelli's contemporary, Giuseppe Torelli, who settled in Dresden, bringing the Italian violin style to the German courts, influencing Bach, whose solo sonatas and partitas exploit the full potential of the solo violin in all its technical virtuosity, while remaining towering works of music.

Two artists made the very best violins ever; Antonio Stradivari and Bartolomeo Giuseppe Guarneri del Gesù. Sometimes they are known by the Latin versions of their names, which they used themselves when they signed and dated slips of paper to glue inside the backs of their instruments: Stradivarius and Guarnerius. Del Gesù is so named because he dedicated all his violins to Jesus, right on the label.

Stradivari made over one thousand violins by his own hand, as well as many violas, cellos and basses. The earliest we have is dated 1666, the year of the Great Fire of London. Stradivari was twenty-two then, still apprenticed to Nicolo Amati. The last is dated 1737, the year of his death at the age of ninety-three. It is the longest violin-making career on record, seventy-one years, and the greatest. His two sons, Giacomo and Omobono, carried on his work, but they died five and six years after the old man. Their instruments are very fine, but Antonio's are better. The very first Stradivarius I ever owned is still with me. It is known as the Prince Khevenhüller, after one of its most distinguished owners, an aristocrat of Austro-Hungarian lineage. Almost all the greatest violins have names like that, just as a fine race horse is called by its given name. By such names, violinists know immediately where and when a violin was made. Stradivari was almost ninety when he made the Prince Khevenhüller. I was twelve when I first played it, and it was to be my steady companion.

Recently I fell in love with another Stradivarius called the Soil. It is one of a pair owned by the Belgian consul in Moscow at the end of the last century, and both still carry his name. Mine was made in 1714 when Stradivari was seventy and at the absolute peak of his powers. It has brilliance and body which make it ideal for concert performances and for most solo work, whereas the Prince Khevenhüller now seems to me wonderful in chamber music. Playing a Strad is a great and unforgiving discipline. You do not dare betray it. The slightest excess or miscalculation is heard immediately by the player, and if he strays only a shade further off it will be noticed by the audience.

I played for quite a time on a violin by Guarneri del Gesù during my very first American tour in 1928. About Guarneri del Gesù we know surprisingly little, considering he came after Antonio Stradivari, and that the Guarneri family was by that time far better known. It was del Gesù's grandfather, Andrea Guarneri, born in 1626, who founded the dynasty. Apprenticed to Nicolo Amati at the age of ten, the first violin known to be of his hand is dated two years later. By the time Antonio Stradivari came to the Amati workshop, Andrea Guarneri was already successfully established as a master in his own right. His son was also a fine craftsman, but is known today far more for being the father of Guarneri del Gesù. Del Gesù was born in August 1698, a few months before his grandfather Andrea died. He was apprenticed to his father, but set out as a young man to make his own way. That way seems to have been occupied in part by drink, women and high living. We see great variations in the quality of his work in these years. He did not maintain the impeccable standard of

The skills of instrument making improved rapidly in the eighteenth century, as the demand for larger and more resonant, well-tuned ensembles increased. This maker of wind instruments carries a work-bench, hatchet, borer and saw, as well as an oboe, bassoon, zinke and other instruments of his trade.

Stradivari. Some of del Gesù's violins look almost careless, but always genial—each one has a unique character. The f-holes are hardly graceful, and the left and right sides are not always perfectly symmetrical, although accoustically the balance is ideal, and their sound is extraordinary. Del Gesù may have been exuberant in his life as he was unconventional in his workmanship, but his achievement may be heard in the playing. The Guarneri del Gesù at its best is a magnificent instrument. Whatever I have to give, it can take and improve on it. I can lose myself in it without restraint. For the music of the romantic repertory, it cannot be surpassed. After owning two Guarneri del Gesù, one of 1748 and one of 1730, the Ebersholt, now in the hands of a collector, I have finally acquired the most beautiful of all, the Lord Wilton 1742. This outstanding instrument is to the life work of Guarneri what my Soil 1714 is to Stradivari.

Guarneri del Gesù died in 1744, a year after the second of the Stradivari sons. His father had died four years earlier. Within less than a decade, the five finest violin makers of their age had perished. With them went the glory of Cremona. Violins were still made there, of course. They still are. But the secrets vanished with the standard bearers. The varnish and its exact composition have never been duplicated and neither has the process of aging the instrument. A violin might hang on a hook in the Stradivari roof-top veranda for years before it was considered ready for sale. The masters of Cremona achieved their results through extraordinary patience and intuition. Each violin was made to its own specifications, the right shape and thickness being found in the very grain and life of the wood. Decoration aside, the violin is made up of some eighty or more separate pieces. The top is usually pine or spruce, for strength. We refer to it as the belly. The sides and back are curly maple, if the maker can afford it, or poplar, lime or beechwood if he can't. In the great days of Cremona, some of the finest maple came from Venice. The sides of a violin may be reinforced with willow, inside their graceful curves. The bridge is maple, the fingerboard ebony. Many of Stradivari's instruments are exquisitely decorated with inlaid woods and mother of pearl. This is in the lutemaker's tradition, for instruments made for princely purchasers were expected to appeal to the eye as well as to the hand. It was also a matter of taste. Some violin makers found joy in decorating their instruments lavishly. Others, like del Gesù, seemed content to fit them together and send them on their way without the fancy dress.

In my love of the violin, which is the greatest, most mysterious achievement of the instrument maker's art, I yield pride of place only to the human voice. The keyboard may have had everything to do with the perfection of harmony, but the violin is at the very core of the creation of what we have come to call classical music.

Plain or fancy, the violin was also part of the life exported to the New World by the French and English, who were now settling in large numbers in North America. The Virginia Colony of 1607 and that in Massachusetts of 1620 were the Pilgrim strongholds, but by 1608, the French, under Champlain, pushed past the St. Lawrence into the interior, and then swept south. There was a continuing exchange of music between French and English, in contrast to the almost ceaseless conflict over control of the territory, a battle which also went on in Africa. Both continents were also areas of missionary zeal. The colonists for the most part held onto music which they knew from the Old World, rather than creating their own. A surprising amount of the music the French farmers and trappers brought with them is still sung and played to this day, especially in the province of Quebec, while the game song "Alouette, Gentille Alouette" is probably known to every North American school-child. The settlement of this vast continent, with its cruel extremes of temperature, was quite a different challenge from that of Africa. The proud Indians were on home ground and could not be enslaved. The colonists' response over the ensuing two centuries was steadily to exterminate these original rightful inhabitants, whose traditions and way of life were swept aside as if valueless. By 1682, the French colonists had occupied and claimed the entire Mississippi valley to the Gulf of Mexico, and in honor of Louis XIV, the Sun King, they named it Louisiana. French colonies exist on the gulf still; the inhabitants, now called Cajuns, are descendants of the Acadians who first settled in Nova Scotia and were subsequently exiled by the English.

The English had been through a great political upheaval during the first part of the seventeenth century, which was also the time of the Thirty Years War (1618-1648). English music had by this time been flourishing for a thousand years, and had developed a great choral tradition under such masters as Thomas Tallis, William Byrd and Orlando Gibbons. There was a setback under Cromwell, some of whose followers, in their zeal, smashed the organ pipes at the great cathedrals in Chichester, Canterbury, Norwich and Winchester. These great instruments were considered to be an invention of Satan. Cromwell suppressed the theater, the maypole, horse races and cockfights; but he did not intend to injure the music of the church, and intervened to save the organs at Ely and Lincoln, and the beautiful one at Magdalen College in Oxford.

As secular music began to return slowly to favor, the publisher John Playford could by 1652 profitably print airs and dances for the violin for the delight of private musical enthusiasts at home. Efforts to organize the printing of music in England had been tried earlier by Tallis, Byrd and Gibbons, all members of the Chapel Royal; but they failed. By the time

Playford went into business, the cost of printing music had finally become reasonable. His collection, *The English Dancing Master,* is not only a treasure-house of folk and popular music of the day, but it gives us a clear idea of the style of violin playing that prevailed. These tunes were meant to suit the fiddle, especially the dancing master's little portable version, called the *pochette.*

As the seventeenth century drew to a close, no figure better represents the changes that were taking place in Western music than did Henry Purcell, whom many still call the greatest of English composers. Purcell was probably born in 1659, a year after the death of Oliver Cromwell. Westminster, where the Purcells lived, suffered terribly in the plague and fire, and the family may have taken refuge from the flames in the waters of the Thames nearby, along with so many of its neighbors. Young Henry's father, also called Henry, was himself a busy musician, master of choristers at Westminster Abbey and a composer to His Majesty's violins, a duty he was soon to share with Pelham Humfrey. King Charles II had sent young Humfrey, whose gifts were noticed early, to the much admired court of Louis XIV to train under Lully and others. Samuel Pepys tells us he came back in 1664 at seventeen "an absolute little Monsewer." The Purcells may have rejected such extravagant behavior, but they could not escape the French and Italian music Humfrey brought back with him, which gradually became the rage of Restoration England.

An unknown painter depicted the Great Fire of London which devastated so much of the city in 1666.

Young Henry Purcell was initiated into the complete musical life right from boyhood. It was typical of the age that the musicians were expected to be skilled in several instruments, able to repair them, and to compose and teach besides. Henry's talent showed early, for he was a superb boy soprano who was made a member of the Chapel Royal before the age of ten. His choirmaster was Captain Henry Cooke, himself considered one of the finest singers in England. Cooke died in 1672 and was succeeded by Pelham Humfrey, who must certainly have taught Purcell and the other boys the "better" music from abroad. Purcell's voice broke the next year and he left the choir, taking with him, as was customary, his royal livery and thirty pounds. He quickly found employment as assistant keeper,

Henry Purcell is at the height of his powers in this celebrated portrait, done in the early 1690s, a few short years before the composer's death.

maker, repairer and tuner of the regals, organs, virginals, flutes and recorders to His Majesty; he worked without pay for John Hingston, and cared for instruments not only at the Chapel Royal but at Whitehall, Hampton Court and Windsor. Maintaining a number of organs was also one of the chores, and within a year Purcell was entrusted with the tuning of the organ at Westminster. At eighteen he was invited to join his father as a composer to the King's violins. This may seem precocious now, but it was not unusual then. Careers often began early and ended early; Purcell's was no exception. The early death of Pelham Humfrey in 1674 enabled Purcell to become King's composer at the age of only twenty-seven.

Henry Purcell knew and admired Italian music greatly, as is made abundantly clear in the preface he wrote for his first collection of trio sonatas:

> Its author has faithfully endeavored a just imitation of the most famed Italian Masters, principally to bring the seriousness and gravity of that sort of music into vogue, and reputation among our countrymen, whose humor, 'tis time now, should begin to loathe the levity and balladry of our neighbors.

That last remark was a dig at the French manner which Charles II so admired; Purcell did not mean to put down the English tradition, which he knew and loved. After he became organist and choirmaster at Westminster, he kept up the established practice of writing anthems, welcome songs, catches and glees. English music was still governed by the human voice, a glory of the Renaissance which held its own far longer in England than on the continent. Even Purcell's works for strings, his fantasias and chaconnes, show a concern for the writing of every part which belongs to this tradition.

Purcell also wrote much glorious music for the theater, and it is instructive to compare this with the music of Lully. The French master paid attention to the top line and the bass, rather like Monteverdi, and let his assistants fill in the harmony. Purcell wrote out all his own inner parts, and each one makes itself felt, each player contributes his share. Any viola player who has performed this music will admit how much more satisfying it is for him than a number of more celebrated works of the Italian Baroque, whose inner parts are little more than filler. In this respect, Purcell can be compared to Bach.

What I especially admire in Purcell is his unconventional mind and his freedom of phrasing. Purcell arrives on the scene by the time the bar line had regimented Western music into a stable series of two, three or four beats to the measure. The beauty of Purcell is that he knows how to ignore the bar line. It never impedes his flow and is merely a convenience, not a mathematical division. His harmony is exceptionally resourceful, and you have to look to Bach to find his match. That powerful effect, the suspended dissonant note, brought to such intensity in Italy by the Gabrielis, Monteverdi, and Gesualdo, is multiplied by Purcell. He can arrange a series of suspensions in different voices, each of whose resolutions intensifies the emotional effect of the whole, while lending nobility and force to the rhythm. Purcell gives you surprises in his harmony, though it is more correct to speak of it as counterpoint, by not taking a suspension to its expected resolution but around the corner to another vista. He will shift tempo in the middle of a movement for dramatic contrast, and then not return to the original beat. He will devise one rhythm in the bass in an odd number, deliberately forcing the upper voices to free themselves from regimentation. It only seems to refresh his inspiration, and ours.

For a composer who so loved the voice, it is curious that Purcell wrote only one opera; but that one is a supreme masterpiece which still holds the stage today. It is *Dido and Aeneas*, and this is music that does not age. It displays all Purcell's harmonic and instrumental skill, his gift for original melody, his feeling for text and purity of style. All the more remarkable is its durability. It was written on commission from a girl's boarding school in Chelsea, where it was first given. In Purcell's day music was usually written for special occasions and practical uses. The idea of music for its own sake, written simply because it was what the composer wanted to say, was another hundred years off. Purcell's sonatas were intended for use by music lovers gathered at home.

The first performer to sing Dido was a teenage girl, and probably so was her lover Aeneas (a reversal of the Shakespearean practice of having women's roles played by boys). There are many marvels in *Dido and Aeneas*, such as the thunder and lightning scene (which he labels "horrid music"), or the syncopation of the chorus "Fear no danger to ensue." There are also moments derived from French or Italian convention that work less well. But in all of music there is no more moving moment than Dido's farewell. It is a scene which unfolds with consummate musical and dramatic force.

Dido stabs herself, and the chorus, which earlier prepared us to endure this final tragedy, twice sings a lament for the dead Queen, comforting her and us, rather like the final chorus in Bach's *St. Matthew Passion*. The lament of Dido is a supreme achievement, a worthy successor to Monteverdi's "Lament of Arianna" written eighty years before. Its construction is unusual, the bass carrying a five-bar repeated pattern, against which the melody moves flexibly, achieving a continuous sense of forward thrust.

Henry Purcell died in 1695 at the age of thirty-six, and was much lamented. England did not realize it, but with Purcell's passing the native-born English composer was to go into a substantial eclipse for some two hundred years. This does not mean that there were no composers, for Thomas Arne, William Boyce and, of course, Sir Arthur Sullivan, among many, are still known today; but they are not of Purcell's stature. Moreover, into English music now came George Frideric Handel (the spelling with which he always signed himself), and for more than forty years it was his sound, his style, which dominated English musical life.

Music in England had by this time become more public. In 1699 the Playfords had introduced concerts three times a week in a London coffee house. Until then, concerts had been home affairs, chiefly for the delectation of the players. The idea of a paying public for concerts was new, though operas were doing well. The coffee house concerts caught on, first in England, later on the continent, and were gaining ground

The Canadian alto Maureen Forrester enacts the role of Dido, Queen of Carthage, for the television series The Music of Man.

quickly by the time Handel arrived in London in 1711. Born in 1685, George Frideric Handel was equipped, like Purcell, with fabulous technique, having studied all the latest Italian models. He was an able violinist, a member of the opera orchestra in Hamburg under Reinhard Keiser, the father of German opera. Handel was not yet twenty when he wrote his first opera there, taking over a commission in which Keiser had lost interest. *Almira* was so successful that Keiser quickly realized how strong a rival he had sitting among his second fiddles. He needn't have worried unduly, for the love of Italy soon took over, and at twenty-two Handel was in Florence courting the Medici, and then in Venice where his opera *Agrippina* took the city by storm.

Other changes were coming over Europe, and the key year was 1714–15. Queen Anne died and the British House of Stuart came to an end. George I

The London of Handel's day is splendidly rendered by his contemporary William Hogarth (1741).

A fireworks display by the Duke of Richmond on the Thames in Whitehall celebrated the peace of Aix la Chappelle in May 1749. Handel composed the Royal Fireworks music for this event.

arrived to establish the German house of Hanover as rulers of England. The new King barely spoke English. Then in France, Louis XIV died and was succeeded by his great-grandson. The way was being paved for the French Revolution. German influence in English music and affairs cannot be underestimated, but Handel would have been formidable at any time. His back was so broad, as it were, no one could see past him. Handel wanted nothing more than to become an English country gentleman, and promptly mastered both language and manners. He was soon taking investment advice from one of the best stockbrokers in London.

Handel could not help but be impressed by the strength of the English choral tradition. He took possession of it and with remarkable swiftness altered the English musical landscape. In addition to turning out forty operas in the next thirty years, he also wrote dozens of sonatas, concertos, cantatas and duets, and the *Water Music*. England offered the kind of society able to support Handel's lavish dramatic style, and his operas were wildly popular. Handel had been his own opera producer, and he faced financial difficulties when his audiences turned fickle, preferring comic opera and the tart tunes of *The Beggar's Opera*. He extricated himself by his canny handling of his shareholdings. When the famous South Sea Company failed in 1720, in which hundreds, including George II, lost huge sums, Handel had managed to sell all his shares just a week before the crash.

After 1741 Handel wrote no more operas, recovering his musical standing through the English love of choral singing. He had already written several oratorios on Old Testament texts, and these had done well in Ireland. In 1742 in Dublin, he produced *The Messiah* and upon its performance in London, the English were once again his until the end of his life, in 1758. The German presence in English music remained unbroken, for Handel was succeeded in public favor by Johann Christian Bach, youngest son of the Leipzig master, and by the 1790s the symphonies of Josef Haydn were the talk of London.

The Renaissance to all intents and purposes was over. With its waning, the center of political and musical power moved northwards. Yet, as the seventeenth century gave Western civilization its control over new territories and scientific method, so in music it provided the composers with full control over all the technical and artistic resources of the medium, the instrumental and composing skills of harmony and counterpoint needed to achieve the ultimate heights that were reached in the eighteenth and nineteenth centuries by Bach, Mozart and Beethoven. Western music had come of age. The music of Handel is frequently joyous, an affirmation of life, as in the "Hallelujah Chorus" from *The Messiah*. It is also a celebration of his own skills and of the achievements of Western music itself.

Vivaldi, Bach, Mozart, Haydn, Beethoven and Schubert establish music as an idiom commonly understood throughout the Western World. The production of the towering masterpieces is begun, works which continue to dominate our present-day concerts. Bach establishes the tempered scale and perfects the art of counterpoint; Mozart speaks of human passion with a last gesture of elegant restraint; Beethoven announces the composer as creator of his own personal idiom; Schubert addresses the inner man.

4. The Age of the Composer

WE HAVE SEEN that the evolution of the very techniques by which composers are able to function took several hundreds of years, beginning with the flowering of harmony through the Middle Ages and the Renaissance. As we enter the eighteenth century, in music as in world affairs, the period of Western exploration and exploitation of new territories was beginning to give way to a consolidation of knowledge gained and battles won. It was also a time when the many voices of the people began to demand a hearing. England had established the principle of a constitutional monarchy with her Glorious Revolution of 1688, and some one hundred years later France and America were to abolish and repudiate monarchy altogether. The composer began to speak increasingly for the larger mass of the people throughout this period, whether in the noble, unifying voice of Bach or the proud, defiant one of Beethoven. It is also in this century that we leave behind a society built around the great courts and kingdoms, moving toward one which relies on individual initiative. It is natural enough that the composer should be part and parcel of this gradual transformation.

The seeds of change can be seen in Venice, for this city of wealth and diversity, founded upon the sea and its commerce, was a symbol of Italy's dominance over Western music during most of the Renaissance. Toward the end of the seventeenth century, as the Baroque era was dawning, power was moving north and Venice was in the sunset of her world influence. Here in 1678 one of the last of the long line of outstanding Venetian musician-composers was born, Antonio Vivaldi.

Opposite:
The splendor of a Venetian concert by the young ladies of the Ospedale Santa Maria de la Pieta, trained by Antonio Vivaldi, is preserved for us in the painting by Guardi.

Of all my illustrious predecessors, perhaps none was more gifted or enviable than the Venetian violinist, Antonio Vivaldi. The son of a brilliant and well-known violinist, he started his virtuoso career at an early age. He was an ordained priest at the age of twenty-five, known as the "Red Priest," in those days a benign title referring only to the color of his hair. He was entrusted with a musical seminary for young, orphaned illegitimate girls, the Ospedale Santa Maria de la Pieta. These young women became the most proficient and well-known instrumentalists and singers of their day. They even played the bassoon and the double bass, not to speak of conducting the orchestra with elegance and precision. For these inspiring young women, Vivaldi composed no less than five hundred concertos and symphonies, and innumerable other works of a musicality and verve, charm and warmth which delight us today as much as they did his devoted wards and his enthusiastic audiences.

Vivaldi, a Venetian, inevitably composed a great many operas as well, which are today virtually forgotten, though one or two have finally appeared on recordings. Toward the end of his life, as his music was fading from favor in Venice, and hearing that he was known to the Hapsburg emperor, Charles VI, Vivaldi travelled to Vienna hoping to find fresh employment. Soon after he arrived, the Emperor died, and the next year, in 1741, Vivaldi also died and was buried in Vienna, far from the scene of his triumphs. His music was to lie neglected for two hundred years, until the response to passion tempered by order brought him back to public favor. It was a rebirth which would have surprised nobody more than Vivaldi himself, for he wrote his music for immediate consumption rather than for posterity, a point of view which only began to change with Beethoven.

The violin and the singing voice were Vivaldi's chief means of expression, as they had been throughout the long evolution of Western music since the Middle Ages. Many composers owe a debt to Vivaldi, beginning with Bach, who adapted and rewrote many of his concertos. Later, Mozart and Mendelssohn acknowledged his influence. Vivaldi is the champion of emotion immediately translated into pure melody. But the violin was also nearing the end of its leadership role in Western music.

Although the violin dominated the music of the Baroque, as the voice had done in the Renaissance, the keyboard represented a unique resource for the composer. It was a research tool, a means of testing and measuring musical ideas. In the seventeenth century, it also became an instrument for highly skilled improvisation, especially in the hands of such northern organists as Pachelbel and Buxtehude. In the eighteenth century, the

harpsichord began to take over from the violin as leader, determining dynamics, tempo and harmony. Within the compass of ten fingers, the keyboard performer held the whole gamut of separate melodic lines, counterpoint and rhythm—little wonder that the Western composer usually has been a pianist also. With the advent of the keyboard, the violinist was demoted, intellectually and creatively; and as political and musical influence moved north, the keyboard was on the rise, along with the music of the Germanic culture, a music of discipline and order, premeditation and power.

By now, music in the West had become an interchangeable commodity, with musicians and composers everywhere adopting each other's style. Handel's music is a consummate blend of German, Italian, English and even French idioms. It was in its popular forms that music in German lands retained a local flavor, a quaint turn of phrase, which varied like the dialects from area to area. It seems to have been a way of holding onto the past, even as a national spirit was beginning to emerge. We can hear it still in the traditional dance music of such districts of Switzerland as

The Baroque painter Canaletto gave us many impressive views of Venice, but none reveals more vividly the pageantry of processions by waterway on the feast days. The gondolas are as lavishly outfitted as were the floats of the défilades of Renaissance times.

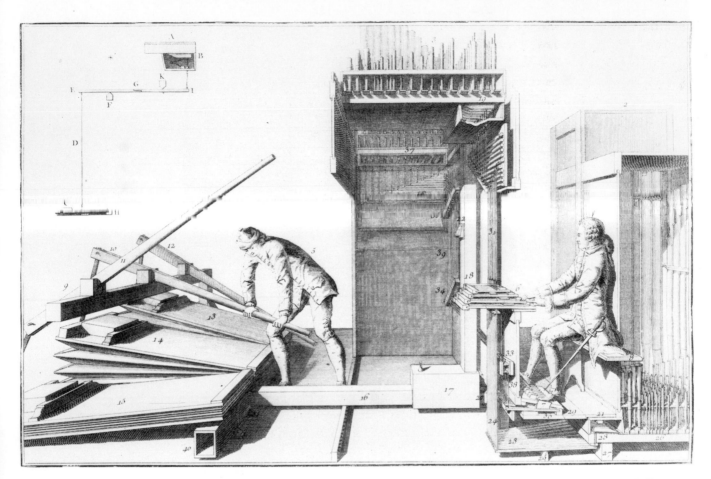

Appenzell, one of the most conservative in that nation of fiercely independent cantons, located near St. Gallen, whose monastery is one of the oldest and most eminent seats of learning in all of Europe.

We have seen that the concept of harmony evolved slowly out of rules for the agreement of separate voices. No manifestation of harmony is more impressive than the resonance of a great church organ. In parish churches from the province of Casamance in Senegal to Oka in Quebec is to be heard that unique sound, the sound of harmony.

This is the great Western musical achievement, a multitude of voices each carrying its own melody, yet sounding together as one. Perhaps the origins of that harmony lie far back in the medley of races moving across the Eurasian continent, following the setting sun, only to find themselves trapped in the European peninsula, each clamoring to be heard in its own tongue, yet having also to learn how to coexist. Not for a long time had such a diversity of cultures met in so small a space. For Western music it meant that sooner or later a truly universal spokesman would appear, and for me that man is Johann Sebastian Bach, composer, organist, violinist, teacher, theorist, and servant of God.

Bach has passion as well as serenity, for in his day religion was the center of the life of sentiment. Biblical events were seen as symbols, replicas of events in the daily lives of people who were truly in love with the life of Christ. The birth of every child was to be compared with His pain and sorrow, His exaltation and resurrection, His love. The passion of Bach's music is the passion of humanity. It is not music which says, "I feel, I hurt, I suffer"; it says, "We feel, we hurt, we suffer—and we accept."

In the same way that language was becoming a unifying factor amongst the Germanic peoples, composers like Johann Sebastian Bach were narrowing the gap between the music of their church and that of the people. The *Brandenburg* Concerti, evolving largely from folk dances, are a good example of that evolution. Bach was a German, a devout Lutheran, but if ever there was music in the world that can be described as belonging to all time, to my mind that of Bach is first in line. He is a servant of music, but he is also its sovereign.

One might say that the Bachs were almost the *griots* of northern Germany. What other family has produced a larger number of eminent composer-performers over so long a period? The family was of pure German stock, although some of its members may have lived in Hungary during the Middle Ages. Pablo Casals used to say he was sure there was gypsy blood in Bach, such is the inspired passion in his improvised fantasies. The father, uncles, grandfather and great uncles were all musicians, as were Bach's cousins, sons, nephews. Only nine of his twenty children survived him. The influence of the Bach family lies at the heart of the formation of German musical taste, reflecting the time when the name of Bach had become almost synonymous with music throughout northern Germany.

Johann Sebastian Bach was the clan's greatest product. Like Henry Purcell, he was a complete all-round musician. He too started as a choirboy, reputedly possessing one of the finest, truest soprano voices anywhere in Saxony. By the time he was eighteen he was making his living as a violinist and organist. His life is actually rather uneventful. There were none of the scenes of triumph, as with Handel in England. He was a hired court musician for twenty years, applying at last for the post of head of music and education at St. Thomas School in Leipzig. Bach won the job, but he was the third choice, selected only after two others had turned it down. He kept the job for the rest of his life. For his acceptance test he had offered the city fathers no less than his *St. John Passion*, which

they considered a little stodgy and old-fashioned. In a way they were right, for Bach knew and admired the music of many older composers, notably Cabezon, Lassus and Palestrina, by then considered antique.

We have the benefit of hindsight; we know that with Bach we are dealing with a giant. We must not blame the good burghers of Leipzig for failing to recognize a miracle. For one thing, in his day Bach's style was considered heavy compared to the Italian and French. And when he came to the St. Thomas School, much of his greatest work was still to come. Besides, he was famous as a performer and scholar, but as a teacher he was an unknown quantity. What could he do with five dozen boys, aged eleven to seventeen, with whom he was expected to provide the music for Sunday services the year round in four churches? Actually, the city fathers need not have looked further than the job Bach was doing with his own sons. Nowhere is his teaching skill more evident. He gave them a profession with which they could make an honest living and bring pleasure to their employers, a life of service in the best sense. Karl Philipp Emmanuel Bach, the second son, became attached to the court of Frederick the Great in Berlin. Despite his fame and wealth, he remained devoted to his father's memory, and it is thanks to his care that a great many of Sebastian's scores have survived. Johann Christian Bach, the youngest son, became the darling of London after Handel. When Mozart

first speaks of the Great Mr. Bach, it is to Johann Christian he is referring, for as a boy he sat on his knee to play duets. Christian Bach was ruined trying to maintain the production of his operas, unfortunately not possessing Handel's superior flair for wise speculation in the market.

The sons of Johann Sebastian Bach helped to train another generation of musicians, as the father had trained them and so many of their peers. The impact of Bach's teaching is only now being fully recognized. Bach is a perfect example of what Western music had been moving towards for five hundred years. Here is a composer-performer who can do anything with his material that he pleases. He can take simple dance rhythms and turn them into elaborate suites or variations. He can turn his themes upside down, inside out, backwards and sideways, as he delights to do in the fugues. He can combine many independent voices, each heard clearly, as in the opening chorus of the *St. Matthew Passion*. He can test the skill of the best players on every instrument, as in the *Brandenburg* Concerti. He can turn the organ into a match for the finest orchestra. He did his best to pass these skills along to his boys, in the school and at home.

Once there, the orchestra begins with a "Solemn Vivat to the Old Regime," proceeding with a serenade or divertimento; if this were Bach's orchestra in Leipzig, the choice might have been one of his Suites or a Brandenburg Concerto.

When our Western music began to grow in medieval times, composers were mainly content to add a layer of melody at a time, usually over and under a basic chant taken from plainsong, or blending a dance rhythm with a lyric to produce a two-part song. The procedure is not unknown elsewhere; you find its counterpart in Africa, the Near East, Indonesia. In the West it led to a different result. By the time we come to Bach, the process had undergone a striking development. Not only is each separate part beautiful in its own right, as with Purcell, but Bach interlinks them all so as to form a complete harmonious whole. In this respect it is difficult to compare Bach to anybody else, for his ability is so far superior to others.

Bach's musical structures seem dictated by the primeval powers of the universe—almost like the earth's own landscapes which are fashioned by the opposition of elements and temperatures. To me, Bach represents the ideal toward which Western music had been striving for a thousand years. Bach is a rule to himself, virtually self-taught, and the creator within an established convention of an unmistakable personal language. The quality of his mind is dazzling. We can reproduce what he wrote down but we cannot duplicate, much less surpass, his feats of invention. There is that troublesome word again, invention. Did Bach invent, did he create, or discover and combine? He did more than this, for he made music which joined art and science, thereby moving people's hearts and disciplining their minds in a compelling, living experience *in time*, such as had never been achieved on such a scale or intensity before.

We can see this clearly in a Bach fugue, one of his most rigorous and at the same time most ingenious disciplines. In a fugue the theme appears again and again in different registers and keys, sometimes moving from major to minor or the reverse. In its classic form, the main thematic idea is most often introduced four times in succession, once each in voices equivalent to soprano, alto, tenor and bass. Once launched, each of these voices continues independently while complementing the others as they enter. The theme can also be inverted or reversed, given at half or double speed. The other voices fill out the harmonic pattern while retaining their separate identity, as if each voice had a will of its own. The form does not originate with Bach, for many composers had been developing it for nearly two centuries. The fugue owes something to the idea of theme and variations as in the *tientos* of Cabezon, but still more to the canon, that form made popular among singers even before "Sumer Is Icumen In."

To me a fugue is like our own process of thought. We think by comparison, by analogy, by going back over our tracks, by reversal, parallel, by comparing angles and speeds. We say, "If this is true, then that must follow." We obtain results by experiment. We remember and we think ahead. A fugue is like that. The various episodes are developed according to principles of logic and brought to a closing climax or result. The wonderful thing with Bach is how natural all this was to him. He was such a master of the form that he could improvise his fugues, tossing them off on the spot even on themes suggested by others. Among those Bach committed to paper there were many in which he introduces two or even three separate musical themes, all fitting with each other, and developing simultaneously. His last and greatest set is called *The Art of Fugue* and is his master's thesis on this form of music. It is as universal, true and inevitable as the motions of the stars. Such pure music is not conceived for any one instrument in particular. It is an exercise in construction, testing whether indeed it is inhabited by life. Repetition of the theme offers a security, but the form is not rigid, it can contain the personal and spontaneous, as in chess. The theme can be presented in double time, half time, like the many speeds of our heartbeat. Its nature corresponds to human biology, as it does to human thought.

In the nineteenth century some teachers warned students to stay away from Bach fugues because they did not follow the rules. Of course they did not, for the rules were invented later, and, in any event, imagination reigns in Bach's fugues as in all his music. Rules are the composer's servants, not his masters. There is another aspect of Bach's work which represents the Western musical synthesis, and that is the use of the written note. Bach relied far less on a kind of musical shorthand than did his predecessors like Purcell or Monteverdi, who counted on instrumentalists to understand and to fill in as needed, whether middle parts or ornamentation. There are still uncertainties in Bach which modern scholarship has done a great deal to clarify, such as the grace notes and turns which Bach certainly loved as much as any musician of his day, but which were played by convention rather than written out. Nonetheless, an original Bach score is a remarkably reliable guide as to how his music should sound.

I was raised with a feeling of innate respect for the intentions of the composer, and the effort to discover them sometimes takes unusual paths, even to examining the composer's handwriting. Its tracings may show impatience, agitation, calm, serenity or cheery exuberance. The musical handwriting of Bach is wonderful in its liquid flow, its unrigid pattern. Since he used a quill, the lines start thick and end thin, which only add to the fluidity. You could frame a Bach manuscript as a beautiful abstract etching. Bach is also frugal to a fault. When he wrote out his six solo violin sonatas and partitas, for instance, at the end of one colossal piece he begins the next on the same page. He does this even at the close of the staggering D Minor Chaconne, the longest of any of the movements in his set of six works for solo violin. I use the word "set" advisedly, for in these sonatas and partitas we can see that using up all the paper was not simply good household economy. The sonatas are composed in a sequence of related keys: G, B, A, D, C, E. Clearly, Bach had the whole set planned from the start. Continuing from the end of one work to the beginning of the next was a logical step in a unified process, a single gesture. Bach's handwriting does not have the impetus of the turbulent Beethoven; it is just as strong, but more fluid because the creative powers were more disciplined. In these violin works he shows us the thoroughness of his method, never writing multiple violin notes as chords, but always as individual voices. He is constantly thinking in terms of counterpoint.

The D Minor Chaconne is for a violinist one of the most rigorous tests imaginable. Its difficulties lie entirely within the idiom of the instrument, for Bach was a lifelong professional fiddler, and it is that very knowledge which allows him to exploit to the fullest every technique available to the instrument. The Chaconne comes at the end of a long work, crowning four preceding movements. All that has gone before is preparation for this supreme effort. The form of the movement is repetitive, rather like an Indian raga, in the sense that it springs from the same underlying sequence of bass notes and intervals. You do not feel the recurrence, just the growth. Bach helps hold your attention by beginning the rhythmic pattern of many variations in the final bar of the one just ending. It is like some modern films in which you may hear the sound belonging to the next scene begin while you are still watching the action of the present one. All Bach's works for solo strings use forms based on our ability to do a thing twice, to repeat an experiment, drawing on dance rhythms familiar to his listeners: the louré, gavotte, bourrée and gigue, the sarabande. I believe that the Chaconne carries its dance rhythm to a height no other composer has attained.

Bach was intent throughout his life on providing music with still another tool, one whose usefulness he clearly foresaw. We refer to it as the tempered scale. What do we mean by that, and why did Bach think it was so important? If you look at a piano keyboard you will see that each octave contains seven white notes and five black ones, making a set of twelve semitones. The sequence repeats across the piano's seven octaves. That convention of design took some time to evolve. Now tuning any keyboard, whether piano, harpsichord or organ, is a tricky thing, for in any given key the distances between the twelve semitones are not equal. If you tune the keyboard to work best in one key, you will not get into trouble, so long as you stick closely to that key and its near relatives. But tune it to C major, let us say, and then try to play in F-sharp major, and it is more sour than lemon and vinegar.

Musicians devised all kinds of compromises, the easiest of which was to avoid writing music in any "distant" keys, those with many sharps or flats in the signature. In the sixteenth century Nicola Vicentino created the archicembalo, in which every black key had a separate upper and lower half, tuned for flat or sharp keys. That lasted about as long as the triplane in aviation. It was too easy for things to get out of line, and too hard to handle. Vicentino knew, however, that an F-sharp and a G-flat are not actually the same note, nor an A-sharp and a B-flat. Their tuning depends on their function within a given key. F-sharp is actually tuned a shade higher than G-flat. To accommodate the difference, a halfway house called mean tone tuning was introduced, reconciling the sharps and flats just enough to help the keyboard join in all the commonly used keys. This form of tuning lasted well into the nineteenth century, especially for church organs.

Bach's musical temperament demanded freedom. He felt one should be able to compose, play and move easily in and between any key. He supported the idea of equal temperament, a system of tuning in which all the semitones on the keyboard are tuned an equal distance apart. That sounds simple enough, but in fact it involved modifications that many musicians felt went deeply against the grain. The only interval that was to remain in perfect tune was the octave. All the fifths would be a bit flat, thirds a bit sharp, not enough to bother, but off true pitch nonetheless. It was a form of cheating of which many purists disapproved. Bach's standing among musicians of his day was so high that when he lent his support to equal temperament, it caused ripples far and wide. But Bach went further: in 1718 and again in 1744 he composed two separate sets of twenty-four preludes and fugues, one each in every major and minor key. They became a cornerstone in his teaching, for he was interested in establishing not just the principle, but the practice of playing in all keys with ease. For voices and strings that is natural enough; the adjustment of sharps and flats is automatic if the ear is keen; brasses and winds have leeway through the use of lip pressure and other aids. The keyboard is the culprit, and Bach's efforts prove the importance of the keyboard to music in the eighteenth century. It is not that the violin had lost its place, far from it, but the keyboard was challenging the violin for leadership of the orchestra, both in concert music and the opera pit. It was becoming the foundation of the sonata, alone or in partnership with other instruments

in a phenomenal array of chamber music, and it simply would not do to have everybody else playing in tune except for the keyboard-leader.

Other musical systems do the same. To allow harmony to become what it now is in the West, the tempered scale was indispensable. It is that element which allowed us to discover how to move freely within a piece from one key to any other by a process called modulation. We tend to forget how recent all this has been. Yet how quickly it led to the dense harmony of Richard Strauss and the twelve-tone system of Schönberg. I sometimes wonder if our ear will ever regain the ability to savor a pure fifth or fourth rather than the tempered one, as the singers of plainsong clearly did; and if it does, will we have to give up all the music which depends on equal temperament?

Bach never used technical devices just for their own sake. He was always making music to communicate through emotion and image. Georges Enesco drew the parallel for me most clearly in the Chaconne, comparing that moment when the music returns to the tonality of D minor at the end, with the image of the suffering Madonna, tragic and weeping, carved by Tilman Riemenschneider, the great medieval Bavarian sculptor. Indeed Bach's music corresponds perfectly to those archetypal images of sorrow, faith, pain and resignation present in the entire altarpiece of which the Madonna is a part, as these emotions are forever part of human existence. The music of Bach is an exalted bridge between the eternal and the everyday, between the sacred and the temporal.

In the small parish church of Saanen, Switzerland, site of the Yehudi Menuhin Festival since 1956, the artist joins with the English alto Norma Procter in a performance of the aria "Erbarme Dich Mein Gott" from Bach's Saint Matthew Passion, *accompanied by the Accademia Alberto Lysy.*

When Bach intertwined his many musical lines, he was trying to turn form and meaning into the same thing. In the *St. Matthew Passion*, when Christ states that one of the disciples will betray Him, the chorus cries out repeatedly "Not I." They do so just eleven times, thus accounting for Judas, though it happens so quickly we are not aware of it. But Bach and God knew. The aria "Erbarme Dich, Mein Gott" from the same work, meaning "Lord have mercy on me, look upon my bitter weeping," written for alto voice, solo violin and strings, is not unlike the laments of Monteverdi or Purcell, except that the voice and violin blend above the supporting strings, each one keeping its own character, yet adding up to a larger and more poignant whole, each commenting on the other. Indeed, for Bach, the devout Lutheran, putting notes on paper was itself an act of faith. He initialed his scores "D. G." (usually at the end) meaning "Deo Gloria," or "To God Alone Belongs the Glory."

If Bach had been a statesman, perhaps he could have helped to reconcile the opposing forces of his time. Lutheran Protestants and Roman Catholics were still at war. Bach waged his battles not on a partisan basis but through music for Christ and God. He went so far as to compose a complete setting of the Catholic Mass, one of his finest works, apart from the more than two hundred cantatas and several Missae Breve for the Lutheran church. Tolerance, the human "equal temperament," remains a goal towards which we struggle.

In Bach's day, Vienna knew little or nothing of his music, and yet it is to Vienna that we must turn for the next stage in our story. This city was the heart of the nominal Holy Roman Empire, where the marrying Hapsburg emperors made their home when they were not in Prague. Here music has always been as natural as breathing; for Viennese were committed to the joys of the senses as well as of the mind, elaborately courteous and forgivably spoiled. Here life was an art, a play, a sacred activity to be pursued within the rules of taste, as much in music or the theater as in the city streets. Here the most musical races of humanity met, for Vienna was a musical crossroads as once Venice had been.

Through Vienna flows the Danube, once almost impenetrable to navigation because of its dangerous rapids and shoals, but whose banks were always a route of travel for a true human melting pot. German is spoken in Vienna with an unmistakably soft southern twang. The Viennese often use a word, *gemütlich*, which is almost untranslatable. It means comfortable, nostalgic, yet stimulating—the opposite of severe. That is Vienna. In this city nobleman and commoner mixed more easily; the quality of life itself was derived from the interweaving of separate

Castello d'Athene comme si ritrova nel presente anno 1670

parts. People served one another with greater tolerance, and the arts flourished because that was the way the Hapsburgs decreed it. They demanded the best and could afford it, nowhere more so than in music.

It should be stressed that four emperors in a row, Ferdinand III, Leopold I, Joseph I and Charles VI, reigning between 1637 and 1740, were skilled composers and performers. In fact, Charles VI liked to conduct dress rehearsals of operas, and did it well. The works by these Hapsburgs fill many volumes, which is remarkable considering the cares of state which intervened. One does not think of emperors carrying music notebooks about. But one of the Hapsburg mottos, after all, is "The lyre is more powerful than the sword." Thanks to these emperors, the best musicians were gathered in Vienna, which by Mozart's day was on the way to becoming the musical capital of Europe.

It was in Vienna that the wars between Moslems and Christians came to an end, at least on European soil. The Moors had been gone from Spain for almost two hundred years, but the Turks were still in possession of an important part of the Balkans and Greece. The armies of the Ottoman Empire reached the gates of Vienna for the last time in 1683, and their defeat was managed by the unusual alliance of Poland, Russia, Austria and Venice, powers usually at odds with each other. In Vienna the Turks nonetheless left their mark—from the breakfast croissant which later migrated to France, to the highly decorated whipped cream iced cakes

In 1670 the Parthenon still stood virtually intact, as this Italian drawing shows, after two thousand years of life on the fortified Acropolis. Only a muezzin's tower betrays its new function as a Moslem mosque. Here in 1687 the retreating Turks took refuge, using the Acropolis as an ammunition depot.

VEDUTA DEL CAST: D'ACROPOLIS DALLA PARTE DI TRAMONTANA

which are not unlike the Moorish confections found in Spain and Portugal, and to the exotic sound of Turkish music for which the Viennese retained a passion for years. We find their influence in the music of Mozart, Haydn, Beethoven and many other composers who made Vienna their home, though the bits of Turkish color with cymbal and drum introduced by these masters had no connection with real Turkish music.

Out of the defeat of Turkey, the German-speaking world emerged with renewed prominence (as well as coffee). It is well to remember the German King George I ruling England and Handel ruling English music. The coffee house concerts which had started there late in the seventeenth century now spread to the whole German world. Bach played his share at Zimmerman's coffee house in Leipzig. Indeed, Handel may have dominated music in England, but as we have seen, the entire Bach clan had an immense influence on the continent. Coffee house concerts

The Venetian cannoneers were unfortunately good shots, and their shells found their mark. The Parthenon was devastated, and the shock was felt across Europe. The appalling sight is rendered in the famous Fanelli engraving of the period.

took longer to catch on in Paris, where, in 1725, the *Concerts Spirituels* were started on Sundays when the opera house was closed. In Vienna the Italian influence was strong, there was far less division between the popular and the refined, and opera was a widely accepted entertainment, competing at times with the wine bars and beer gardens.

It is in this climate that we encounter Wolfgang Amadeus Mozart. Though born in Salzburg in 1756, he spent most of his mature life in Vienna. Mozart's versatility is unique, though comparable to that of Bach or Purcell, both as instrumentalist and composer. He could live within the discipline and order exemplified by Bach without losing the easier sentimentality of Austria or the lyric gifts of Italy.

Mozart's was the courtly style, reflecting the more sentimental and stratified nature of Austria, yet growing in an unbelievably brief span to a mature musical language able to convey the most heartrending emotions without ever transgressing the bounds of elegance. Enesco, my teacher, likened Mozart's music to smiling vineyards on the slopes of an active volcano. For Mozart, with the most urbane of voices, speaks for the anguished heart. All his music is operatic in conception. When Mozart was born, Handel was still living. When he died almost thirty-six years later, Beethoven, who had wanted to become his pupil, was already shattering the conventions of his time. And so Mozart was the link between the structured formality of Bach and the eruptive defiant power of Beethoven. Mozart's music brings us to what we have come to call the

In a tinted engraving dating from 1781 we see Vienna as the twenty-five-year-old Mozart would have seen it, the year before he composed his Haffner *Symphony (No. 35). The scene is the* Graben, *the city's commercial heart, looking toward the* Kohlmarkt *(coal market).*

Romantic era, into the nineteenth century, with a last gesture of elegance and restraint.

Mozart was a prodigy from the age of three. His father Leopold, not an ungifted composer and violinist himself, proudly showed off the boy to unbelieving patrons in such elegant gathering places as Salzburg's Marmorsaal, the marble-lined concert room of Mirabell Palace. Mozart accompanied his older sister Maria Anna, nicknamed Nännerl, who played violin. They were the only two of seven Mozart children to survive

Leopold Mozart took his two gifted children to Vienna in 1762, where they were received by Empress Maria Theresa and Emperor Francis I, and their many children (among them Marie Antoinette, just two months older than Wolfgang). In this detail from a painting by Meytens, the six-year-old composer stands in a box with other musicians at a concert in Schönbrunn Palace.

infancy. It may be that their early start is due simply to the astute business judgment of their father, who recognized immediately the bankable properties of his children. It is a measure of how far the world had moved since Purcell's day and of a change in parental attitude, for the English genius, born a bare century earlier, was almost as precocious, but never marketed.

Surely no prodigy has ever been more lionized than Mozart. He was equally at home with the harpsichord or the newly introduced instrument called the pianoforte, and was almost as good as Nannerl on the violin. He wrote sonatas at five, his first symphony before he was ten, his first opera at twelve. This was music in the solid Germanic tradition, but Mozart spent a few crucial months in Italy, days which were to change his life. There can hardly be a greater contrast in environment between the red-tiled rooftops and inky green poplars of Tuscany and the café-au-lait flow of the river Salzach. Mozart made several trips to Italy as a teenager, and fell in love with the rhythm of that especially singable language. He adored Italian opera, and came to write some of the best we have, *The Marriage of Figaro* and *Don Giovanni*. But Mozart never lost the Austrian common touch, as his German operas *The Abduction from the Seraglio* and *The Magic Flute* attest. He was delighted whenever some of his best opera tunes were whistled in the streets. *The Magic Flute* (like his last opera *Idomeneo*) displays a reverence as well for the operas of his great predecessor Christoph Willibald Gluck, as it does for the lofty ideals of Freemasonry which Mozart had adopted, demonstrating his ability to live in two worlds at once.

We might describe Mozart as the first completely independent Western freelance musician, but that would only be to put a label on unavoidable circumstance. Mozart knew his worth, and did not favor the idea of working for a single patron. He felt that commissions and reward should come to him, even though he was hardly the most adept at courting princely favor after he grew up, any more than he was at managing his finances wisely. Mozart had started life at the court of the Archbishop of Salzburg, where he was but a humble servant in a lavish environment. All his adult life he sought to establish his independence from such servitude. Had he lived as long as Josef Haydn, he might at last have succeeded.

Here let me point out something which had happened to Western music in the short time between Monteverdi and Mozart. The bar line, the regular rhythm in two beats, three or four to a bar, had become the rule. Gone was the easy flow of the madrigal, which pauses only for breath, and which helped to give rise to the free singing in Monteverdi's operas as to the decorated sonatas of Corelli. It is true that metre had been a highly defined aspect of Western musical art as early as the twelfth century, and by Monteverdi's time works of great complexity were being performed in clear measured rhythms, even if without bar lines. Gradually through the eighteenth century, all over Europe music began to settle into what I feel is a metric cage. The flexible melodic phrase, the rhythmic groups of five, seven, eleven or other odd numbers so often encountered in folk music, disappeared from the music of the concert hall. This is partly due to a Germanic passion for order, but also has to do with the rise of measured dances such as the minuet and the waltz, both in three-four time, and both popular in Mozart's day. It also has to do with the increasing need to keep the many parts of a score moving in a predetermined order, to assure coordination in complexity. Without a bar line, how might a conductor be expected to get all the players to keep together? Orchestras of as many as sixty players were not unusual by this time, and the unity of massed strings achieved by orchestras such as that in Mannheim became the marvel of the age. To my mind this served to make Western music less elastic.

Unwritten folk music with only a few musicians playing by ear does not have this problem; and its rhythms have remained freer, less bound by the restrictions of notation; and so we still find in Greece, the Near East, Central Europe, as we do in the ragas of India, tunes based on five beats or seven, or even more complex combinations. In their way these rhythms are rigid, too, being part of a tradition established long ago. We will find them later in the music of Stravinsky. But they give this folk music an imbalance, an unpredictability, an elastic quality, a greater latitude for improvisation, which Western classical music has largely lost. It is a loss I regret, for I feel we have lost touch with an important heritage, part of the pagan in music, a natural freedom to which we are all born. It is also the imposition of what we fondly imagined was a superior order on an inferior chaos.

In Mozart, as in the Strauss waltz, what keeps the rhythm alive is his humanity and flexibility. His music simply must breathe. The beat must be ready to change all the time, a little faster here, a little slower there. This tenderness, compassion, humor and sympathy are qualities which mark Mozart throughout his life, qualities which never forsook him despite his struggle to make ends meet.

Mozart wrote his most lasting works as an adult, harried by overwork. By 1776 no longer was he the prodigy, no longer was he fawned over by adoring adults. Finding the next patron, the next paying concert, was an

Mozart was born in this room on January 27, 1756, and here Yehudi Menuhin sits at Mozart's own piano, under the watchful eyes of his father.

unending struggle; and though Mozart made a good deal of money in his day, he did not spend wisely and died leaving debts behind. Buried in an unmarked pauper's grave, his bones have never been found. Fortunately, he was a prolific letter writer, and almost all his letters convey a sense of cheer and commitment which is all the epitaph he needs, besides his imperishable music.

Mozart mastered the art of modulation which the tempered scale made available. He could move far from his starting point without ever losing the ability to locate an exact path back to home base, even though he might return by another route, intensifying our feelings along the way by his adroit turns. In his harmonic adventures he foreshadows Chopin, even Wagner. Behind the ruffles and powdered wigs there is a paradoxically rebellious, yet melting personality. Let us not forget that Mozart was twenty when the American Revolution began (which England so long referred to as the Secession of the Colonies). When he died in December 1791, just short of his thirty-sixth birthday, the French Revolution had begun. A century of thought and political movement had altered men's

To Peter Giffard *Esq: Son and Heir to* Peter Giffard *of* Chillington *in the County of* STAFFORD *Esq.* *and to Master* Thomas *his Brother this* PLATE *is most humbly inscribed by their much obliged Servant.*

minds. Citizens proposed to choose their rulers as they would their destinies. Mozart himself had done no less. The Age of the Individual was about to begin.

One of the last of the court musicians, a man who lived through that change from dependence on God and King to a faith in the power of the individual, was Josef Haydn. Even he, twenty-four years Mozart's senior and called Papa Haydn in his day and since, freely admitted he had learned much from the younger man (as of course Mozart did from Haydn). Writing to Leopold Mozart, he states, "I know of no greater

The effort to preserve dance patterns through notation had also begun by the eighteenth century, although this English example would hardly have been legible to amateurs. Eventually the pavanne, passe-caille and chaconne were given up in favor of the more regular waltz and minuet.

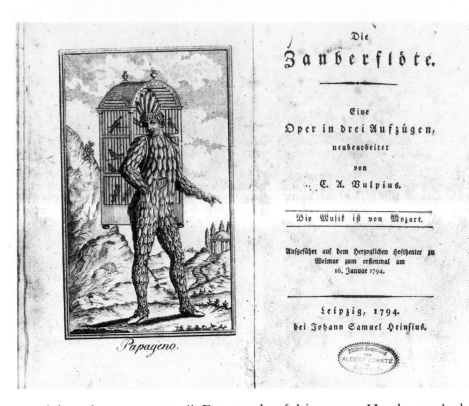

Die
Zauberflöte.

Eine
Oper in drei Aufzügen,
neubearbeitet
von
C. A. Vulpius.

Die Musik ist von Mozart.

Aufgeführet auf dem Herzoglichen Hoftheater zu
Weimar zum erstenmal am
16. Januar 1794.

Leipzig, 1794.
bei Johann Samuel Heinsius.

Papageno.

When Mozart's The Magic
Flute *was produced and published in Leipzig in 1794, three
years after its première, the late
composer got scarcely a line on
the title page under the name
of the arranger of the new
version, Vulpius. Of Mozart's
original librettist, the ebullient
Emmanuel Schikaneder, there
is no mention. The figure is the
folk-hero Papageno.*

musician than your son.'' For much of his career Haydn worked at
Eszterháza in what used to be Hungary, for the lord of that place, Prince
Nicolaus. It was quite a different life from Mozart's, and Haydn really
achieved his best work after Mozart had come onto the scene, though he
was already the unquestioned universally admired founder of the
classical style. Haydn outlived Mozart by seventeen years, and his last
twelve symphonies, his most popular today, were begun the year Mozart
died and finished five years later, becoming the rage of London. These
two composers completed the centralization of musical influence in the
German-speaking world.

The development in Western music which produced Mozart and
Haydn was a slow one, but its pace was to accelerate throughout the
nineteenth century. Until the end of the eighteenth century, composers
made use of a musical idiom commonly understood throughout the
European world. Of course each great composer evolves his own recognizable style, yet Purcell, Bach and Mozart reflect the heroic age of the church
out of which so much in Western music had been forged in a millennium.
As the Romantic age begun, an idea took root which has profoundly
affected the music of the past 150 years. That idea is the establishment of a
personal idiom for each composer. Ludwig van Beethoven is both the
seed and the first flowering of this idea.

The emerging doctrine of egocentric, personal self-realization could not have found a more vigorous expression than it did in Beethoven, which may be due in part to his eventual deafness and isolation. This tendency has continued to our day when every literate composer feels obliged to invent a new style, rather than simply evolve a distinctive personality. The result has been a great number of disappointments and blind alleys. No composer has ever refined his raw material to the degree of purity Beethoven achieved. Wrestling with it until he transformed it into concentrated statements of intense meaning, he focussed his fire in the process. Today, when composers so often begin with their raw material already in an advanced state of abstraction, there can be no such process of distillation, of self-immolation, in the creative act. In Beethoven, more than in almost any other creative artist, we are allowed to witness the struggle for the ideal of beauty, purpose and truth.

Beethoven's achievement is that universality of utterance which partakes alike of the rigors of mathematical equation and the emotions of human experience. I have often asked myself what it is that guides us

Josef Haydn was popular at Eszterháza as a composer of stage works, creating over a dozen between 1762 and 1783. He usually conducted from the harpsichord, as in this performance of his opera L'Infedelta Delusa *in 1773.*

toward this ideal, for such creation is the opposite of study, occurring before rather than after the event. I think we can explain it in part by that psychical intuition of the true self which we sometimes call revelation or fate: a state of being in which we may observe, yet remain quite separate from, the accumulation of information or the daily work routine.

Most living things are aware of the polarity of darkness and light. The tree, though blind, grows toward the life-giving light, drawing upon the dark earth for physical sustenance. In the same way, the human being normally *knows* when something is right, when something is true. The tragedy of our day is that our civilizations are competing with each other most rapidly and effectively to destroy man's innate sense of the good, that good which is a composite of living purpose, fairness and equilibrium

It was Beethoven who gave to the symphony orchestra the final basic shape we know today. While he inherited the orchestra of Haydn and Mozart, he extended its range and variety, added the trombones which were more commonly reserved for the opera, and experimented with the use of the piccolo and the contra-bassoon. It may seem a contradiction to seek the definition of the age of the individual in such a collective musical body, but this institution is directly connected with the idea of a personal musical idiom, and Beethoven found new ways to make use of it to express the power of the individual in music.

Beethoven had been a student of Haydn, and hoped to study with Mozart, but by the time he settled in Vienna in 1792, Mozart was dead. Beethoven was then twenty-two, only fourteen years Mozart's junior, but what a difference separates them. Mozart must have sensed it, for Beethoven was also a brilliant pianist and an even more striking extemporizer, even as a boy. On his first visit to Vienna at sixteen Mozart heard him and said, "Watch that fellow, some day he'll make quite a noise in the world." Handsome, if graceless, Beethoven endeared himself to all of Vienna. Named for his grandfather Ludwig, head of music for the Elector of Bonn, Beethoven was raised by a drunken father and by a mother who died of tuberculosis before Beethoven was seventeen. At eighteen Beethoven was on his own without the support of intelligent, perceptive parents which Mozart had enjoyed.

It was just at this point that another influence made itself felt in the world: Napoleon Bonaparte, the Corsican, the people's general, was leading the armies of France and almost singlehandedly remaking the image of Europe. Even Vienna could not afford to ignore him. Beethoven was similarly assertive, self-willed, unbending. That spirit of rebellious resistance is already felt in his Second Symphony, written in 1802, which did not please every music-lover in Vienna, as a review from the *News of*

The portrait is anonymous, but Beethoven's intense uncompromising gaze is unforgettable. This painting now hangs in the Liceo Musicale at Bologna, and probably dates from around 1810 (the year Chopin was born).

the *Elegant World* makes clear: "The Second Symphony is a filthy monster, a wounded dragon writhing hideously, refusing to die, and in the finale, even though bleeding from every pore, still thrashes about with upraised tail." To our ears the symphony sounds exuberant, irrepressible, but its energy did run counter to the decorum of upper-class Vienna, which seemed inclined to hang a sign on its door reading "Do Not Disturb." Neither Beethoven nor Napoleon heeded the warning.

Up to the time he was thirty, Beethoven's music followed older models, but then broke away with extraordinary suddenness. The change came at exactly the moment when he had to admit, first to himself, and then to his brothers, in his famous letter known as the Heiligenstadt Testament written in 1802, that he was going deaf. Beethoven had already known something was wrong by the time he was twenty-six. Now he was thirty-two and the music he was writing was to be some of the last he would ever hear reasonably clearly in performance. His ears were closing to the

A project for the invasion of England by Napoleon, printed in 1801, shows the plan for a tunnel under the channel; while feigning attack by sea and air, the main force would be sent through the tunnel (of which the English were apparently to be unaware).

sounds of the natural world. George Marek in his splendid biography states that for some time Beethoven's deafness was like a veil which would occasionally clear, but before he reached fifty it was total.

We know from the Heiligenstadt Testament that Beethoven seriously contemplated taking his own life. Instead, he went on in 1803 to compose another symphony, the third, known today as the *Eroica*. He had planned to dedicate it to Napoleon, but when the General decided to become Emperor, and had the effrontery to place the symbolic crown on his own head with his own hands, Beethoven angrily scratched out the dedication. Until then Napoleon had been for Beethoven a champion of human rights. Even he could hardly suspect that within a few years Napoleon's armies would be standing at the gates of Vienna.

Beethoven's tragedy has been compared to blindness in a painter. That is only a half-truth; the blind painter may no longer be able to paint, but blind musicians compose and perform, like Cabezon in Spain. And while the deaf performer cannot play, the deaf composer can still write, creating by a process of inner conception, drawing on aural images etched onto his mind and heart; for music is finally an inner experience, a happening occurring within ourselves. Beethoven needed only his eyes and his hand, and they continued to serve him well. And yet, how are we to assess the depth of tragedy in the monumental despair of this colossus, facing so fateful and shattering a curse? It was as if Beethoven were Prometheus, who stole fire from the gods and gave it to man; then, like Prometheus, the gods punished him by chaining him to a rock, the rock of his deafness.

To the uninitiated, Beethoven's axiomatic statements may seem misleadingly simple and self-evident, until one interprets their symbolism. The most powerful element in the first movement of his third symphony (*Eroica*) is undoubtedly the two-bar unit, two great E-flat major chords, which rivet our attention and propel the action. The passionate intensity is quickly revealed in the sixth bar as the melody drops to a C-sharp against a breathless syncopated accompaniment in the violins. But it is the implacable basic three-four beat (soon challenged by a two-four unit within it) as pronounced by the opening chords which, like the measured distance between great waves, carries everything along with it.

Whether it is the solemnity of the epic funeral march, or the feverish drive of the scherzo, Beethoven engulfs us in torrential purpose and direction, a single man's purpose, embodying, symbolizing a whole nation's raging energies, emotions, ideals and frustrations. Never before had mankind heard music with such single-minded drive. The more I think of Beethoven, the more he recalls for me a Hebrew prophet, some

The General became Emperor on December 2, 1804 in an extraordinary ceremony held at Notre Dame in which he took hold of the crown from the hands of Pope Pius VII himself. Painted in 1806 by the twenty-four-year-old Jean Auguste Dominique Ingres, the portrait failed to please, and Ingres moved to Rome. It now hangs at the Musée de l'Armée in Paris.

great figure of the Old Testament: unresigned, castigating, menacing, pleading and demanding.

The *Eroica* was the longest symphony any composer had yet attempted; it took its listeners on a voyage well beyond the safer waters of its predecessors. The E-flat theme is like the chromosomes of a living cell, transmitting information for the reproduction of other cells, which gradually form themselves into and sustain the life of a unique entity, unlike any other. Beethoven was once asked what his symphony "meant," and his answer was to walk to the piano and play the first eight notes of his theme that simply outline the key of E flat. It was all the answer he gave.

By nature man is an explorer, one of the most consistent characteristics of the human race. Beethoven is an explorer in search of first causes. His nature was not an accepting one, but challenging, defiant and questioning. Indeed, his incomparable stretches of utmost serenity were very dearly bought, and so often were followed by bucolic festivity, as the celebration of inner creative struggle leads to serenity, thanksgiving and celebration. Nowhere in his volcanic temperament can we see this more clearly than in his sketchbooks, of which hundreds survive. These are like the sketchbooks of Leonardo da Vinci, only without their neatness and precision. Beethoven was too impatient, struggling constantly to reinvent music itself, working under pressure, to make form emerge from recalcitrant material. Beethoven started as a disciple of Haydn and Mozart, but soon he no longer quoted others, as a scientist like Darwin might quote ideas and techniques learned in the course of setting forth an argument. In the final analysis, Beethoven is like Moses, an intermediary between Divine Will and human recalcitrance, leading us out of bondage into the Promised Land, a mortal become immortal, no longer quoting others. God perhaps said it first and Beethoven was content to quote God.

One of the most striking aspects of Beethoven is his use of silence. His pauses are among the most pregnant voids in the universe; like the emptiness of space, they are filled with the power of magnetic tensions, set up in like manner by the mass of each heavenly body. Those pauses are essential to the music. When we experience them we find the pulse is never absent, and the way the music then continues is quite wonderful. If the following phrase comes in a trifle too soon or too late, the magical effect is lost, for the length of silence is predetermined and fateful.

Once the *Eroica* was finished, Beethoven set to work on another symphony, which was to take him a long time. Mozart wrote the last three symphonies of his life in a single summer. Beethoven was to struggle with this new one for five years, during which he finished yet another (it appeared as his Fourth), completed his opera *Fidelio*, the sublime violin concerto, the fourth piano concerto, two piano sonatas and three quartets. All the time he circled back on his tracks, working at this monumental symphony which he could not let go. Finally in 1808 he felt it was ready to send to his publishers to appear as the Fifth Symphony.

The classic symphony is one of our most extended pure musical forms in the West. Emerging from the sonata, whose four-movement form Haydn perhaps more than any other composer helped to bring to its final shape, the symphony usually begins with a strong, decisive opening movement, then two gentler middle movements (one slow and one fast), and a lively finale. Such works are not built by formula—except among lesser composers. The great masters proceed from an intuitive sense of perfect continuity generated by the thematic and harmonic material. The key to the form lies in that of the opening movement, traditionally cast in the sequence of "exposition-development-recapitulation," referred to as sonata form. The composer states his initial melodic idea, continuing it to the point where he is ready to introduce a contrasting theme. Once they have been stated fully they are given as inventive a development as the composer can devise. Yet however far afield he may travel, the composer knows his eventual goal is to return home to a reassuring restatement of the opening theme. We recognize the familiar landscape and are brought home to safe harbor after the journey.

Sonata form is like the womb, and we ourselves are the development within its walls, putting our own personal views into the sonata as its content. The form may be repetitive, but the content is original. We sense this in Haydn, more clearly still in Mozart, and nowhere more forcefully than in Beethoven. He takes sonata form and puts into it a personal "development" that bids fair to eclipse "form." It does not remain for him simply a container, for each phrase grows organically with seeming spontaneity from what came before. In an academic symphony of the time, the recapitulation in the opening movement was dictated by convention, often after an insipid middle section whose lack of real inventive spark we might have foreseen from the exposition itself. In fact, musical form had once been but two repeated identical expositions with nothing in between, no doubt of repetitive folk origin, which survives most clearly in the scherzo.

Beethoven simply cannot leave either the form or his first melodic idea as fixed and final. His sketchbooks are full of themes twisted and turned every possible way. The form is like a sculptor's metal armature in clay or plaster. Unless it is exactly right, the sculptor's work will not stand up; there will be an imbalance, a lack of proportion or of energy. In fact,

Beethoven reduces, compresses and makes an essence, as it were, out of his raw material, first simplifying it to the utmost, and only then treating it as a seed to germinate and flower.

The American composer Charles Ives once remarked that Beethoven could have made a lot of money "if he had only written symphonies *for* the people instead of symphonies *to* the people." But when Beethoven tackled the Fifth Symphony he set himself a task in the realm of form greater than any he had previously attempted. He not only changed what had been accepted as material for a symphony, he sought to unify the themes of all the movements so that their development would reflect a total unity as the work progressed. In fact the scherzo continues without a break, an unheard-of liberty, straight into the striding sunburst finale where Beethoven, always a deft orchestrator, brings in the opera-house trombones for the first time in this score and in the history of the concert orchestra. It is a masterstroke, a shaft of light whose noble theme is a transformation of those found in both the slow movement and the scherzo.

Beethoven's greatness of soul transcends craft while illuminating it. As he became increasingly locked inside his deafness, he devised elaborate hearing aids so that he could pick up vibrations from his piano directly, applying a stick against the sounding board and pressing the other end directly against the side of his head. Beethoven's isolation emphasizes something new in Western music: the separation between composer and performer that had begun at the turn of the nineteenth century. The two had always existed separately, but composers had in the main also been performers, even virtuosos, like Mozart and Bach. Beethoven's deafness forced on him methods of composing on paper only, starting a process which helped to lead to a dissolution, a fragmentation of Western music, the opposite of the heritage which he hoped to pass on.

At the emergence of the Romantic era, Beethoven was one pillar of Western music; the other was Franz Schubert. He was as modest and humble as Beethoven was overbearing and arrogant, as intuitive as Beethoven was philosophical, as true to man's subjective inner turmoil, passions, even nightmares, as Beethoven was true to man's social and personal struggles. Like Beethoven, he never heard many of his greatest works performed—Beethoven because of his deafness and Schubert because his great works were largely ignored. Yet the phenomenon of Schubert lies in the fact that he marks one of those apparently inevitable milestones along man's path toward self-realization, a conscience answerable to itself rather than to some higher power. The voice of Schubert is

suddenly the voice of Everyman. Beethoven is cataclysmic, speaking to a million, while Schubert speaks one to one to the individual human heart.

Born in 1797, a generation after Beethoven, Schubert was a fine singer as a boy, but with adolescence his voice broke into an indifferent croak. He was adept as a pianist, but without the temperament to become a celebrated soloist. The larger works may have lain unrecognized, but Schubert's dance tunes, his *Ländlers*, were as popular as those of his contemporaries, Josef Lanner and Johann Strauss Sr., and his songs were adored from the very first. They are perhaps the most moving and valid documents about man the orphan, at times joyful and free, at others abandoned and suffering, without parental comfort. Schubert was quite simply the first composer to be humanly himself.

Schubert's career as a composer began when he was fourteen and lasted until his death, tragically early at thirty-one. In that time he wrote not only operas, theater music, sonatas and symphonies, and exquisite chamber music, but over six hundred songs. Sometimes he turned out half a dozen songs in a day. He was a highly individual judge of poetry, sometimes choosing Goethe, Grillparzer, Heine, even Shakespeare once

The crowd at Beethoven's funeral on the afternoon of March 29, 1827 was estimated at nearly 20,000. Among the torch and pallbearers were Kreutzer, Hummel, Linke, Czerny, the poet Grillparzer, and, of course, Franz Schubert. The wealthy watched from their carriages, the people pressed for a glimpse from their windows, or ran ahead to find better places behind the restraining railings.

The street before St. Michael's Church in Vienna appears here as it looked to Beethoven and Schubert toward the end of their lives. The orderly grace of the city blends beautifully with its informality.

or twice (his setting of "Who Is Sylvia" works as well in the original English as it does in German), but he also used much indifferent verse which survives today only because Schubert chose to set it to music. His sensitivity to the blend of words and melody is almost flawless, even when he uses the simplest means. His facility amazed his contemporaries. There are countless tales of his glancing at a poem, studying it for some moments, and then, saying "I've got it!," dashing away to return later that day or soon after with a completed setting. In this sense Schubert is much more the bohemian artist struck by instant inspiration, a view of the life of genius made popular later by countless Victorian stereotypes but almost always far from the truth.

Schubert's music, except for the songs, dances and some chamber music, took a long time to become part of the repertoire. This music was not in the heroic Beethoven vein or in the extroverted manner of the operas of Gioacchino Rossini or Vincenzo Bellini, whose virtuoso vocal style dominated public taste for much of the first half of the nineteenth

century. Some of Schubert's finest music in the larger forms lay hidden in drawers for decades and some was lost. The truth is that Schubert was unable to fight for his music in the way that Beethoven did, negotiating stiff terms with publishers and protecting his copyright, though it was not for lack of trying. Like Guarnerius's violins, most of Schubert's works finally had to make their way in the world without the embellishment of contracts or patrons. It is difficult for us to credit that the *Unfinished* Symphony was not given its first hearing until 1865, thirty-seven years after Schubert's death, and only weeks after the première of Wagner's *Tristan und Isolde*.

Never previously published, this anonymous portrait of Franz Schubert was probably painted around 1816 when the nineteen-year-old composer's Ländler *and other dances were at their most popular. By this time he had already completed five symphonies, four masses, and countless other works.*

The composer as promoter-entrepreneur on behalf of his own work is an idea that finally took hold in the nineteenth century. Handel, Bach and Mozart had made their start in that direction; for Bach, music was most often made for immediate practical reasons (as it was for Purcell). Bach pushed his predecessor's music off the shelf when he arrived in Leipzig, and fully expected much of his own to vanish in the same way after his death. Contemporary music was for the most part the only music played, and the composer-performer faced a horde of active competitors. Mozart wrote so many piano concerti in order to have new works to present in concerts for which he was the principal conductor-soloist. The piano parts of some of these were not even written out completely, partly because he was so busy and knew what he wanted to play by heart anyway, and partly so that he could keep their secret safe in a day when works were stolen so much more easily. Schubert simply had no salesmanship, a quality not formerly essential to composers.

Appearance in public has been admittedly a vital part of every musician's life, including composers, right to our own day. Beethoven still appeared as a pianist long after much of his hearing was gone, and his difficult concerti and piano sonatas were written partly to display his keyboard gifts. Even after his hearing was totally gone, he still attempted to conduct, the last occasion being the première of his Ninth Symphony, so important to him was his public role. That hugely publicized event in 1824, anticipated by all Vienna as it had been seven years since the last Beethoven symphony was premiered, was nearly a disaster. The performance was saved because a competent conductor was discreetly officiating behind Beethoven's back and the performers watched him rather than Beethoven. Yet Vienna's love for this man and the impact of the symphony were such that the audience, finally realizing that Beethoven could not hear their applause, waved a sea of white handkerchiefs at him. The twenty-seven-year-old Schubert may well have been in that audience. Within five years both men were dead. But their legacy was to dominate Western music throughout the remainder of the century, and into our own. The composer had unmistakably become the warming sun around which the other musical planets would henceforth revolve.

Schubert's is the plea that dares at times to be hopeless. Before Schubert's time every musical emotion, even the most impassioned, echoed a social order. Defenseless and unprotected, this rather ordinary man became through his music the incarnation of mortal pain, singing to an almost unbearable degree of that anguish, that yearning of love that was neither religious nor heroic, but which lay within the experience of us all. The idea of service to God, sovereign and father is an arrangement which must inevitably tremble when its structure is attacked by the passions and doubts of its servants.

Unlike Beethoven, Schubert doesn't proclaim, he contemplates. His songs, quartets, symphonies and masses amble and stroll with a natural human gait. In his songs he makes speech and music into a single expression, as if this were the only way we human beings could truly speak to one another. He reunites worship and love, a unity he makes self-evident in the "Ave Maria," a reverent love song to the Blessed Virgin not far removed from his equally tender-hearted *Serenade*.

Schubert, this first Romantic since the marriage in Vienna of Mediterranean with trans-Alpine cultures, remains a phenomenon we may claim as *ours*. Schubert was born in an age of clashing philosophies, the master of a vast musical imagination, always on the edge of poverty, carefree by nature and tragic by circumstance. It is engrossing that Schubert could evoke the hallucinatory, the spectral, as an essential part of man in the selfsame city where later Sigmund Freud was to pursue the same dread side of man with such foreboding and concentrated persistence. Schubert's is the mortal voice achieving the transcendental, and immortal by the only means known to him, the bird song become prayer. Had he not died at thirty-one, in 1828, would he have been able to maintain this rapture?

I believe that there is something constant in us all, a sense of what is right, a sense of balance, of harmony with ourselves and the world in which we all must live. Yet we also need a sense of hope for something beyond ourselves, which helps to give our lives proportion and direction. Music lives and breathes to tell us just that: who we are and what we face. In Bach, as in Mozart or Schubert, it is a path between ourselves and the infinite. I want to end this chapter, however, with the memory of what is to me one of the finest moments in all music, the slow movement of that sublime Beethoven violin concerto. Such music is that which is best in all of us, and which we call humanity.

On November 1, 1755, All Saints' Day (and only weeks before Mozart's birth), the city of Lisbon in Portugal suffered a devastating earthquake in which thousands died, many in the very churches in which they worshipped. The catastrophe shook the faith of Protestants and Catholics alike, and helped speed the search for natural causes. No longer could one ascribe everything to God.

The industrial age brings with it the modern grand piano, the huge symphony orchestra, the massive grand opera. Paganini, Chopin and Liszt become the embodiment of the romantic solo virtuoso. The cities grow, popular and folk music becomes urbanized, the national anthem emerges. Verdi is the cultural hero of an emerging Italian nation, and Wagner cuts Western music loose from its moorings. Nationalism takes musical shape in Tschaikovsky and other composers, and in popular forms such as the flamenco. Brahms retains his sense of contact with folk roots, and the waltzes of Strauss sweep Europe.

5. The Age of the Individual

THE ROMANTIC AGE, running from 1800 into our own century, is sometimes labelled *Sturm und Drang* by German historians (roughly, "storm and stress"), a broad term covering political upheaval, cultural transformation and personal liberation. The paintings of Turner and Delacroix are characteristic of the spirit of the time, as are the novels of Scott and Goethe, the poems of Blake and Coleridge, the plays of Schiller, the operas of Bellini and Weber. It was also the moment when industrial growth truly began in the West; the cities took on an ever greater importance, and practical applications of James Watt's steam engine proliferated. In this era of social and artistic expansion, the composer's creation of an idiom belonging only to him became as much a part of the proclamation of his identity as language itself identifies a people. For many composers after Beethoven, the symphony orchestra became an ideal battleground on which to test their strength.

Like opera, the symphony orchestra is one of the most costly assemblies in Western music. Admittedly, opera was created for an age of aristocracy, where the trappings of ceremony on stage matched the expectations and display of the audience. By contrast, the orchestra is more restrained and more heroic.

Assembling many instruments was an old practice, as we have seen, but the orchestra as an expressive instrument in its own right came to be used during the nineteenth century for some of the most highly personal music yet known, the symphonies and concerti of the Romantic composers. This is the age dominated by subjective experience, when the individual life became the center of interest for society and art.

The Schrammel family in Vienna created both a literature and a tradition in their garden music of the early nineteenth century, which is still played in the charming wine bars of Grinzing on the outskirts of the city.

Opposite:
The burgeoning romantic spirit of the nineteenth century is beautifully rendered by Johann Erdmann Hummel in a canvas painted in 1823 depicting the joys of spring in Naples.

Drawn by Rich.ᵈ Westall R.A.   Page 74   Engraved by Cha.ˢ Heath

LADY OF THE LAKE.

IN LISTENING MOOD, SHE SEEMED TO STAND,
THE GUARDIAN NAIAD OF THE STRAND

Canto I Stan XVII

LONDON, PUBLISHED DEC. 1. 1810, BY JOHN SHARPE, PICCADILLY.

The novels of Sir Walter Scott, Kenilworth, Ivanhoe, The Lady of the Lake, *were widely translated in the early 1800s, and became favorites among artists, writers and the educated class. One novel,* The Bride of Lammermoor, *became even better known later in its version as an opera by Donizetti.*

There had occurred in the Romantic age that profound shift from the worship of God to the exaltation of the individual and, by the same token, from the fear of God to the fear of man. The change had begun in the Renaissance with a powerful fascination with the idea of man as the measure of all things, and the creations of man as the measure of purest order and absolute beauty. The implications of this shift unfolded and flowered during the nineteenth century when, as had once been the case in Greece, the artist, poet and philosopher resumed their role at the center of things.

As the cities of Europe expanded, the mass of people demanded cohesion, purpose and leadership. The great symphony orchestra is a microcosm of this evolution. It assembles a powerful but unformed mass of every kind of sound and noise, which demands to be given shape, texture and creative purpose. That may be one reason why the orchestra has achieved such widespread acceptance, even popularity, in the United States.

The celebration of the artists' emotions for their own sake was the hallmark of Romanticism, and the arsenal of the symphony orchestra is a formidable weapon for its realization. In the hands of the French master, Hector Berlioz, for instance, the orchestra assumes a musical character which is not to be confused with the music of anybody else, a sound whose splendor expresses individual exultation in his sense of power. Many consider Berlioz to be the father of the modern orchestra, as he is of the art of conducting, though, of course, there were many precursors. His music revealed a new vision of society.

Louis Antoine Jullien (1812–1860) was one of the first star conductors, appearing first in France and then with great success in England, where his concerts at Covent Garden drew the attention of the Illustrated London News *(1846).*

Hector Berlioz sometimes enlarged the size and resources of the orchestra somewhat beyond what his contemporaries thought proper, as Grandville's cartoon (1846) makes clear.

Hector Berlioz was the virtuoso of the orchestra, a composer and conductor who rejoiced in amassing 150 players or more. He developed the art of orchestration to a level it had scarcely known before, beginning with such works as the *Symphonie Fantastique*, the *Roman Carnival* Overture, and also in his operas, especially *Benvenuto Cellini* which created a sensation in Paris at its première on September 10, 1838. Berlioz prepared the way for the huge orchestras required by the music dramas of Wagner and the symphonies of Gustav Mahler.

Orchestration, the designation of specific instruments for each separate part in a score, was a practice begun in the late Renaissance. We have already seen how this art flourished under the Gabrielis in Venice. In orchestral music of the Baroque period, in fact until Mozart and Haydn's day, scores were often written by giving the principal melodic line to the first violins and using the other instruments to fill in the harmony. In his last symphonies Haydn gave the woodwind instruments far greater prominence, which brought a particular wit and sparkle to his scores. Beethoven enlarged the technique of orchestration immensely, especially in his handling of the brasses, percussion and kettledrums. In the scherzo movement of his Ninth Symphony, the use of two kettledrums tuned an octave apart as a solo instrument in the first statement of the theme brought gasps of admiration from his audience at the première. Berlioz learned much from Beethoven and, in turn, handed on to others an approach to the orchestra in which each instrument is given its own place, and none need ever be considered subservient.

Within a few years of the death of Beethoven, Western music in all forms began to break with the ordered conventions inherited from the Classical and Baroque periods. Berlioz was one of many musicians to respond to a new sense of freedom of expression, a liberation of feeling that brought with it a revolution in opera, dance and concert music. The Romantic age was certainly the age of the virtuoso, and if Berlioz was the star of the orchestra, no composer-performer was more celebrated in the first third of the nineteenth century than the Italian violinist, Nicolò Paganini. He was a friend and patron of Berlioz, and it was for Paganini that Berlioz composed his symphony *Harold in Italy*, with its solo part for the viola, Paganini's alternate instrument.

Paganini was born in Genoa in 1782, and made his violin debut at the age of nine. By 1805 he had embarked on a career destined to turn him into a legend. Certainly, no artist created a greater sensation through his performance, not even Franz Liszt. We have no recordings of Paganini's playing, but we do have the music he composed for himself, and it tells us unmistakably that he was one of the most extraordinary violinists in history. Part of Paganini's appeal lay in his cadaverous appearance, and he did nothing to dispel rumors of his pact with Satan, knowing well its promotional value. Paganini was his own best agent; he handled his career almost as masterfully as he played. The first truly commercial artist, he made his way across the continent of Europe from one engagement to another, moving from triumph to triumph like a great general or a prizefighter. Consumptive, gaunt, dressed entirely in black, his huge hands belying the delicacy of his chosen instrument, he cut a dramatic figure. Schubert may have heard him perform, for Paganini first played in Vienna in March of 1828, half a year before Schubert's death, outstripping in one concert the earnings Schubert received from an entire series. Paganini was only fifty-eight when he died, wracked by many ills, his voice completely gone.

Nicolò Paganini is seen in 1812 at the age of thirty, at the height of his career, and in 1838 at the age of fifty-six, two years before his death from cancer and other ailments.

I have always been an admirer of Paganini, an enthusiasm due in great part to my master, Georges Enesco, and now shared by my wife Diana, who has assembled a most wonderful collection of Paganiniana. Among these is a French portrait painted when Paganini was thirty years old, showing a sensitive, secure, yet visionary man, no doubt thinking up more effects and hurdles for lesser violinists. Another canvas, deeply moving, painted in England when Paganini was fifty-six, shows an old man suffering from cancer of the throat, and near death.

Perhaps among all his works, including the many extended concerti for violin and viola and the variations on popular airs, the most important for the violin is the set of Twenty-Four Caprices, the violinist's *vade mecum*. Paganini's technical imagination was without precedent and, among many other effects, he developed the use of artificial or stopped violin harmonics to an astonishing degree. This is a technique in which a finger (first or second) of the left hand stops the string at one point, and another (third or fourth) touches it lightly at a critical distance beyond, allowing the bow to set the string vibrating in several sections rather than as a whole—in the manner of the skipping rope to which reference was made earlier. One harmonic at a time was not enough for Paganini: he

would play harmonics on two strings at once, shortening them with the first two fingers and touching lightly with the other two at the correct distances. Violin harmonics have an eerie flute-like resonance, a whistling sound with which Paganini loved to transfix his audiences.

Paganini was also a skilled guitarist, and liked to combine the techniques of the two instruments, plucking the accompanying harmony with some of the fingers of the left hand (usually the little finger) while articulating the melody with the others. It is a difficult trick, but not nearly so hard as it sounds if the work has been skillfully composed. A good example is Paganini's Variations on "Nel cor piu non mi sento." The simultaneous sounding of plucked and bowed notes is a sensational effect on the violin, and contributed to the general talk that Paganini was somehow in league with the devil.

Like Guarneri del Gesù, one of whose violins he owned and championed (it came to be known as "The Cannon"), Paganini preferred at first to spend his time at cards and other distractions. He was given the Guarnerius by an admirer, a French tradesman, who had lent it to him, then insisted that Paganini keep it after he heard him play it—a fortunate happenstance,

The popular journals of the day outdid themselves portraying the fantastic, seemingly supernatural aspects of Paganini's personality and skill.

since Paganini had recently pawned his own instrument to pay his gambling debts.

Paganini lived the life of the popular romantic hero. His addiction to gambling cost him many a loss, but when he won a Stradivarius by playing a difficult concerto at sight without making a mistake, it was hardly a gamble. It was as if the 250 years of great Italian violin making from Amati onward, and of great Italian violin playing as well (for his role was well rehearsed), had all been in preparation for him. In a way Paganini was the captive of his own fame. He loved chamber music, which he usually played with friends at home. He also loved Beethoven's Violin Concerto, but he did not make it a regular part of his repertoire as his audiences came to expect display and fireworks.

Paganini is one of the few virtuosos of the age whose music has survived his reputation. Much of his music he did not publish, preferring to keep its secrets for himself. The Caprices are virtually the only works written in Paganini's own hand in the kind of elaborated detail that must have characterized his concert platform manner. His five Concerti, several of which lay forgotten after his death, are rather more like outlines for his improvisatory gifts—though the First Concerto is essentially complete in its solo part and accompaniment. Paganini himself once wrote to a friend, "The desire to hear me again will always persist. How many Paganinis do you think there are on this earth?"

With the rapid growth of the cities, the soloist stood out as a potential individual hero, an ideal toward which the revolutionary progressive spirit of the age could aspire. The soloist could also cater more effectively to a greater number, in halls holding two thousand or more. The aristocracy may have been the first to fill these halls, but the bankers, lawyers and merchants were not far behind. Finally, the soloist's prominence was the outcome of several hundred years in the perfection of technique both in performance and in the manufacture of instruments. In the late eighteenth century, the violinist Jean Baptiste Viotti had already made known the Stradivarius, as Paganini did later his Guarnerius, but both drew on methods of performance which had started with Alessandro Striggio and others, three hundred years earlier.

The arrival of the virtuoso soloist augmented the role played by improvisation. In the opera house the singer had always been considered free to embellish any aria or ensemble, but this freedom came later to instrumentalists. Mozart is one of the first true masters of that moment in a concerto called the cadenza, arriving before the final *tutti*—Italian for "all"—when the orchestra ceases and the soloist is left to improvise on

themes and figurations from the preceding movement. Concerti are
most often in three movements, fast-slow-faster, sufficiently varied to
allow a full display of the soloist's skill, with a heady dash to the finish.
The cadenza was usually inserted in the first and last movements.

The contrasting of a soloist and the entire orchestra is a practice which
goes back to Handel and Corelli. From Mozart onward the soloist was
given a chance to display his ability to improvise. If he did a brilliant
job, the return of the principal melody could seem like the composer's
bow to the soloist, figuratively speaking. Composer and soloist were
usually one and the same person, but later, as the virtuoso became a breed
apart, the challenge for supremacy was initiated. If the cadenza failed to
please, the composer's superiority of invention would be clear to all. The
soloist had to try to beat the composer at his own game, for in this final
moment before the end, the composer had already played his round of
cards, and the soloist could show off tricks of the instrument which few
composers would know how to set down on paper.

Even my teacher, Georges Enesco, himself a splendid composer, would
not have thought of improvising every cadenza, any more than would a

*As private wealth increased, to
appear and be seen at the best
places became important to a
widening circle. One of the
events of the season in England
for young ladies and their
dandies was the Hunt Ball.*

Private gathering places of great elegance were created, for instance the Grand Salon maintained in Paris by the Frascati family, portrayed here in the 1820s.

great soloist like Joseph Joachim, who composed cadenzas to fit the violin concerti of Beethoven, Brahms and Mozart. Violinists travelled the length and breadth of Europe perfecting their performances, including all their cadenzas—which one might suspect were often borrowed. Few of the audience could remember from one performance to the next how a given cadenza was supposed to go, so the soloist was usually safe. As such music became better known, the best cadenzas predominated. Yet as compositions became totally integrated and predetermined—and, concomitantly, the performer less creative—composers began to write their own. Beethoven did so for his last piano concerto, the *Emperor*. Eventually little was left to the performer's imagination, and the slavish adherence to the printed note became too much of a prison. In our day we are learning to breathe once again, to try our wings.

In the twentieth century, the audience is increasingly familiar with a large body of music. Therefore, everything depends on the quality of the performer, though nowadays even a badly played work may well enhance the self-esteem of a demanding and critical audience. We know the work well enough to recognize that it will come to an end within a given time, and we do not feel impaled forever on the point of a musical lance. Quite the opposite happens when we listen to Indian music to which we are meant to surrender as we follow the performers through creative flights of fantasy. If they do not improvise creatively and rivetingly, relying rather on conventional prefabricated sequences learned by rote, the music becomes intolerable. The listener recognizes infallibly that originality and beauty are ultimately more compelling than any perfect performance, mechanically and perfunctorily executed.

The Romantic music of the nineteenth and early twentieth centuries is still that most often performed in the concert halls of the world. At no previous time in musical history has so much old music been kept current. I quite understand the frustration of composers of our day before this fact. It is pointless to say to them that in Beethoven's or Paganini's day it would not have been tolerated; the fact is that the idea would not even have arisen then. Bach was right; music was a constantly self-renewing source, just as rivers absorb the melt from new snows every spring—sometimes it comes in torrents. For an extraordinarily long time, we have been dwelling in a strong musical past. However, we need only recall Bartók and Stravinsky, among others, to realize that musical giants are not confined to past ages.

What is this fascination with the past for us? It is simply that we reach for the life-giving sources of music as we would gasp for oxygen and thirst for water, rejecting substitutes. I believe that much of Western music has become synthetic, experimental, arbitrary, over-intellectualized, perhaps glorious to the initiated, but undecipherable to the rest. In faithful reflection of our times, it is noisy, aggressive, disjointed and often ugly. Nonetheless, exotic music and contemporary music do often flourish, particularly among younger people—nor can we, any more than previous generations, select the masterpieces from the plethora of "assembled," derivative or fashionable music, some of which may be catching, and even useful, but not of lasting value.

Romantic music usually suggests great expression and freedom, soaring elation and plunging gloom. Music can convey or induce an immense range of feeling. How it does so is connected with the process by which we perceive music and sort it out in our brain. We know now, for example, that the right half of the brain controls the left side of the body and vice versa. What is more, we have discovered that the two halves of the brain each play an entirely different role in relation to music. The discrimination of pitch, melody and rhythm lies primarily in the right half, which is also the reservoir of our emotional life. The left half of the brain comes into play by offering a capacity for analysis and decoding, performing the

In 1851, the thirty-two-year-old Victoria had been queen of the British Empire for just four years when she officiated at the opening of one of her favorite projects, the Crystal Palace.

same function in handling mathematics, science and also speech. This seems to be true, by the way, whether we are right- or left-handed.

This shorthand description oversimplifies a highly complex process of the human individual learning through training to achieve a synthesis of left and right. One of the earliest manifestations of that synthesis is depth perception, the coordination of eyes and hands in a baby, adorable to watch and vital to the child's development. Another is walking, an infinitely more subtle harmonizing of the entire left and right hemispheres of the body and brain. And in regard to hearing, tests by F. L. King and D. Kimura in 1972 show that right-brain dominance seems to apply to all non-verbal sounds, such as laughing and crying. Other tests in 1974 by T. G. Bever and R. J. Chiarello demonstrate that untutored listeners perceive melody chiefly in the right brain as a general shape, whereas experienced listeners involve the left brain in the analysis of sets of relations. In fact, these tests also show that trained musicians recognize simple melodies more easily in the right ear than in the left, showing left-brain dominance since the nerve path of the right ear is to that area. The analytical function converts music into a language for these professionals; the untrained listener continues to do better with the left ear.

These and similar tests have also shown that the ability to recognize music can be suppressed, as can the ability to deal with speech. The latter condition, called aphasia, is familiar in persons who have suffered a stroke affecting the left brain. What is much less commonly observed, though it exists, is amusia, the loss of musical discrimination by those with right-brain damage. Because it is a less critical loss, it has been overlooked. If the right brain is anaesthetized, it will produce amusia, a condition in which the ability to recognize or sing a sequence of notes vanishes; the tune comes out a monotone. Speech will generally remain— at least for Westerners; there are African and Oriental forms of speech which depend on pitch differentiation, which could be more seriously affected. Repeat the process on the left side and the subject cannot articulate words, though he can sing a tune. In fact, he cannot speak at all or even recognize language. It would seem that syllabic language is a structure independent of pitch for most people, and thus independent of tone deafness.

Part of the pleasure in music lies in this synthesis of right and left, of emotion and analysis. In Western music, the composer first writes down the notes which combine expression with his ability to manipulate his chosen materials. The performer then contributes his share. For both, the

By the mid-nineteenth century the opera house was becoming the focus of upper-class social life in all the major European cities. The colonnades inside and out were ideal places to display one's cultural appreciation and expensive fashions. Many were erected alone on great plazas, as in Dresden, Germany.

balance of right and left is the synthesis of form and meaning. It penetrates to the deepest levels of our awareness. That is part of what makes the performance of music so exhilarating, for the message must be conveyed at both levels. The music becomes as much the performer's as the composer's; and in the nineteenth century this pairing of skills in separate individuals combined to produce works which finally established Western music as one of man's greatest achievements.

The interplay of right and left is particular to my instrument. The right hand sets the bow to the strings, and this is like the act of breathing and the pressure of lungs for a singer. It is also where analysis and meaning come in, for the physical movement of this hand and arm is controlled by the left half of the brain. The bow measures intensity, color, attack and release. It governs the whole line and shape of a phrase, as a poet chooses words to express feelings. Moreover, the violinist is entirely dependent upon balance in every part of his body, the relationship to the vertical, to gravity; the position of the head must be vertical, though not stiff. It is my belief that the special power of the violin is due in part to the way it blends heart and mind, feeling and meaning. These separate functions of right and left are part of the difficulty inherent in playing the violin well. It is rather like trying to pat your stomach and rub your head at the same time. The body that is not fully liberated tends to want both halves to be doing the same thing at once.

Social novelist Bettina von Arnim, friend to Beethoven and Goethe, regularly brought the best chamber music performers into her home in Berlin. The scene was painted in 1855, near the end of her life, in a watercolor by Carl Johann Arnold.

I place special emphasis on this problem when I teach the violin, on what I call "the dissolving of mental adhesion." Orchestral conductors know it well, for so many of them conduct with both hands beating the same time, often in mirror image. I have seen Pierre Boulez maintain a steady beat with the right arm while executing the most complex rhythmic subdivisions with the left. Children who have taken the Dalcroze course can do much the same. There are still other conductors who use the left arm and hand only to turn the pages and mop the brow.

With my violin students I try to help them become aware of these "adhesions" and to break them down. I have developed a number of special exercises of the head, trunk, arms and hands which encourage the freedom and independence, as well as the coordination, of the parts. There is a tendency for violinists, as the right arm brings the bow up on the string or into the air, to prepare a downstroke, to turn the head or even dip the body a bit to meet the arm in motion. I find it useful to experiment in the opposite way. The head balances the violin on the collarbone, adjusting with the aid of thumb and fingers the angle of its level to the left-hand position along the strings. These exercises give the players surer control, for the wrong automatic reflexes no longer interfere with arm or finger action. It is equally important to work from the fingers backwards through the arm, the shoulder blades, all the way to the toes, as it is to follow through in the opposite direction.

Not many years ago I recorded some programs for French television about the role of the violin in Eastern Europe. We filmed a troupe of gypsy musicians in Budapest, and I remember how fascinating I found the coordinated "breathing" within the music on the part of the entire ensemble. Their control was total; they could speed up and slow down simultaneously and instantaneously within every phrase. The leading violinist, Lajos Boros, set the pace, and the range and color of his vibrato and slides with the left hand were even more remarkable than the flashing bow of the right. Boros performed some of the tunes which Brahms used in his arrangements of the *Hungarian* Dances. I have played this music since I was a boy, but I still play it in concert style, the notes all in place with more or less the right feeling and sound. This violinist went into an amazing rendition of the original, as Brahms himself might first have heard it, complete with the richest, most extravagant ornamentation and lightning changes of pace. The only way you could possibly figure out what he was doing would be to put it all through a computer, or slow it down five times. It was simply beyond my mental dimension, and it came from an entirely different impulse than mine.

In his playing of a *czardas*, in which the dancers start slowly and finish with a rapid twirl, the dance used by Brahms, and also by Pablo Sarasate, the late nineteenth century virtuoso violinist, an intuitive technique had been developed to satisfy a vision, and to give that vision exuberant expression. It was a technique bred over hundreds of years. The gypsy Lajos Boros told me he was the seventh son of sons all descended from a violin-playing forebear, all violinists in turn, rather like the Bachs. He could even demonstrate for me how his father used to play certain tunes, incidentally quite unlike the way he himself preferred.

The artist develops what he needs, whether he wishes to paint or sculpt or play an instrument. Our Western classical string playing has grown out of many centuries of practice and training. Those of us who are trained in that way can no more step into the gypsy's world than he into ours, much as we might appreciate one another. I think this distance has everything to do with the difference between the written and unwritten. (How much we have lost with the written or printed score). In the gypsy's playing, there was an elusive inflection which we must surely lose the minute we follow notation. It is a subtlety of expression which can only be compared to a player of the Indian sarangi, with all its sympathetic strings surely one of the most difficult bowed instruments to master.

The distance between unwritten and written traditions grew as the nineteenth century wore on. The pattern of life was changing as the general standard of living in Western Europe rose, along with the level of education. The concept of the audience was evolving also: a general public for the music of an artist or composer was quickly becoming a feature of urban life and prosperity. That audience included the formal and informal, in the concert hall and opera house, alongside the outdoor garden restaurant and park band.

In the Romantic era, the Age of the Individual, the worship of star performers was evident above all at the opera. Composers such as Gioacchino Rossini (1792–1868) and Vincenzo Bellini (1801–1835) tailored their comic and lyric operas to suit the talents of Giuditta Pasta, Maria Malibran, Adolphe Nourrit and Luigi Lablache. It is from such works as Rossini's *The Barber of Seville*, *Semiramide* and *William Tell*, and Bellini's *Norma* and *I Puritani* that we have inherited the term *bel canto*, meaning, simply, beautiful singing. Attending the opera house was at once a source of intense emotional experiences in music and a means of displaying one's superior cultural and social attainments. The new style of romantic opera was not limited to Italy; in fact, Carl Maria von Weber (1786–1826) is credited with composing the first opera that can truly be given this label, *Der Freischütz*. In France, the gargantuan operas of Giacomo Meyerbeer (1791–1864) called for huge casts of highly skilled singers and lavish scenic effects, notably in *Les Huguenots* and *L'Africaine*. The transformation of opera made possible the later innovations of Verdi and Wagner.

On a more casual level, music was welcomed increasingly in a wide variety of settings. Dance music, serenades and village bands had provided for part of the musical needs of the people since the Middle Ages. Now opera tunes, the latest marches and waltzes, arranged for garden bands or played by ear by two or three musicians, were encountered everywhere. Schubert and Beethoven both wrote such music, as Mozart and Haydn before them had written serenades and *divertimenti* for the pleasure of noble patrons. As the appetite for music grew, many composers provided a supply of popular tunes, expressly written for light entertainment; in Vienna, Joseph Lanner and Johann Strauss Sr. were rivals. Later, Mendelssohn and Brahms were to contribute their share.

Mozart was the peak of the earlier Classical era; the music of Johannes Brahms was the fruition of the late Romantic age. Both drew inspiration of a high nature from that unique city, Vienna. Mozart lived there much of his adult life, and Brahms was drawn to spend his last twenty years in its seductive embrace. Vienna today is still marked by its very great past, still elaborately courteous and charming, and there is no better place to feel the irrepressible gaiety that is Vienna than in Grinzing, a bucolic suburb on her outskirts. Here we may still hear a strain of music as unexportable as that heady aromatic new autumn wine, the *Heuriger*. It is a music compounded of troubadour and Romany gypsy, of elegance and abandon; in this case it is unexportable *not* because it is difficult to understand, but because, like a flower picked from the living plant, it must wilt when in alien hands, in an alien location. It is called *Schrammelmusik* after the Schrammel family who first created this local form of entertainment. Its intrinsic worth may be rather poor, and the term is now somewhat pejorative, which I regret, for to me it reflects unashamed and wholesome joy in the memory of the best of times in the old Austro-Hungarian Empire. Today it is but an echo, a somewhat threadbare tapestry, the original exuberance unable to fulfill the span of its initial impulse. In this musical tradition of Johann Schrammel, we have a half-way house between the improvised rural folk music, always played by ear, and the domesticated urban concert music of set written pieces. Schrammel and Strauss were contemporaries, and the village of Grinzing was the rustic realm of Schrammel, as it remains to this day. In this engaging music, we hear the spirit which continued over two centuries to inspire the great composers of Vienna.

Easygoing, good-natured music for dancing and conversation was to be heard throughout German-speaking lands in many forms, and any celebration or social occasion was unthinkable without it. In Switzerland,

The sophistication of the modern orchestra is evoked by Edgar Degas, who for once placed his ballerinas in a secondary role.

one of its most appealing forms is found in districts such as Appenzell, where traditional dances have been composed by local musicians for more than two hundred years. It should be mentioned that there was far less arbitrary distinction (at this time) between popular and classical music. The great composers knew that folk music belonged organically as part of the whole, and willingly borrowed such tunes. Johannes Brahms made use of dance rhythms in his symphonies, both in the gentler middle movements and the lively finales—earlier the minuet had been part of the symphonies of Mozart and Haydn.

In the nineteenth century Germanic tradition, the writing of a great symphony was one of the noblest tasks a composer could set for himself. Mozart and Haydn had been extraordinarily prolific, writing 41 and 104, respectively. But Beethoven wrote only nine. Robert Schumann wrote but four, between 1841 and 1851, though his output of piano music of every kind was as abundant as Chopin and his songs almost as numerous as Schubert. Brahms took the symphonies of Schumann and Beethoven as his model, but the shadow of Beethoven was so intimidating that it was not until 1875 that Brahms completed his First Symphony—a labor of twenty years. Brahms was then past forty. The relief must have been great,

for he finished another within a year. The Second Symphony is as cheerful and friendly as the First is somber and aspiring. Tracing the common language shared by Brahms and the folk music of his time—even the *Ländler* of Schubert or the waltzes of Strauss, and the abandoned music of the Hungarian gypsy—helps us to understand better how their romantic ardor came to be tempered by the sobriety of the North-German master. In both we respond to the structure of the music as well as to its feeling.

In the hands of Berlioz and Brahms, the symphony orchestra grew, competing in volume with the ever-stronger noise of daily life. By the 1830s when Brahms was born, the railroad had begun rattling through the once quiet countryside. Soon steamships would whistle in the harbor and factories would clatter. The long and noble peasant tradition was being overtaken by urban culture. What could be more natural to the industrial age than the piano, which became the heroic voice of the concert virtuoso.

Mozart and Beethoven had favored the piano, but the instruments on which they played were lightweights compared to the instruments which now began to appear. The piano firm founded in London by John Broadwood in 1795 was one of the leaders, along with that of Ignace Pleyel in Paris in 1807. Sébastien Erard in Paris was another, and his double escapement action patented in 1821 came to be widely used. This gave the individual piano-key hammer far greater flexibility and avoided the annoying rebound in loud playing by which the hammer might bounce to hit the strings a second time. The piano became popular very

Industrialization was growing swiftly, and the deep mining of coal became vital to railroads and shipping as the steam engine improved. The Hetton Colliery in England was one of the earliest to make use of the latest in technology (portrayed here about 1825).

The display showroom of the Leipzig piano manufacturer Blüthner offered the opportunity to advertise instruments whose glitter and finish make them comparable to the Cadillacs and Rolls Royces of our own day.

quickly in the United States, where Jonas Chickering began production in 1823 and William Knabe in 1837. Steinway and Sons set up shop in New York in 1853, after their success in Hamburg, Germany. In Vienna Ignaz Bösendorfer began producing in 1823, Friedrich Bechstein in Berlin in 1856, and Joseph Blüthner in Leipzig in 1851. Theodore Heintzman launched his firm in Toronto in 1860.

The piano's new voice was brought to life first by Frederic Chopin. Born in Poland in 1810, at the very dawn of the Romantic era, at nineteen Chopin made his professional debut as a piano virtuoso, and two years later settled in Paris. Actually, Chopin preferred the older English Broadwood, but the music he created has survived splendidly in our day of the concert grand. This is due in part to his having unlocked the secret of making the piano sing like an orchestra while sustaining an entire harmonic underpinning. It is also due to his superior harmonic imagination. Beethoven may have been bold in a work like the *Appassionata* Sonata where he created extraordinary drama out of subtle shifts between F minor, C major and G-flat major. But even he could not surpass the astute wizardry of Chopin, who could make listeners sense the ambiguity of notes which might at one and the same time have two different

functions, leading out of one place and into another by shifting meaning from C-sharp to D-flat, all the while being sustained by the fingers or the pedal. This was the art of *enharmonic* modulation for which Bach had so thoroughly prepared the way with his *Well Tempered Keyboard*.

Chopin almost alone transfigured the technique of writing piano music into its romantic expression. Of course, there were contemporaries like Sigismond Thalberg and the Irishman, John Field (who settled in St. Petersburg), but none had the instant effect of Chopin. If Chopin's writing is to be taken as a reliable standard of his playing, we know he possessed an extraordinarily fluid technique, although he did not have the stamina or force of Franz Liszt, achieving his effects rather by shading of tone and color.

The skill of Paganini served as an example to Chopin; the violinist was also the first musician to deeply impress Franz Liszt. Liszt began his solo career in Vienna at the age of ten in 1821, then preceded Chopin to Paris by eight years; he was already an adored favorite there when the Polish expatriate arrived, and they became fast friends. The new, heavy keyboard artillery was ideally suited to Liszt, for here was the true pianist counterpart of Paganini, a cult figure worshipped and admired in all the great capitals of Europe. Liszt embellished his formidable piano compositions with coloratura effects as astounding as those of any diva. Other virtuosos attempted to follow suit, and piano manufacturers were driven to improve and reinforce their instruments so that they could withstand such an unprecedented onslaught.

Hungarians consider Liszt their own, but musical history cannot do so, though he did not escape the influence of Hungary as his many

Frederic Chopin was a supreme pianist, but far more the poetic dreamer than the thundering keyboard virtuoso. Here he plays for Prince Radziwill and his daughters Elise (standing) and Wanda (seated, foreground) at their home in Berlin about 1830. The prince was also a singer, cellist and composer.

RECITAL CAGE OR THE
FEMALE-KISS-FENDER

MY HAIR
HELP
YOURSELVES

His abundant auburn tresses and digital wizardry made of Ignaz Jan Paderewski the most romantically appealing concert figure of the late 1800s. Later Paderewski became a Polish patriot, and in 1917 was named Prime Minister of his newly liberated nation.

Hungarian Rhapsodies attest. Liszt was born in Raiding, now in Austria, and though the area then belonged to Hungary, the school where Liszt was educated was German-speaking and he never learned Hungarian. How this growing Austrian world loved show and display—one rested on Friday to get ready for Saturday, and took Monday off to recover from Sunday. Crisp uniforms, polished buttons, full dresses made an ensemble beautifully suited to the new urban popular music, the waltzes of Johann Strauss, father and son, who together between 1800 and 1900 established a hold on Vienna, indeed over all of Austria.

By the mid-nineteenth century, peasant and merchant were being caught up in a rising tide of nationalism, as the long rule of dukes and princes began to be swept away. The Strauss waltz has been called the national anthem of Austria, but it is not so much nationalistic music as it is the expression of a zest for life, for beauty and taste. It has far more rhythmic freedom than most Germanic music, and borrows some of its ebb and flow from the gypsy. Like the Hungarian *czardas* it gets faster and slower, quite quickly, within the same phrase. The waltz has that curious antici-pation of the second beat and delay of the third which gives such charm to what is otherwise plain three-quarter time. The Austro-Hungarian Empire may be gone, but its perfume remains.

The examples of Mozart, Beethoven, Chopin, Liszt and others drove many young people (and their parents) to seek acclaim as prodigies. The trio formed by the Neruda children, Victor, Wilhelmine and Amalie, was an unusual instance of balanced planning (engraving by Moritz Galisch, 1848).

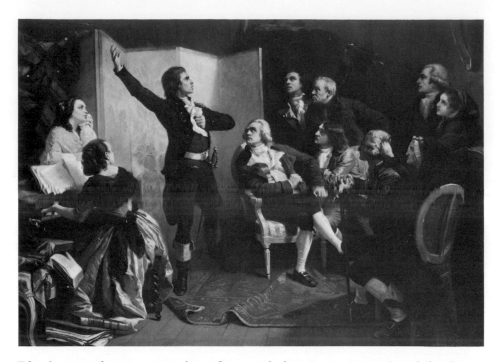

Rhythm can be an expression of a people in many ways: take plain three-quarter time, put a strong accent on the first beat and an almost equal one on the second, and lift the third; play it slowly and regularly, and you have the basis for one of the other great national dances of the period, the *polonaise*. Chopin wrote several of these for the piano, as he also wrote many waltzes. Each of these dances, though in three-four time, is quite unlike the other. The *polonaise* expresses pride and honor, fiery independence, and just a hint of what poles call *zal*, as untranslatable a word as Vienna's *gemütlich*, but meaning a mixture of regret, defiance and surrender. In some ways the *polonaise* is Poland's most characteristic expression of her national identity.

National pride and honor receive their most widely recognized musical expression in a form widely accepted by the mid-nineteenth century, the national anthem. This is not to say that previously there were no anthems. Haydn had written one for Austria when she faced the forces of Napoleon; Germany later appropriated it with new words as "Deutschland Über Alles." Britain's "God Save the King" is known in a number of versions dating back to the seventeenth century, taking the form we know around 1745. Without having to raise its voice, the anthem affirms Britain's pride, as much a prayer as a national statement, upholding the long tradition of a deeply respected monarch. Amazingly, that same tune served equally well as the first anthem of a united Germany, and in the United States as "My Country 'tis of Thee," as well as for the anthem of Denmark and Switzerland. It is in slow three-four time, and cannot serve

A romantic conception of the first singing of Rouget de l'Isle's patriotic song "La Marseillaise" was painted by Isidore Pils at about the time the song was officially adopted as France's national anthem. Originally called "Chant de Guerre Pour l'Armée du Rhin," it acquired its present name when sung in Paris by troops from Marseilles.

as a march. The same is true of "The Star Spangled Banner," adopted as America's official anthem only in 1931, though it became popular quickly after it was written in 1814. Francis Scott Key grafted his words onto what had been a jolly three-four drinking song, "To Anacreon, in Heav'n," by John Stafford Smith, an Englishman. That tune in turn was derived from an eighteenth century ballad of the Enniskillen Fusiliers of Northern Ireland. Such are the tortuous paths nations may take to proclaim their spirit in music.

The anthem which offers the most striking contrast to these is one born directly out of revolt. France's "La Marseillaise" is in two-four time, clearly suitable for marching. The tune can be traced to an aria from the opera *Thésée* by Gossec. Rouget de l'Isle, author of "La Marseillaise," was a young Army engineer and composer, member of an aristocratic Royalist family imprisoned during the Revolution of 1789. Gossec's melody evidently penetrated de l'Isle's subconscious, for when he wrote his anthem in 1792 he did not think it anyone's but his own. Le Comte de l'Isle shifted the tune and harmony around a little, pairing them to a series of highly inflammatory rhetorical verses, of which the first concludes:

Citizens, to arms!
Tighten your ranks!
Let us march, march,
So that impure blood shall water our land!

Like some of Schubert's songs, "La Marseillaise" is harmonized in alternating major and minor. The shift saddens the middle lines, but leaves room to recover for the march onward to triumph.

It was Napoleon who said, "One good march is worth one hundred cannon." He would sometimes speed up their tempo so that his troops might cover ground more swiftly. Militarism has rather lost public favor now, and the French anthem is played more slowly, conveying greater majesty and dignity. Hector Berlioz made a striking orchestration of "La Marseillaise" which Rouget de l'Isle lived to hear at its Paris première in 1830. The anthem was finally placed under copyright in 1850, in the arrangement by Colonel Pierre Dupont, and became the official anthem in 1857.

Anthems in two-four time may serve as marches, but Canada's anthem "O Canada," and Haydn's tune for Austria, for example, tend to require a tempo too slow for anything but a dead-march. In the effort to impress, some national anthems have reached absurdity, not least those composed by foreigners for newly emerged nations. The smaller the country, the louder and longer the anthem. The Swiss, however, have a conception all their own. There every one of the cantons has its own "national" song,

for instance the anthem of Appenzell, which speaks of a quiet pride in mountains and fertile valleys, in peace and independence, in a sense of native worth.

Actually I am not much in favor of music in the service of nationalism. In the Middle Ages, Europe's boundary lines were much looser and people could move about more easily. Passports and frontiers erect barriers, glorify nations, and risk the loss of much that is local. It may be that patriotism, like religion, works toward the fulfilment of our needs for great purpose; but when barriers are artificially imposed, they become a reflection of nations arbitrarily enlarging their dominions. European colonizers decided how to divide Africa and Latin America, often parting human families as savagely as the Berlin Wall divides Germans.

Conventionally we tend to think of Beethoven or Brahms as German, Paganini or Bellini as Italian. In fact, before the 1860s, these nations were unknown under such names. The drive toward unity began with the need to defeat Napoleon. His example nonetheless inspired others, for he brought a cohesion to French law and administration which the Revolution had failed through internal dissent to achieve. Clearly, Napoleon could not have accomplished what he did without a unified nation behind him.

When one looks back, the nineteenth century sometimes appears to rumble like a volcano in constant eruption. In the turmoil of the 1840s two nations were struggling valiantly to be born: Italy and Germany.

The prevailing Swiss sobriety is alleviated by the liveliness of their folk and dance music, performed here by the musicians of Appenzell, one of the most conservative of all the cantons of Switzerland, and one of the proudest.

Quite early, two opera composers became identified with this process: Giuseppe Verdi and Richard Wagner.

Much of northern Italian land was then still under Hapsburg control. Verdi, born in 1813, was a fiery partisan of independence and national unity, and his early music owed its popularity as much to this fact as to its vigor. One example can be taken from the 1842 première of his opera *Nabucco*, composed when Verdi was twenty-nine. The chorus of the Hebrew people in exile sing of their yearning for a national homeland in the noble tune "Va, Pensiero, sull' Ali Dorati"—"Fly, Thought, on Golden Wings." The singing of "Va, Pensiero" that night caused a great demonstration; the audience came close to storming the stage.

Verdi became the hero of the day, his name scrawled over city walls like graffiti, not just because of his music but because by happy chance his name V–E–R–D–I spelled out the acronym for Vittorio Emmanuele, Re d'Italia—Victor Emmanuel, King of Italy. (Victor Emmanuel II was King of Sardinia at the time.) Italian patriots wrote it out in the slogan

The Fighting Temeraire towed to her last Berth *by J. M. W. Turner (1775–1851) is a symbol of the arrival of the industrial age. Turner's foggy, swirling canvases were a foretaste of impressionism; this one was painted in 1839.*

After the unification of Italy, Giuseppe Garibaldi was welcomed as a hero on his entry into Naples in 1860 (from a contemporary newspaper account).

Viva Verdi, proclaiming their sentiments in a safe musical form. When Italy finally became one nation in 1861 with Victor Emmanuel as King, Verdi reluctantly became a deputy in the first Italian parliament at the invitation of Count Cavour.

The operas of Verdi displayed a virile, passionate, even aggressive, style, far from the lyrical sweetness of Bellini or the bounce of Donizetti. In the early part of the century, opera was still a place for the display of costumes and of vocal prowess. With Verdi we reach a high-water mark of Romantic opera, where dramatic impact is as important as anything else.

At this stage in our journey it should be abundantly clear how inextricably intertwined are music and man, whether for good or ill. Modern states like Chile and Greece have at times suppressed some popular music because it was felt to pose a threat to established power. In Ireland there was a time when you could be jailed for singing "The Wearing of the Green." In our own day, anthems like "We Shall Overcome" and "Blowin' in the Wind" have become both spurs and symbols. Artists are often caught up in the swirl of politics, as in 1956 when Zoltan Kodaly inadvertently became a hero in the short-lived Hungarian uprising against the Soviets. Verdi in his turn was forced by Italian censors to change the locale of his opera *Un Ballo in Maschera*, set in the court of King Augustus III of Sweden. He was urged to substitute a far-off, little-known land and time, so that Sweden might not be offended. Verdi chose Massachusetts under the Puritans.

While Italy was in revolt, the German people were also clamoring for unification. Wagner, already famous for *The Flying Dutchman, Rienzi* and *Tannhaüser*, became so embroiled with the revolutionaries in 1849 that he had to flee, first to his friend Liszt at Weimar, and thence to Paris and Switzerland. This exile lasted thirteen years. In Switzerland he completed *Lohengrin*, and began sketching a text for his only comic opera, *Die Meistersinger*. It took him almost two decades to finish the music. By that time, Germany had united under Bismarck to form a single nation.

Born in Leipzig in 1813, Wagner was obsessed with the history of the German race, far back to the myths of antiquity. He was equally influenced by the example of Carl Maria von Weber, whose *Der Freischütz* had transformed public taste in 1821. For *Die Meistersinger von Nürnberg*, Wagner took as his hero a troubadour, Hans Sachs, a sixteenth century maker of shoes and songs. Sachs had lived in Nuremberg, one of the centers of early German musical life. A member of the guild of Mastersingers, he was an able composer and a fine poet. More than six thousand of his poems are extant, some having survived with his tunes. Wagner used one of these melodies as the main opening theme of his opera. It recurs throughout, and forms the final chorus of the people.

When Wagner wrote the text of *Die Meistersinger*, he was concerned with the need to preserve and defend German art and culture against the threat of alien intrusion, from within or without. Prophetically, he had his hero admonish and exhort the people to remember their duty to honor all that is German. At the opera's close Hans Sachs is crowned, to his surprise, with the laurel wreath of victory in the Mastersingers' song contest. No doubt Wagner secretly saw himself as Sachs, mythically crowned with laurels, deserving of praise and glory. How ironic it is that Wagner should be the one to bring his people such a conservative message. What Wagner could not have foreseen was that his undeniable genius helped to accelerate the dissolution of the bonds holding Western classical music together.

While that may seem an extreme statement, Wagner's harmonic experiments had profound consequences. The impulse for this is already found in the music of Chopin, a debt not usually acknowledged. Liszt and Berlioz are far more frequently cited as Wagner's forerunners, and it is true that in orchestration and heroic lift both men brought much to Wagner's spirit. But in terms of pure harmony, Chopin is the greater

influence; he had the ability to modulate from suspended chord to suspended chord, avoiding settling on any clear key. He even avoided at times the return to the home key. Such techniques profoundly affected Wagner's thinking.

In Wagner this becomes the stretching of the suspended tone, that famous dissonance of the Renaissance, to the absolute limit. It is part and parcel of the aesthetic stretching of sexual sensations, the prolongation of the ecstatic, the unreal, the mysteriously dark and visionary. It is a totally un-Mediterranean attitude. Wagner's achievement lay in his mastery of the elements that were at hand in this emerging Germany with its wealth of Nordic myths, its philosophers—Schopenhauer and Nietzsche—its great literature and its musical heritage.

The founding of the German Empire was officially pro-claimed on New Year's Day in 1871, and two weeks later, officers and delegations from nearby battalions and districts assembled in the Hall of Mirrors at Versailles to salute Kaiser Wilhelm I as Emperor.

Wagner experimented with three harmonic techniques in the four operas constituting the cycle *The Ring of the Nibelung: Das Rheingold, Die Walküre, Siegfried* and *Die Götterdämmerung.* He toiled over the text and music for some twenty-five years. The legend is the medieval epic of the Germanic people, one which captured Wagner's imagination in boyhood. There is perhaps no other example of such sustained creative energy devoted over so long a time to a single obsession. Wagner had reached the music of the second act of Siegfried when he broke off the work to concentrate on his greatest harmonic breakthrough, *Tristan und*

Isolde, completing the music in the surprisingly short time of one year. It is all of a piece, and like no other music before or since, even for Wagner, despite its celebrated influence on so much that was to follow.

In 1862 Wagner received an amnesty and returned to Bavaria. The next year the Vienna Opera attempted to put *Tristan* into production, but had to abandon the effort after twenty-seven rehearsals, considering the opera unperformable. It was not until 1864 in Munich, thanks to the enthusiastic support of King Ludwig II of Bavaria, that *Tristan* was rescheduled, and at last produced in 1865. It immediately raised violent comment: Eduard Hanslick, the leading music critic, said it reminded him of an Italian painting of a martyr whose intestines are being unwound from his body. Gioacchino Rossini, still revered as a composer of some thirty lively opera comedies, perhaps had the last word. He said, "Wagner has good moments, but bad quarter hours."

No composer ever suffered more critical abuse in his own time than Wagner; his operas were bigger and longer than those of anybody else except perhaps Meyerbeer. He used a huge orchestra, and made unprecedented demands on the capacities of voices. Today we no longer find his musical language so strange, and the opera house he planned and supervised himself at Bayreuth, in northern Bavaria, has become the shrine of Wagner-lovers. The *Festspielhaus* was paid for by King Ludwig despite the objections of his treasurer. The King was only eighteen, and probably mad even then; certainly he was neurotically obsessed by Wagner's music.

Wagner's theater in Bayreuth remains an acoustical marvel, and its masterstroke is a huge orchestra pit sunk deep under the stage, entirely separated from the audience. In this pit over one hundred players can sit; the many horns, trombones and trumpets are at the back, alongside four harps, two sets of kettledrums, with dozens of winds and sixty strings in front. The whole orchestral space under the stage acts as a sounding box: the blended sound of the orchestra mixes with the voices and is projected into the fan-shaped amphitheater like one vast horn. The singers say that they can feel the great orchestral blasts in their feet, all but levitating them, when the players unleash their maximum force.

This house broke with the elegant conventions and traditions of Italian and French theater, so fashionable in the German principalities. It remains a symbol today, as much for the power and strength of Wagner's music as for the deep emotional impact of the ideas he expressed. It is amazing to me that no theater has ever imitated Bayreuth since Wagner conceived and built it. Perhaps the simple explanation is the invisibility of the conductor. Wagner would sit or stand on his podium, towering

The pure Germanic legendary hero Siegfried became the central figure in Wagner's cycle of four operas, The Ring of the Nibelung. *The painting by Ferdinand Leeke dates from the time of the first performance of the cycle in 1876.*

above his orchestra, his head and shoulders just visible to the singers when he stood, and to the rear brasses when he sat. But the audiences could not see him at all, hidden behind the high orchestra ramp like a sinister black sausage. Wagner wanted his spectators to concentrate on the musical drama. It was a composer's dream come true. But conductors these days have much to say about the shape of opera houses and, no doubt being exhibitionists by definition, would hardly tolerate being reduced to a mere musical presence.

What Wagner did to music was fundamental; ever since Mozart and Bach the driving force in Western music had been vested in the idea of the home key. A piece of music, a movement of a sonata or symphony, was announced in a chosen key, the safe harbor to which the music would always return no matter how far it might stray. Richard Wagner changed all that, for his mature music displays no permanent home key, though it remains tonal—even in the feverish modulations of *Tristan*, aptly called by one scholar "the crisis of our harmonic system." In Wagner there is instead an endless thread of melody running through a limitless change of keys, rather like Alice walking through all those mirrors and never turning back. Wagner cut our Western music loose from its moorings, with unforeseeable consequences.

If Beethoven launched the idea of the composer as hero, writing in his own personal, inimitable style, Wagner is its most prominent nineteenth century champion. He also marks one of the points of greatest distance between what the French call *musique savante*, meaning roughly "artistic music," and the music of the people. The split has developed in our day into full-fledged schizophrenia. Wagner's music is full of sexuality and is obsessed with death, not only in *Tristan* where the references are obvious, but in the whole of *The Ring*, which is built on the long-recurring climax. His late operas epitomize the state of slightly hysterical fantasy which the Romantic era had reached, taxing the endurance of both the performers and the public. The symbol of the hero, Siegfried, betrayed and slain, and of the goddess Brünnhilde who in the end laid down her life for him, was not lost on Germany. In 1883 Wagner died, less than a decade after completing the Ring cycle. His death—in Venice—seems strange, for the Latin colors and elegant immorality of that city hardly agree with the paranoia and fogbound myths of the Wagnerian music drama.

Music did not change all at once, of course, for many of the old ties were still strong. The symphonies of Anton Bruckner are proof of this, as are his works for organ. It simply was not possible for the old European world to give up centuries of accumulated expectation so easily. When we listen to Bruckner we may hear instrumental techniques pioneered by Wagner, but we also hear musical impulses rooted in Bach, and even further back, in the Renaissance. Bruckner was organist at the magnificent old monastery of St. Florian in Austria, and though a disciple and admirer of Wagner, he could not have been more different in nature. A simple man with boundless faith, his nine long symphonies and many masses have a countrified quality, an elegiac purity. This music is rooted in the sound of the organ, for Bruckner could truly make that noble instrument the anonymous voice of God.

The burst of harmony in a great Bach chorale-prelude or a Bruckner fugue heard on the organ is a splendid thing, displaying an immense versatility, with a unique power and range from the lowest of audible

frequencies to the highest, and a rich mixture of overtones. For me the sound of the organ is like the sound of nature itself, attuned to prehuman laws of proportion, a vast breath filling vaulted spaces with ease. Some say the organ shakes us physically to impress us with God's power. Others say it cries out in order that God might hear us more clearly, and take pity. Bruckner continues Bach's tradition of the composer as servant of God, and his symphonies are in part an extension of the resources of the great nineteenth century organ with its multiple keyboards and stops.

Bruckner makes use of Wagner's chromatic harmonic language, but keeps the home key clearly in mind. Yet the Wagnerian tidal wave was unstoppable. His innovative harmonic style even penetrated to France, where the operas of Gounod and Massenet were enthroned, despite Bizet's upstart *Carmen*, with its bow to the south. One can trace the influence first in the music of César Franck (himself, like Bruckner, an organist). His only symphony, his many tone poems for orchestra and his piano and organ works all bear the unmistakable mark of the German master. Franck's Sonata for Violin and Piano, composed in 1886, three years after Wagner's death, may have a moody passionate thrust, but it has none of Wagner's bombast. As with Brahms, the music of Franck is a harmonious

Fascinated by displays of extravagant and huge machinery, people flocked to the Paris Exposition Universelle in 1889, where the Eiffel Tower was the brand-new landmark, and Alexander Graham Bell's telephone and Thomas Edison's phonograph the great sensation.

combination of structure and feeling, a surge of what one can only call "musical meaning," a sweep entirely free of the self-conscious. It is the essence of Romantic musical style, the marriage of composer, performer and audience.

There is also in this music an extraordinary sense of control over the passage of time; a moment will be held still as if suspended, and then released with a rush. Einstein has told us that time is relative, flexible and elastic; I have noticed these qualities whenever I have tried to play to the tick of the metronome. It literally seems to change its pace. Some notes seem longer and others shorter, though I know in my rational mind that the beat of that instrument is automatic and even. In music, memory governs the sense of time, from the individual notes, to the phrase, to the overall contour. Living in music is like living in a family of time relationships corresponding to the physical states of the body and the emotions. For the performer this communication with the listener is one of life's most satisfying experiences, for if a mood of serene acceptance is established, an audience can be held there for as long as four or five minutes, as in the slow movement of the Beethoven Violin Concerto. The larger the audience, the more intense is the sensation. I have no feeling that I am responsible for the music, somehow addressing the listeners and urging them on; rather I am the means whereby a common meditation becomes possible.

Free open-air concerts of light music were a popular attraction throughout Europe by the late nineteenth century, the expense incurred usually paid for by the consumption of food and drink. The "Vauxhall" in Naples emulated London's famed garden concert spot (from the Illustrazione Italiana, 1878).

As ever, there is no action without reaction. One of the most striking musical evolutions of the later nineteenth century was the emergence of a recognizable national element in classical music. Some parts of Eastern Europe were only just awakening from the Middle Ages, and composers like Dvorák and Smetana did for the Czechs and Slovaks what Grieg achieved for Norway and later Sibelius for Finland. They made extensive use of native melodies and dance rhythms in their work. Nowhere was this national pride stronger in its musical voice than in Russia, where so many and diverse races had lived for so long. The Russian musical tradition is very old and very deep, and was still divided at this time into the same two basic parts as that of Western Europe at the time of plainsong—that of the cultural elite and that of the people. Among the latter there were folk songs and peasant dances of vigor and variety. There was also the music of the Eastern Orthodox Church, which had taken shape by the time of Charlemagne and had since changed little. The unquenchable Russian spirit survives in the music of its faith, with its deep male voices singing with longing and passion of union with Christ and God.

The Opera house in St. Petersburg was the home of the classic ballets staged for the Russians by Marius Petipa, a former dancer from Marseilles, whose reign lasted nearly fifty years until his death in 1910.

Russia had not experienced the refining urban fires of the Renaissance, and was now racing toward her encounter with the modern world. The first wave of Western culture had already come to Russia under Peter the Great at the end of the seventeenth century. He deeply admired Louis XIV and French was the official language of his court.

The Russian passion for French elegance also extended to the dance. Tsar Peter had imported ballet masters and musicians directly from the court at Versailles. Later, teachers and musicians came to Moscow from England and Italy. Around 1860, a choreographer and dancer from Marseilles,

Karen Kain has been called by many critics the prima ballerina of Canada. She performs here with Yehudi Menuhin and cellist Donald Whitton a solo moment from the White Swan pas-de-deux, from the Tschaikovsky score Swan Lake.

Marius Petipa, arrived to build the Russian Imperial Ballet at the Maryinsky Theater in St. Petersburg. He molded it into one of the finest companies in the world, and through it Russia began at last to make incursions into the West. Russia has always produced outstanding dancers. Their display of stamina still astounds us today in such touring companies as the Moiseyev Ballet. In Russian farming villages, the tradition of exuberant folk dancing still continues.

While Wagner was splitting Western music into two camps, the impact of Russia was felt through the music of Peter Ilyitch Tchaikovsky, who wrote many scores for Petipa, among them *The Nutcracker*, *Sleeping Beauty*, and perhaps the best known, *Swan Lake*. The discipline of Russian dancers calls for the ability to work long hours without a break or complaint, a national characteristic. Their standard in the dance remains a model, and was carried to America by Georges Balanchine, Diaghilev's last and perhaps greatest choreographer, whose highly sensitive musical mind is married to a painter's eye and a poet's vision.

How well I remember, at the tender age of five, my first experience of unattainable love. It was engendered by seeing the inimitable Anna Pavlova dancing in San Francisco, a miracle of lightness in the title role of *The California Poppy*. She remained my ideal, my Dulcinea, until she was superseded by my wife Diana, herself a dancer trained in the Russian tradition in England. The melody of the White Swan pas de deux from Tchaikovsky's *Swan Lake* is one of his most sublime, a heavenly violin solo which I longed to perform for Pavlova. You may well understand how transported I was when accompanying Margot Fonteyn and, more recently, Canada's fine prima ballerina, Karen Kain, and premier danseur, Frank Augustyn. Knowing that one's music causes people to dance is a great satisfaction and I have also experienced the pleasure of it when leading polkas and waltzes at the Bath Festival. This helped me to understand the gypsy fiddler for whom the dancing of others is the ideal fruit of his labors.

The dance may have been imported first from France, but Russia made it her own. There is no flower without a root, and if it is to bloom it must be fed by something strong and steady. Western music was fed for a thousand years by a richly inventive folk tradition, from as far away as Mongolia. This element has always been strong in Russia, where the people retain a great sense of identity with the earth, a sense most of us have lost.

Russia was nearing her own Revolution; the introduction of French and Italian literature, painting and architecture by the Tsars had only widened the gulf between the people and their leaders. Composers such as

Borodin, Balakirev, Rimsky-Korsakov and a host of others drew inspiration from vital popular sources. Modest Moussorgsky tried hard to establish a truly Russian music, especially in his opera *Boris Godunov*. Many of these composers managed to hold onto the peasant love of uneven rhythms. Tchaikovsky himself was much criticized for introducing a five-four movement into his Fifth Symphony, when it seemed "apparent" to academics that it would have been much better as a waltz. Tchaikovsky remains the consummate blend of the Russian East and the European West.

A particular natural talent for rhythm in dance and music has always been part of each nation, whether Russian, Austrian or Spanish. Brahms recognized this when he once signed an autograph book with the first notes of the "Blue Danube" waltz, adding, "Unfortunately not by—yours, Johannes Brahms."

Toward the close of the century the national musical idiom of Spain was suddenly rediscovered by all of Europe. There is no truer voice of a people than the art of flamenco, a music characterized by forceful, often improvised, rhythms. It is like a blend of the many streams which become the Danube or the Rhine. Flamenco is a development of the Romantic age, deriving its form in part from France's *café chantant*—which may be one reason why this music became so fashionable in France; Bizet's *Carmen* is one of its finest flowers. Flamenco springs from old sources. It has Moorish roots, and Andalusia on the southern coast of Spain, where the Moors lingered the longest, is the flamenco homeland. It also contains the spirit of the gypsies, those nomadic people who may first have come from central Asia and who entered Spain just as the Moors left.

This perfectly coordinated music and dance of the flamenco is proof of the need never to wander too far from the organic roots of our being. As the nineteenth century drew to a close, urbanized man was being alienated from the soil. The Romantic era was giving way to new forces, unleashed by the struggles between nations, and by the artist's constant search for renewal. The choice was between the sanctity of life and the fear of man, between total control and total freedom, in music as in our very lives.

It is fortunate that I am writing at a time when we have been freed from the inclination to idealize and romanticize historical trends and events, merely because they belong to our own background. And although we have our own inescapable blindnesses and prejudices, at least we are capable of seeing that revolution is often no more beautiful or sacred than repression. It is merely a reaction released by accumulated energy. A Napoleon is no more enlightened than a Frederick the Great, and the rule of a majority can be as liable to excess and shortsightedness as the rule of the minority. What counts are qualities, not labels; content, not form.

Immigrants, the willing from Europe and the unwilling from Africa, become the population of North America, where a new music begins to take shape. The songs of Stephen Foster, the rags of Scott Joplin, the marches of John Philip Sousa are part of an America coming of age. Edison's invention of the movies and the phonograph revolutionize the shaping of musical taste. In Europe, the old conventions break up under the impact of the impressionism of Debussy, the splendors of Strauss and Mahler. Charles Ives foreshadows the inevitable, and Igor Stravinsky brings on the revolution in music with The Rite of Spring.

6. The Parting of the Ways

IS IT THE FATE OF ALL CIVILIZATIONS to become exercises in abstraction? Our culture is like a woven fabric, itself an abstraction of our former animal fur—as a house is an abstraction of a cave, and the law is an abstraction of a practical code of mutual conduct. Mathematical equations "describe" the fusing inferno of solar hydrogen. All of these abstractions relate to verifiable realities; yet there is a danger, for when human imperatives become vested in legal codes and dogma, we may, in fact, legitimize the very impulses we seek to control. It was Winston Churchill, speaking in the House of Commons in 1947, who declared: "It has been said that democracy is the worst form of government, except for all those other forms that have been tried from time to time."

The whole of man's history is a gradual coming of age; the conflicts, inner and outer, are concerned with the assumption or rejection of responsibilities, the exercise of authority. The Bible may be a noble and glorious record of human history, but it has been used to justify some questionable behavior. The Greeks, the highest pagan civilization, fought hard and succeeded at last in maintaining the unity and wholeness of man, ensuring that the good and the beautiful, body and soul, would never part company. All the arts were one vast, united discipline.

Today there are many signs that we are emerging from the era of conflict as we search for wholeness, an awareness of the ecology of nature, of our dependence for life on the meanest insect and plant—just as many others recognize the spectre of the alternative: annihilation. Survival of life on earth is our responsibility. That remains the message of democracy, a powerful idea, tangible yet intangible, which offered in the

By the 1880s the mechanical piano was becoming a fixture at fairs, in taverns, and was soon to be joined by the mechanical violin; eventually these devices grew to become mechanical orchestras.

Opposite:
The Paris workshop of sculptor Frédéric Auguste Bartholdi was a busy place in 1883, as construction proceeded on the Statue of Liberty; France paid for the statue and America for the pedestal. The unveiling was in 1886, ten years behind schedule.

New World the possibility of a new beginning. For more than three centuries, millions came, white or black, willing or unwilling, bringing with them the varying seeds of their many cultures.

When the Pilgrims arrived in 1620, they found an indigenous music and culture which was then at its high point, stretching across the entire North American continent. They found not one homogenous people, but many nations and tribes, each with its own beliefs, language and tradition. It is as false to speak of the Algonquin and Cherokee, the Pueblo, Natchez and Mohican, the Inca, Maya or Aztec as one people, as it is to speak of all Europeans, east and west, as one people. Yet this native American culture and its music were strangely not included in what was to become the American musical mainstream. In fact, within little more than two hundred years, the Indian heritage in North America was not absorbed, but nearly decimated.

Aside from the Vikings, the English were the first white men to settle the coast of what is now Massachusetts, the name itself derived from the local Indian nation. The songs the English brought with them are still sung from Eastern Canada, to New England, to the hills of Appalachia; their ballads of love and honor were shared as companions to the hymn book. The force of Western harmony, already introduced to the East and

The slave trade flourished in Latin America from the time of the Spanish Conquest until the mid-nineteenth century. Those being disembarked here in Brazil around 1810 were doubtless destined for the sugar and coffee plantations which abounded in the tropical climate.

Africa by colonists and missionaries, ruled the music of the New World; the French brought it to Canada and the Spanish and Portuguese carried it to Mexico and Latin America, and to the idyllic islands of the West Indies, where they shared space with the French and English. Today in Jamaica the steps of the French quadrille are danced by the descendants of slaves, yet with an unmistakable Spanish lilt and body rhythm. The slaves mated with the Carib Indians native to the area, and although the local Indian population was wiped out, a few fragments of their culture still survive, preserved by the offspring of those marriages.

Lying off the coast of Senegal is the tiny isle of Gorée, where the complex of buildings and prison cells serve as a memorial to the days of slavery. Its festering walls, chains and rings speak mutely but implacably their terrible, callous tale. From here the French, English and Spanish

The bowed string was part of the musical life of the Apache Indian, as this photograph taken by A. F. Randall in the early 1880s demonstrates. The music of Native Americans was nearly a lost tradition by the 1920s, but has seen a remarkable revival in our own day.

The grinding of corn was celebrated among the Pueblos by an elaborate ceremony, one of many homages to the fertility of the land, captured in the 1930s by painter Alfonso Roybal. Some rituals would have been entirely lost if it were not for such paintings.

ships collected their human cargo, hundreds of thousands passing through the cramped cell blocks, the able-bodied culled first, while the old and infirm, even small children, often were tossed onto the rocks below to drown. All through the seventeenth and eighteenth centuries this cruel treatment continued. We may still hear in the revival meetings of North America and the West Indies, and in the spirituals which have become part of our musical life, the mood of those unjust times, voicing man's unquenchable hope for a better life, the hope that has sustained the African in the New World for so long, and which today finds its expression in the nobility of the hymn "We Shall Overcome."

The spiritual took shape slowly, influenced by the developing black music and the huge camp meetings which became part of popular social life in the first half of the nineteenth century, as America spread west after the Revolution. These spontaneous gatherings brought a comforting sense of community to courageous pioneer families, thousands of whom left their isolated homesteads to join in camp meetings that sometimes lasted for days. Here they could trade songs, goods and stories, and escape

from the solitude of the wilderness. One observer wrote of these meetings: "As the excitement increases, all order is forgotten, all unison of parts repudiated, each sings his own tune, each dances his own dance, as he leaps, shouts and exults with exceeding great joy." A native American music was beginning to form out of these elements which had never been brought together before. Although white and black were kept separate, their voices and music could mix, echoing from camp to camp, feeding a musical union whose product would sweep the world.

In the New World, the rhythm and melody of Africa joined with the harmony of Europe to produce many distinctive musical forms. One of these, closer to our own time, is the blues. As the spirituals speak for a whole people, so the blues speak for each individual, yearning for the comforting touch of another, or for relief from the injustices and tribulations of life.

Emigration to the New World increased immensely throughout the nineteenth century. In 1800 the population of the United States was just five million. By 1850 it had grown to twenty-three million and by 1900 to seventy-six million. Ireland launched a huge human tide from her shores during the potato famine of the 1840s. Thousands of German and English immigrants followed in the 1860s, even during the upheaval of the Civil War. By the 1880s the yearly count including Scandinavians, Austrians, Italians, Mexicans and Canadians had passed half a million.

The New World offered space and opportunity for a new life; it became a symbol for the experiment of democracy at work. In music America

The camp gatherings which had begun by the 1820s remained popular gatherings throughout the nineteenth century, and led to such institutions as the permanent tent in Chautauqua, New York, where great orators, brass choirs and cultural entertainment were welcomed.

offered diversity, a taste not yet fully formed. The piano was responsible for part of that diversity, becoming a fixture in the parlors of North America. As the West was tamed and settled, the possession of a piano became the symbol of respectability and cultural achievement. But America was still taking in Europe's cultural washing. The Europeans brought the fruit of their great culture. No home could claim to be refined without the musical classics, and young ladies applied themselves, as they did in Europe, to learning piano versions of the symphonies of Mozart and Beethoven, and the latest novelties of Felix Mendelssohn and Giovanni Bellini. This music became as popular as the music of the phonograph and radio were later to become, and it spawned an immense printing industry—the amateur had no choice but to provide his own music.

The extraordinary phenomenon of these United States lies in the fact that the entire early culture is a transplant. By the beginning of the nineteenth century the elements out of which a native American music would form were all present. Many of the immigrants brought with them little more than their memories and the clothes they could carry, but they could all bring their music, a possession of the heart and mind. It took root in a new and distinctive way, flowering in music of extraordinary diversity and color, from which were to spring ragtime and jazz. While America pursued a progressive development, Europe was heading toward an inevitable break with a way of life built over the centuries.

The four-hand piano music which became part of American households was largely music of a Europe still secure, blissfully unaware of the tremendous upheavals that were about to overturn long-established traditions and conventions. There were two main streams of population coming to the United States: the willing from Europe, the unwilling from Africa. Here the concept of human domination over others was already evolving from the quantitative derived from brute force to the qualitative derived from selection. From this unprecedented mixture evolved the compelling moral obligation to spell out an equal justice for one and all (with the unfortunate exception of those truly native, the Indian). It was therefore inevitable that the final confrontation over slavery should occur in America.

The first musical signs of that confrontation were seen in the vaudevilles and minstrel shows which had begun before the Civil War. Blacks were not yet permitted to assume the role of legitimate performers, and were considered mainly as a labor force. The first minstrel shows were all by white men and women in blackface, who had listened and learned from

The minstrel shows were for a time the most widely accepted form of acknowledgement by white Americans, north and south, of the impact of blacks on society and music. The practice of blackface entertainers (of whom Al Jolson may have been the last) yielded a huge literature of sheet music and helped to give rise to ragtime.

this new musical voice. It is here that the blend of cultures began to generate something permanent and prophetic, a rhythmic vitality and melodic gift that would produce ragtime and jazz. We find them in the songs of America's first great native composer, Stephen Foster. Born in Pittsburgh in 1826, on the fourth of July, no less, he was destined for West Point and a military career when he began to write the first of his more than two hundred songs. Though Foster lived all his life in the North, he so absorbed the plantation spirit that those songs which he called

From "Oh! Susannah" in 1848 to "Beautiful Dreamer" in 1864, Stephen Foster composed more than two hundred songs including "Camptown Races" (1850), "My Old Kentucky Home" (1853), "Jeannie With the Light Brown Hair" (1854), "Old Black Joe" (1860).

"Ethiopian" are now often taken as traditional Southern tunes, for instance "The Camptown Races" (1850), "Massa's in the Cold Ground" (1852) or "Old Black Joe (1860). The minstrel shows helped to bring Foster's songs before a wider public.

The minstrel in medieval times was the people's entertainer, juggling and dancing in every town square; in America, he became the white man's homage to the blacks who shared this new land, an uncomfortable coexistence made symbolic, for the spirit and personality of the black world were seeping into white culture long before blacks themselves were admitted to white society. Stephen Foster sensed this and seized upon it for some of his finest inspirations, and his songs sold in sheet music by the thousands. Always extravagant though, Foster mortgaged away his future earnings for immediate cash. These songs became America's first popular hits, and at least two dozen of them remain well known and are sung today. His musical background may have been more limited than that of a genius such as Franz Schubert, but his output of songs was comparable, and at their best, as in "Jeannie with the Light Brown Hair" (1854) or "Oh, Susannah" (1848), Foster's melodies have an eloquence and charm which Schubert would not have disdained.

Undoubtedly the true hybrid of the day, and a contemporary of Foster, was Louis Moreau Gottschalk, a Creole born in New Orleans in 1829. Gottschalk studied in Paris with Berlioz, and Chopin attended the boy's debut at the Salle Pleyel in 1844. P. T. Barnum tried to hire him to play piano ten years later and failed. Gottschalk was a superior pianist, and in New York in the winter of 1855–56 he gave some eighty concerts; later he appeared not only in other large cities, but in towns and villages, even in mining camps. Gottschalk also spent much time in the West Indies, and his mature music reflects the mix of black, white and Indian cultures of the New World in a unique way. Gottschalk is considered the father of the cakewalk and other dance rhythms which were to develop into ragtime by the end of the century. His piano pieces, including such sentimental ones as "The Last Hope" and "The Dying Poet," were heard in American homes as often as Foster or the classics. Gottschalk died under mysterious circumstances in Rio de Janeiro in 1869 while taking part in a festival of his own music.

The music of Foster and Gottschalk is music of a young America, still composed of farms and country towns in a continent not yet industrialized. In the South the great plantations flourished, with a way of life made leisurely by temperament, climate and abundant free labor. Inevitably, all this had to change, for towns were being linked by railroads and becoming big cities, and immigration was providing the North with an equally large, albeit hired, labor force. The issue of slavery threatened the

union of states, which had been based on the unique idea that diverse people living autonomously could nonetheless survive as a single nation.

It was in America that music became part of public education sooner than elsewhere, for music was considered a cultivated accomplishment assisting in the formation of character, as it had in ancient Greece. Thus, the traditions of Europe could be absorbed all the easier after the Civil War. The Italians had brought opera, the Irish and Scandinavians their folk songs and fiddle tunes, and Germans symphony orchestra music. Murray Schafer, the Canadian composer of soundscapes, has said that the symphony orchestra is typical of the growth of industrial civilization. He has a point, for like industry, orchestras often began as ad hoc ensembles convened for special purposes—an expensive luxury. For some time opera did not catch on in America. It is a form of ritualized drama which enlarges the range of human expression, and some North Americans tended not to wear their heart on their sleeve in quite that way. In any event, such arts have always required wealth for their support, as in the days of the Medici in Florence, and rich American patrons were scarce.

France brought to America its *café chantant* and the brilliant tunes of its operettas, England sent the music of Gilbert and Sullivan, together with church music still in wide use, all of which made its way into the music of another American, the father of the American military march, John Philip Sousa. Born in Washington, D.C. in 1854, Sousa was for a time a musical aide to Offenbach, and then leader of the United States Marine Corps Band from 1880 to 1892, when he left to form his own

The Fisk Jubilee Singers were organized in 1871 at Fisk University by George White, who had been active in the movement to provide education for freed slaves. They remained a popular attraction for more than two generations and helped to bring the spiritual into the concert hall.

organization. We should listen carefully to that sound, the sound of "El Capitan," "Semper Fidelis," "Washington Post" and "The Stars and Stripes Forever." We take Sousa's marches for granted now, but while they may have their share of operetta, of Wagnerian grandeur, of the precision of a French military band, they also have a swagger and dash all their own, smacking of Mark Twain and Horatio Alger. The spirit of national pride which so dominated Western life in the nineteenth century is heard here, together with the spirit of the settlers who fought to dominate nature and free a continent. People in ever growing numbers were realizing that they themselves held responsibility for the quality of their lives. All that America symbolized to those who had escaped the rigid social structure of Europe is embodied in this music.

Long-term plans are now under way to turn Ellis Island into a vast museum commemorating the generations of Europeans who came to the New World through this narrow gateway.

I have said before that I wish there were no need for national boundaries. They are compromises, neither true to tribe, weather, nor geography, and sometimes not even to the dominant language. I have often wondered whether what we are witnessing now is not transitional, part of that inevitable evolution toward ever larger and even overlapping administrative units encompassing ever smaller and more autonomous cultural units. In the United States, however, particularly in the late nineteenth

century, a totally different evolution occurred. Many cultures gathered to form one, and a great number of new Americans were funnelled through one port of entry, Ellis Island, located in New York harbor. Indeed my own parents first set foot there. It is hard for us to imagine today this desperate pilgrimage compounded of courage, uncertainty, risk, and hope.

As the nineteenth century drew to a close, many of Europe's poor and underprivileged left for the New World, while the privileged and newly wealthy lived in a generation of peace that seemed impregnable. Let us imagine Paris in 1894. Western culture is surely the center of the world, and Paris is the artistic capital of Europe. Impressionist painting is the vogue, led by Manet, Seurat, Monet, Renoir and Degas. These artists do not paint subjects, but light and color itself. The attempt is not without precedent for, in the seventeenth century, light can certainly be said to be Vermeer's subject. However, impressionism conveys something of the quality of the dream world, a dream from which nineteenth century Europe seemed unable to awake.

The first time impressionism in music caught the attention of the public was in a short orchestral work by a young Frenchman, Claude

Many immigrants also came to North America through the east and west coast ports of Canada. This Dutch family entered via Quebec in 1911 (and the youngest was apparently the most eager).

ORIGINAL NAUTICAL OPERA BY SULLIVAN & GILBERT.

Composer Arthur Sullivan was thirty-six and poet William S. Gilbert was forty-two when their operetta H.M.S. Pinafore *was first produced in 1878. These ebullient stage works represented the best of that mixture of opera and the music hall which England gave to an age already brimming with the operetta tunes of Johann Strauss and Jacques Offenbach.*

Debussy. He called it *Prelude to the Afternoon of a Faun.* Debussy took as his source of inspiration not the work of the painters but that of the poets, especially two who exercised an enormous influence on him at this time. One was Stéphane Mallarmé, whose salon Debussy probably attended on and off in 1887. Mallarmé was the author of the poem *The Afternoon of a Faun* for which Debussy set out to compose a musical setting in three parts to accompany its reading. Only the *Prelude* was completed. The other author was Maurice Maeterlinck, the playwright, who was exactly Debussy's age. His play *Pelléas et Mélisande* had appeared·in 1892 and Debussy set about at once transforming it into an opera, even before he started work on the famous *Prelude*; but the task took him years, and *Pelléas* as an opera was not to receive its first performance until 1902.

The *Prelude* was first performed on December 23, 1894, and by this time Debussy was a fixture in the nightlife of Montmartre, where he became familiar with the work of many impressionist painters. Some years earlier the composer had lived in Russia and had come to know Moussorgsky's *Boris Godunov*; later, in Paris, he was deeply impressed by the playing of

a Javanese gamelan ensemble at the 1889 Paris Exposition (where Eiffel inaugurated his revolutionary tower). He had also adored the music of Wagner, and made two pilgrimages to Bayreuth to hear the master's works, hoping to meet him. This may have happened in Venice, for both composers were there in 1882. Later Debussy became deeply disillusioned with Wagner's music and, in fact, the later piano music of Franz Liszt came to impress him far more, works such as the *Années de Pélerinage*, which carry such a strong foretaste of the impressionism to come.

The music of the day was particularly volatile, an absolute or abstract art, while art and literature were dominated by *isms*. Mallarmé belonged among the symbolists; Maeterlinck was a mystic. Mallarmé said of music, "We must take back our own from music!" In that sense he was looking at music the way we may look today at an abstract painting, as a vision which presupposes a reality from which the artist has drawn the essence, the canvas representing his response to color, shape and contrast rather than to subject matter. Abstraction shows us the principle, the matter out of which life itself is made, and the music of Debussy shares this quality.

Claude Debussy was also a clever, witty, urbane writer of articles in which his invented character, Monsieur Croche, was quick to defend the right of an artist to dissent, to cast ridicule upon fashion.

The *Prelude, La Mer,* and the Nocturnes for orchestra, the extraordinary works for solo piano, even his last work, the sublime Sonata for Violin and Piano, do not display the melodies, harmonies, rhythms and structures to which concert music had become accustomed. In these works, Debussy is writing sounds for their own sake. We may know that Debussy was an admirer of plainsong and of the vocal music of Lassus and Palestrina. He was also an admirer of the French keyboard composers of Louis XIV's time, especially that of François Couperin. We are also reminded that this music casts us forward to the experiments of Edgard Varèse, Debussy's young friend and disciple.

Debussy's adventure, like Wagner's, was a leap into space, and it had its counterpart in Germany, though of another kind. Richard Strauss, heir to Wagner as emperor of German music, offered the West a sound that was bigger and more splendid, more grandiose, more bedecked with medals than ever. Though beautifully melodic, the music is deeply in love with its own sound, as it is with the spirit of a heroic Germany that believed its inevitable destiny was to lead the world. Debussy had sought mezzotints, vistas seen through frosted glass, hints and suggestions. Strauss used his love of sound to express a wholly opposed sensibility, exulting in affirmation, in blaze and blare, and especially in the

The boulevards and parks of Paris were rich, colorful subject matter for the impressionist painters. Photography was already robbing painting of the need for literal realism.

virtuosity of his control over the resources available when 110 players are assembled under a compelling leader.

Strauss's tone poem *Also Sprach Zarathustra* has become well known in recent times through its inclusion as part of the score of Stanley Kubrick's film *2001*. It is curious that Kubrick should consider such music apt to accompany his imaginary voyages to the moon, Jupiter and beyond, for this music has more to do with the dream castles erected by mad King Ludwig of Bavaria on the promontory of Neuschwanstein or the isolated island in Lake Chiemsee where he tried to outdo Versailles.

The music of Richard Strauss, along with so much of the concert music of the late nineteenth century, had become like dreams, encouraging and fulfilling our most private wishes, hoping to keep them alive. However, at the turn of the century the great and overwhelming masterpieces of Wagner and Strauss also carried, no doubt innocently, an ominous undertone which seems to us now to reflect a growing European arrogance and unreality, anticipating perhaps our own age of nightmares made real. Richard Strauss's music has become part of the classic repertoire, separated from the time which gave it birth. When a superb orchestra like the Berlin Philharmonic, whose members have played this music all their

In the twenty years between his showing at the Salon des Refusés in 1863 and his death at fifty-one in 1883, Edouard Manet helped to launch a revolution in painting in Paris with such canvases as this view of a Sunday crowd in the Bois de Boulogne. The impact of impressionism was not to be felt in music until half a generation later.

Most of the major tone poems and several operas were already completed when this portrait of Richard Strauss at fifty-one was drawn by the English artist Edmond Kapp in 1915.

lives, performs it, they can almost convince me of its value. Yet it still seems to me out of place in our world. Bach and Beethoven fit perfectly because they have balance. Strauss's music is of a time period where the sense of proportion was lost.

Today we must find ways to reconcile so many elements of which we were blissfully unaware in the past. We must deal with what takes place thousands of miles away, as well as in our own neighborhoods. Science demands that we come to grips with the moral issues created by technological advances. We can no longer draw the blinds, or pretend to virtue, conveniently performing one noble act within public view. Richard Strauss made a last effort to enlarge the elegance and courtesy, the coquettishness and vanity, of his predecessor Johann Strauss, whose romantic dreaminess is the essence of his style. Richard Strauss, even more than Wagner, builds these elements to climax after climax, in an excess of self-indulgence.

Bach's *Saint Matthew Passion* moves us deeply whether performed with only a modest number of singers and instrumentalists, or performed by hundreds. Strauss, whether he is sad or elated, visits his feelings upon the world with enormous show. His music is magisterially orchestrated, the intricate inner voices are heard, the smallest gesture is exquisitely modelled; however, when the orchestra is cut in half or its quality is less than top grade, we recognize immediately how much smaller the content is than the package. Somehow, to me, the essence of this side of Strauss is his *Domestic* Symphony in which the entire arsenal of the modern symphony orchestra is used to describe, hour by hour, a typical day in the life of a typical middle-class German family. The music describes meals, walks in the park, love making; it even bathes the baby.

The family Strauss describes in the *Domestic* Symphony happens to be his own, and this exaltation of the personally trivial goes hand in hand

The castles of King Ludwig II of Bavaria are a vision of a never-never land such as even Hollywood could hardly surpass. Neuschwanstein, high in the Bavarian Alps, eventually became the model for Disneyland.

with the West's view of itself as master of the world. Artists have always been the antennae of their time, sensing growth and change, grasping a mood, even when working alone, whereas the majority is propelled by habit. The outward appearances remained solid, but Europe was losing her grip. Strauss was born in 1864 when European culture was at its apparent zenith; by the time he died in 1949, two world wars had inevitably changed the balance of power.

A contemporary counterpart to Strauss is the Viennese composer Gustav Mahler, who sought to create music in the image of Beethoven, only longer, larger, more insistent. He wrote of an era that he felt was vanishing, and his music is often on the verge of hysteria. The longest of his nine symphonies takes almost two hours to play. Mahler shouts into the advancing dark, trying to save a way of life that was already lost, smothering his fear of inexorable change.

I know many will not agree with me, for Mahler has lately become a great favorite, but to me the art of Mahler, like that of Strauss, is the loud echo of this self-confident age of colonial empire, with its delusions of limitless expansion and growth—already nostalgic and therefore perhaps more vivid.

This music reflects a taste which can be compared with the rich sweet wine made from the last grapes of the season, those left on the vine to ripen until shortly before the first frost. They have already started to

pucker, to dry up, yet still they hold on. You might think they could hang there forever, getting better, riper, sweeter. But if the vintner does not pick them at the right moment, they are spoiled soon after. Taken in the nick of time they are covered with a grayish mold that the Germans call *edelmost* and the French *la pourriture noble*, meaning noble rot. These late grapes produce the sweetest, finest, headiest wines known. Mahler and Strauss convey something of that unique flavor.

The most endearing aspects of Strauss and Mahler occur at those moments when their music remembers its vigorous roots, the German folksong or the Austrian *Ländler*. It is then that you realize that Mahler is tied as much to Schubert as he is to Beethoven, and Strauss to Mendelssohn as much as to Wagner. A Mahler work like the song-cycle *The Song of the Earth* can be exalting in its perception of the mutability of life. Strauss did not modernize his language to suit changing tastes, and his *Four Last Songs*, the final music he completed in 1947, is music in a style fashionable for 1895. The sentiment is genuine, simple and deeply touching, for the fustian trappings of empire are gone, and the content is finally at one with its form.

If the music of Strauss and Mahler is an expression of the passing of a certain European way of life, a new musical sound, sharp and witty, was a prophetic description of the New World entering a new century. The ragtime syncopations of Scott Joplin, Joe Lamb, William C. Handy and so many others invoke the optimism of an America which was to do more than produce entertainment gadgets or transportation miracles. Rags are city music, a music of emancipation, of the start of a new life. The folk music of the old country might keep the millions who arrived in America in touch with their roots, but ragtime was part of the new beginning.

The Western missionaries brought the hymnbook and harmonium with them wherever they went. Here the Rev. and Mrs. T. S. Smith pose with teachers and pupils of the Udupitty Girls' Boarding School in Jaffna, Ceylon, in the 1880s.

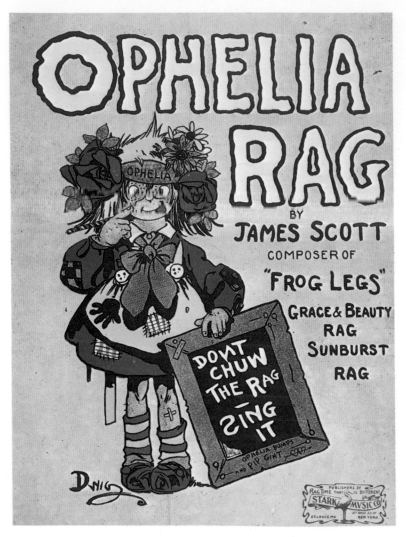

Ragtime is unmistakably piano music, for the piano is the perfect instrument for the mechanical age; as the violin was the instrument which symbolized the emancipation of the Jews, so the piano became the instrument of the Negro in the New World.

Rags are the folk music of the new integrated American cities, and they were written and played by blacks and whites alike. Scott Joplin (1868–1917) is today the best known of these composers. His father was an ex-slave, and although Joplin sought to cast off that inheritance, his roots were there. Ragtime was the fresh blend of Africa and Europe, mixing the sound of brass bands, folk tunes, the Wild West, and the syncopations of the dark continent with a jaunty good humor that had almost vanished from Western music. Just as white Americans heard black music, so

African musicians absorbed what they heard when they arrived in America.

It used to be said that ragtime started in New Orleans, and it was surely played there, especially in the famous red-light district in the old French Quarter—musicians could find steady jobs at good pay in the fashionable houses along Rampart and Beale streets. But rag music was not primarily native to New Orleans. It grew up in a number of places, travelling up and down the Mississippi and Missouri rivers wherever there was a piano. Many of the virtuoso composer-pianists sprang from St. Louis, Kansas City and Sedalia. As their fame spread, some came down to New Orleans. Others went east to Chicago, Scott Joplin among them. Each ragtime musician was determined to outdo his rival, as in the days of Chopin and Liszt, and Joplin made his rags to suit his own style of playing.

The origins of ragtime may have been considered questionable, but it became the parlor music of white, middle-class America, and then, thanks to sheet music and soon after to records, swept the world at the turn of the century. Everybody wanted to learn how to play rags—they were bold, courageous, optimistic, like the marches of Sousa or the phenomenon of flight (the Wright Brothers had finally done it in 1903). The popular has always been one of the counterbalancing forces in music. In the Middle Ages dance tunes and ballads reminded both musicians and people that the purpose of music is communication. In the early 1900s, music played at home by friends entertaining one another filled that same need, and ragtime was the dance music of youth.

The age of modern transportation is superbly symbolized by this photograph taken in 1913.

The movie pianist remained a fixture for more than twenty years, gradually giving way in the twenties to Wurlitzer organs, and even to full orchestras performing scores especially composed, for every showing. Here to accompany Buster Keaton is the pianist, assisted by a violin and percussion.

Ragtime shared the popular musical field with many other forms, among them the male quartet we associate with the barbershop, an American version of the madrigal or four-part hymn. This most engaging form of community singing was an outgrowth of the camp meetings and various other European forebears. Though it has become something of a vaudeville stereotype in recent times, in its original form it had a vitality and warmth that were infectious, displaying some of the same delicious shifts of harmonic emphasis as in the madrigal, notes trading meaning and function, which only voices can articulate when responding minutely to one another. Banker, farmer, professor and clerk together produced these finely coordinated sounds; social barriers fell, as they still do, when singers join whose ears for harmonic intertwining are matched by beauty of tone. Perhaps because this was a popular mode of singing it contributed to the development of a more sensitive ear in the American audience, who might have been intimidated by the music of Chopin or Bach. There is no match for such group singing in Europe, though there is a counterpart in the Viennese operettas of Lehár, Kálmán and Romberg.

In the big cities of America and Europe two technological revolutions accelerated the change from live participation to passive listening, as they did the distribution of music as a commercial product: the phonograph and the motion picture. Both were perfected by Thomas Edison who personified that particularly American capacity to create and be fascinated

with gadgetry. Both changed our lives enormously—for good or evil, depending on your point of view. Think for a moment about the old-fashioned early movie house in North America called the "nickelodeon," the word itself a precise mix of modern slang and ancient Greek, and a grand name for such an unprecedented medium. In the orchestra one found the movie pianist tucked away in a corner. Up on the screen real people moved silently in black and white on a flat surface. As entertainment, this was a great leap forward from the unreality of opera or the stylized theater of the day.

However, there were no voices to help us laugh or cry. Music filled the vacuum, evoking emotion in the viewer and supporting the action. Here the movie pianist performed his supreme role, throbbing away at snippets of Grieg or Schumann, Verdi or Liszt, knitting them together with improvisations of his own. Ironically, a brand-new entertainment medium was reaching back for its musical accompaniment into the classical music written half a century earlier. Such music became instantly familiar as the movie pianist taught a whole generation. At no time has such a medley of periods, styles and purposes existed in a popular medium. Movie music today continues to draw on its nineteenth century heritage.

In the early days of cylinder recording, each one had to be individually tested by being listened to from first groove to last. The din of a hundred different numbers in this sweat-shop factory must have been fearsome.

For thousands of years the visual world had been represented by static paintings, drawings and carvings. Only the Indian, Malaysian and Indonesian shadow plays, like drama, dancing and puppet shows, exhibited a stylized form of action; and music was always the tonal vehicle, measuring and propelling its progress. The New World brought a new attitude to humanity, in which movement and direction took precedence. Unlike the cozy, encircling opera houses of Italian origin, the new movie houses mushrooming everywhere were constructed around the projection of a beam of light. We were learning a new reality, a historically significant and democratic one. The movies were a part of that accommodation, shrinking the globe while opening vistas, educating and uneducating, shaping public taste.

Mechanical music had entered the home before the advent of the phonograph: the player pianos sprayed forth the equivalent of six hands rippling through favorite tunes, waltzes and marches of the day. They could even offer a reasonable facsimile of the great virtuosos, from Paderewski to Rachmaninoff. Legions of amateur pianists followed the ghostly spectral hands, as pneumatic pressure depressed the keys following the perforations in the piano roll. Early models were operated by pedals, like the parlor harmonium, and later, when the machine took over, the speed of the performance could be altered, influencing somewhat the interpretation and the dynamics. But it was the phonograph that brought the performer into the home.

The late Charlie Chaplin once said at the height of his fame, "I am known in parts of the world where they have never heard of Jesus Christ." What the movies did for Chaplin, the phonograph did for Enrico Caruso. To much of the world, the legendary tenor's name and voice still mean opera, and though he died in 1921, his sound remains recognizable to millions. Caruso had the world's first career as a best-selling recording artist, and it is largely thanks to him that the Victor Talking Machine Company became a success. Movie houses on every block and opera arias in every parlor revolutionized our approach to music irrevocably.

To me, an American musician, the most remarkable musical development of the century has been the recording of sound. Until comparatively recently, the voice of a loved one or the sound of the violin of a Paganini were experiences to be evoked only by the memory or the imagination. When Thomas Edison made the first practical phonograph, he thought he had devised a more efficient dictating machine for which both employers and secretaries would bless him. He lived to see both the human ear and eye adjust to and even command synthetic reproduced fare.

The phonograph's impact on music was as fundamental as the invention of written notes and the printing press.

We gain some sense of the importance of the phonograph when listening to the faint echoes still held within the brittle, drying grooves of cylinder recordings made during actual performances at the Metropolitan Opera House in New York between 1901 and 1903. There Lionel Mapleson was librarian, a post he held for almost fifty years. His father had served as music librarian and secretary to Queen Victoria. In 1900 Thomas Edison gave Mapleson a special model of his phonograph, with an immense horn capable of picking up distant sounds. Although hand-cranked and rather unwieldy, Mapleson used it like a home recorder. He would park himself in the wings or up in the scaffolding and capture bits of live performances for the later amusement of the cast. His cylinders contain the voices of many great artists, among them many who never made commercial discs, such as the legendary Polish tenor Jean de Reszke, who retired from the Met in 1901, two years before Caruso arrived. What is more, the audience can often be heard quite clearly, bursting into applause after a particularly brilliant finish to an aria by Nellie Melba or Emma Calvé. These ghostly fragments are quite probably the first recordings of public musical performances. Mapleson stopped making them when commercial records became common; it was simply too much trouble to cart all that equipment up and down the backstage ladders. The collection of cylinders now resides at the Lincoln Center Library of the Performing Arts in New York City.

Early acoustic recording techniques were so limited that many musical instruments had to be modified in order to project their sound into the giant ear. Deep instruments such as the double bass could not be recorded at all, and were replaced by the tuba. Violins were made in freakish models with two metal speakers, one aimed at the recording horn and the other into the ear of the player, perhaps the first example of the separation of sound: one for the public and another for the performer. Fortunately, the system responded well to the human voice, and the best-loved entertainers of the age made the phonograph into a worldwide success almost overnight.

As the American musical industry gathered momentum, one composer, almost alone, sensed that music itself was changing and evolving in a new direction: Charles Ives. This was a remarkably original voice in a land then in love with the music of Victor Herbert. His music is evidence of that collective unconscious which moves us to act together in the way that a flight of starlings wheels as one. Artists may work alone, but they share the same antennae, sensitive to wavelengths which the rest of us pick up later, when the impulses are stronger. Ives was born in 1874 of a Connecticut bandmaster-banker father. Very early he trained his son to distinguish quarter-tones, and to sing familiar hymn tunes faultlessly in one key while being accompanied in another. Charles Ives went on to Yale University where he graduated in 1898 with a complete academic music degree.

However, Ives turned his back on the music of his day, and, indeed, even on a music career. He did not continue his studies in Germany, as did most of his peers, since the old correct rules were inadequate for the new music he heard, and he knew that this music would never earn him a living. He turned instead to insurance, which he regarded as more of a calling than a profession. Ives's innovative brilliance as an insurance man is not the point here, though he built a hugely successful company (predecessor to what is now Mutual Insurance of New York). He drew only enough salary to maintain a modest lifestyle and to publish his own music, which he gave away to anyone who wanted it.

What music owes to Charles Ives can be found in the many compositions he wrote between 1898 and the end of World War I. They contain some of the most forward-looking music from the pen of any Western composer, easily as bold as anything in Gesualdo or the *Ars Nova* of the fourteenth century. At the time, Ives's music seemed too odd to be taken seriously, for he experimented with multiple rhythms and cross harmonies well before any other composer. Consequently, he wrote in a vacuum, and heard few of his scores played while he was still actively composing. Understandably, his productive period was relatively short; he composed for only a twenty-year span between the ages of twenty-four and forty-four. Gustav Mahler was one of the few to take Ives seriously. Mahler was then music director of the New York Philharmonic when he took with him to Vienna in 1909 the score to Ives's Third Symphony (where, it appears, he rehearsed it).

It is interesting to speculate on what might have happened if Ives had moved to Europe and heard the experimental music of Arnold Schönberg and Anton Webern. The fact is that he did not. He had great confidence in an America no longer dependent upon Europe for its culture, an America assuming a new role in the world; but he could not anticipate the horror of the impending war. By the time this music first began to be played in America, soon after the end of World War I, Ives had completely stopped composing. His wife—happily named Harmony—once said that it was the war which was the breaking point for Charlie. It cut so deeply into his belief in the sanctity of human life that he never recovered (though he lived to be eighty). One morning, not long after his first heart attack in 1918, he came downstairs and tried out some sketches at the keyboard. The tears welled in his eyes, and he said, "Nothing I do is any good any more."

In Europe, the painters were once again beginning to produce strange images, no longer tied to past conventions, rejecting mere appearances. Realism had been stolen from them by the camera, and they were left to find new paths, to reveal what lay beneath the surface. Inversion in art and music was the order of the day; basic raw materials were taken apart and combined anew. Some experiments led to dead ends, others to fresh beginnings. What the artists produced was as dislocating as observing the earth from the air for the first time. For some time audiences refused to accept this disturbing new vision of the world, as, in 1906, they could not at first accept Einstein's formulation of the theory of relativity. Inexorably, the expressive canvases of Van Gogh, Cezanne and Munch led to the cubism of Picasso and Braque and the futurism of Boccioni and Duchamp—rags, flight, relativity and cubism, all within less than a decade. The terse, musical epigrams of Anton Webern were heard by only a few, but they were a clear signal that an explosion was about to be ignited. The true musical upheaval came on the eve of World War I with the first three ballet scores of Igor Stravinsky.

The impulse for this development came from that extraordinary Russian, Serge Diaghilev, creator of the Ballet Russe in Paris in 1909, a man whose vision made an immeasurable impact on the cultural life of the twentieth century. This imperious, daring figure had an uncanny flair for choosing unknown but promising talent from among the best

When King Edward VII of Great Britain died in 1910, his funeral cortège included the new king, George V, and the crowned heads of Germany, Greece, Spain, Portugal, Denmark, Norway, Belgium and Bulgaria, the Archduke Franz Ferdinand of Austria, the Prince Consort of Holland, and bringing up the rear, ex-President Theodore Roosevelt of the United States. It was the last such gathering of rulers in Europe.

composers, dancers and designers of the day. Diaghilev was already thirty-seven and had come late to ballet. His initial involvement was with painters, as an organizer of exhibitions in St. Petersburg and as founder of the art review *The World of Art*; but his interest in music had always been strong, and by 1906 he was organizing Russian music seasons in Paris and Berlin, introducing abroad the following year a sensational Russian basso named Fyodor Chaliapin. In 1908 Diaghilev presented Chaliapin in the starring role in *Boris Godunov* at the Paris Opera, a production which launched both the singer and the work on international careers.

Looking for other worlds to conquer, Diaghilev turned his attention to ballet. In Russia many dancers were trained in the French tradition, but there was no Russian company as such. Diaghilev decided to create one out of the younger stars of the St. Petersburg corps de ballet. He recruited Anna Pavlova and Tamara Karsavina, Mikhail Fokine and Vaslav Nijinsky, hastily threw together some orchestral arrangements of Chopin and dubbed the result *Les Sylphides*. The work is still in the repertory of many great dance companies. But Diaghilev also wanted to create new works, to impress Paris with his boldness and daring. Pablo Picasso and Léon Bakst designed for him, Erik Satie and Maurice Ravel composed for him, but no decision was more far reaching than to commission the

Perhaps no two personalities had a greater impact on music in the twentieth century than Igor Stravinsky (1882–1971) and Serge Diaghilev (1872–1929), photographed here in the early twenties, when they were deep into the neo-classic works which replaced the peasant vigor of the earlier ballets.

twenty-seven-year-old Igor Stravinsky to compose a new work for the following year. In 1909 the young composer had little more to show than a good recommendation from his teacher, Nicolai Rimsky-Korsakov, a short orchestral work, *Feux d'Artifice,* and the lovely *Elegy* for violin, both of which showed his teacher's influence.

Stravinsky immediately made his mark with *The Firebird.* Its exotic colors were part of that combination of Oriental flavor and passionate sexuality with which Diaghilev seduced all of Paris. Immediately after came *Petrouchka,* and then *The Rite of Spring,* all three scores completed between 1910 and 1913. *The Rite of Spring* provided the most momentous first night in the history of the musical theater since Monteverdi's *Orfeo.* But far from being a hit, it caused a monumental scandal. The audience was in an uproar, shouting and howling so loudly that the dancers could not hear the orchestra. Nijinsky, by then the most famous male dancer in the world, and both choreographer and star of the production, stood in the wings when he was not on stage and stamped out the complex rhythms with his feet and hands so the other dancers could continue.

A rare and previously unpublished photograph shows members of the Diaghilev Ballet Russe company gathered at the Theatre des Champs-Elysées for the dress rehearsal on the eve of the famous first performance of Stravinsky's The Rite of Spring, *May 29, 1913, just ten weeks after the composer completed the score.*

From absolute anonymity Stravinsky rose to international fame, and though he wrote other scores for Diaghilev, their impact never rivalled the explosion of *The Rite of Spring*.

Why is *The Rite of Spring* undoubtedly Stravinsky's most celebrated work? Simply because it broke like a storm, demolishing the barrier between East and West with an explosion whose repercussions can still be heard and felt in all kinds of music, even in film scores and rock bands. From its origins in Russia, that mysterious Byzantine land as yet mainly unknown, this world of sensuality and fire, of color and new sound, came with the Diaghilev Ballet to Paris and London. My own ancestral roots are Russian, and I think I know how Stravinsky felt. Whenever I look at a new score for the first time, what I want to discover principally is a message, and only then the structure.

To understand Stravinsky better, we might contrast his music to that of the waltz, which is the difference between the organic flexible line responding to changes in temperature, pressure, mood, all within an even beat where subtle inflections and shifts of speed make the music come alive, and the simple unchanging metrical unit like the beat of much African music. Stravinsky's imagination was housed in a precise mathematical mind; a man tight-fisted with his money, there is no "give" in his rhythms either. Like hard, brittle, modern bricks which never bend and adjust, as do old walls (in centuries past the clay was mixed with dung and straw), or like the inflexible unchanging metrical unit of the African musical beat, Stravinsky's rhythms are often complex and assymmetric; unlike the Austrian laissez-faire in waltz or *Ländler*, they are unbending. Stravinsky's acuteness and precision in the spacing and instrumentation of intervals is beyond belief, and the organization of the complex forces at his disposal was no mean task.

The easiest way to run a large society is to reduce its members to identical units which are no longer distinguishable from one another, and are thus processed more easily. However, if people are self-disciplined and realize the importance of imagination and cooperation, they can maintain a much higher degree of individuality through their willingness to adjust. That is another of the differences between the music of Africa and of Europe. The African has individual songs with beautiful melodies, but when he joins with others the rhythm tends to bind the whole. Stravinsky shares that quality. There are other simpler rhythms which are made human by distortion, adaptation, and I find this true of the music of Bartók and of Beethoven.

To many, the music of the young Stravinsky still sounds unruly, dissonant, difficult, even though it is now nearly seventy years old. It is

much the same with the pre-war paintings of Picasso, Braque, Kandinsky. Resistance to the new is common in the history of art. Even so, it is unusual for important work to take so long to win a large audience. Perhaps it is because we are still too close and too much a part of that time to judge it well—we are still living with its consequences. Stravinsky may have become the idol of Paris, living the rest of his life in exile from his native land, but his uniquely Russian voice is as much a part of the revolution that was to shake his nation as it is part of that transformation of Western life brought about by World War I, by technology and by art. The artists knew, well before most of us, that things were changing. Boundaries were dissolving, and we could no longer rely on the protection of natural fences. The artists were telling us to abandon our old dreams and follow them out onto new paths. It was both a warning and a challenge.

The original production of Stravinsky's The Rite of Spring *was conceived by Nijinsky as a Russian folk celebration of the fertility of the earth, emerging from arctic snows into the warmth of white nights. The production was later entirely redesigned by Leonid Massine, because the costumes designed by Nicholas Roerich were too heavy and cumbersome.*

The pace of life in the twentieth century accelerates, and music absorbs new elements with astonishing speed. Jazz breaks like a tidal wave and comes to the concert hall with George Gershwin. Arnold Schönberg formulates the twelve-tone system, Edgard Varèse creates an abstract music independent of conventions. Aaron Copland forges an American music comparable to that of other nations. The era of the big band is concurrent with Hollywood and Stokowski, radio and Toscanini. The music of Bali is rediscovered. Alban Berg sums up and lets go of the past in his final work, the Violin Concerto.

7. The Known and the Unknown

WORLD WAR I SWEPT AWAY a familiar world, changing our attitudes just as surely as it did many national boundaries. It all seemed to happen so rapidly. The Austro-Hungarian Empire, blending East and West, was dissolved, fragmented into its constituent parts. Some old nations like Hungary and Poland reclaimed lands which were historically theirs, while others were pieced together into nations which had previously never existed, like Czechoslovakia and Yugoslavia. Music was also never to be the same again, for it was undergoing its most profound revolution since the invention of harmony.

I think the key to life lies in that very difficult task of preventing the pendulum from swinging too far. Since the Great War, during which I was born, we have all seen some pretty wild swings, for we live in an age of extremes. The swings are so rapid now that, in fact, the extremes coexist. America had not yet entered World War I when I was born, and my first memories go back to a simpler, more innocent time, when Western values still appeared reasonably intact. I could not know or appreciate what was going on under the surface. Yet in music, while Charles Ives was experimenting, George M. Cohan was writing his musicals. Beside Stravinsky, there was Rachmaninoff. In Vienna where Arnold Schönberg composed, there was also Franz Lehár. Music was a true mirror of the age.

In the early years of this century, music began to reveal, as did the other arts, what few wanted to believe: Europe was losing its long-established hold on Western civilization. It may have been the culmination of

At the age of six (1922) Yehudi Menuhin was already intent on a career as a violinist. The following year he made his debut with the San Francisco Symphony under Alfred Herz, performing Lalo's Symphonie Espagnole *as well as any veteran and better than most.*

Opposite:
No popular composer was more beloved at the outbreak of World War I than George M. Cohan (1878–1942). His 1907 musical 45 Minutes From Broadway *had thrust him to prominence, and his tune based on a trumpet call became the theme song of America's doughboys.*

centuries of steady movement, which some still persisted in calling progress; but now, chaos was never far off. Within two decades after the Armistice came the stock market crash and the Depression; then World War II.

Music had long since revealed, as well, that it has the power to alert as well as the power to soothe. But if music has its dark side, it also has a sunny side. There is joy in the songs of America's popular composers, music which lifted so many hearts in those difficult times. For instance, Jerome Kern's irrepressible tune set to Dorothy Field's disarming lyric rightly pointed out:

Nothing's impossible, I have found,
For when my chin is on the ground,
I pick myself up, dust myself off,
Start all over again.

Music manages to give us its message of good cheer again and again, even in the hardest of times, especially when it springs from deep roots. I came to learn this first not just through my love for the violin, that singing Italian instrument, but through two great artists who had a decisive early influence on my life: Fritz Kreisler and Georges Enesco. Both were violinists and composers, and a bridge between the old and the new. For them, as for a fiddler at a square dance, music-making was as essential as the breath of life.

Few of us in the West take part in music making any more, except perhaps in church or at school. Most of us live in big cities, have jobs to do, and are content to let others make music for us. Fortunately for me, I belong to those others, practicing musicians. It wasn't long after the end of the Great War that my parents began taking me along to concerts in San Francisco, when I was about three. I fell in love immediately with the sweet sound which the first violinist could make when he played alone. I did not yet know that he was what is called the "concertmaster," nor that his name was Louis Persinger, nor that he would become my first teacher. I only knew I had to make those same sounds myself. Of course, many others have always responded to music in the same way, and fortunately still do, choosing instinctively to devote their lives to this noble, ecstatic art.

I associate the violin especially with the enchanting tender sound of the *Liebesleid*, composed and played by Fritz Kreisler. I fell in love with his recording of it when I was only five. I had never met Kreisler, and it was another three years before I was to hear him play in person, by which time he was already part of my life. I longed to be able to express myself like him, to penetrate his world. His aristocratic, poised, melting phrases answered all the yearnings of my young heart. This was at a time when

recordings were still made by the acoustical process. The player stood before a megaphone-like horn rather than a microphone, and the physical vibrations of his performance were transmitted directly to the membrane.

Fritz Kreisler was no legend to me, since I could hear him in my own home on the phonograph. We became good friends. He had the typical Austrian zest for everything that life has to offer, as well as their profound musicality. His particular qualities of tenderness and rhythmic lilt, almost like human speech with its lively accented intonations, spoke a universal language understandable to all mankind. I met Kreisler in Berlin when I made my debut there under Bruno Walter in 1929 and had the privilege of hearing him perform the Beethoven Concerto. Unlike most childhood images which shatter in the presence of reality, his presence only etched mine all the more sharply and clearly. He had a natural rapport with his instrument and automatic command, which permitted him to be far more casual about performance than is allowed to most of us. He often warned me, above all, not to practice too much, not

Fritz Kreisler (1875–1959) looked not at all like the willowy ideal of a young virtuoso when this portrait was taken about 1912 when the artist was thirty-seven. Yet his noble performances displayed none of the aggression apparent here.

The sensitive poetic Kreisler temperament is revealed in this lithograph by the English artist Edmond Kapp, made in 1914. Kreisler remained throughout his long life an example not only to violinists but also to other artists.

to destroy that most precious gift, the spark that ignites one's self and one's audience in an act of spontaneous combustion. He feared that too much of the daily grind might take the bloom off that performance—not that it need do so if one keeps *work* and performance separate.

Kreisler himself was loved as much by his fellow violinists as by his audiences, a very great tribute. He was almost equally gifted as a composer and pianist, and his wide interests served as the fuel which fed the fires of his art. His remarkably calm, assured, intense performance of the Beethoven Concerto can still be heard on records. There Fritz Kreisler provides us with one of the last examples of the inspired performer by offering his own cadenzas instead of those by Joachim, which most violinists use. His cadenza to the first movement, in particular, is a rounded self-contained melodic and richly voiced work, towards the end of which he weaves two of the main themes most legitimately together, to the delight of the player and audience alike.

Whether it is preferable to hear a personal cadenza rather than the best available one remains an open question. Originality is better for the stimulation of the performer, but a possible hazard for the audience. I myself have resorted to writing my own wherever the available ones did not appeal to me, for example the Mozart concerti. The reason why I have not done the same for Beethoven and Brahms is because I have not felt confident of improving on those by Kreisler.

For quite a time now, since the Russian Revolution and the First World War, the popular image of the violin virtuoso has been the Russian Jew: for example, the idols of my youth, Mischa Elman, Jascha Heifetz, and then more recently, my beloved friend David Oistrakh. Born in New York, I come of Russian-Jewish stock myself. There's good reason for the assumption of the Russian-Jewish virtuoso, for the Jews were uprooted so often that the violin, travelling easily, became their comforting companion. The Jew is also deeply aware of his heritage. His traditional respect for Holy Law makes him a devoted student and interpreter, good qualities for a violinist. In Russia the Jew was traditionally the village fiddler, belonging there in the same way as did the Italian's singing violin in his native land; by the late 1800s there were also several superb music conservatories in the major Russian cities offering gifted young students a chance to match and even surpass the standards of Berlin, Paris or London. Leopold Auer, the outstanding teacher of violin at St. Petersburg, was a Russian Jew for whom Tschaikovsky had written his Violin Concerto. Auer's students included Heifetz and Elman, and many of the outstanding teachers of the next generation. Moreover, Russians love to sing, so they love the violin as much as any Italian or gypsy. But the violin is neither Russian nor Austrian nor Italian: it has always belonged to the entire world.

When I was nine I first heard Georges Enesco play, and when I was eleven I became his pupil. What I found in Enesco, what attracted me to him from the beginning, was the universal scope of his nature. In a sense he was not even Rumanian: he straddled East and West, North and South. I consider the word genius applicable in his case, though his music has not become well known apart from two potboilers, the Rumanian Rhapsodies nos. 1 and 2, written when he was a young man of sixteen (and on which, incidentally, he never collected a penny in royalties). Wherever Georges Enesco went, he kindled a flame. He was my teacher from the time we moved to Paris in 1927 and for many years afterwards. He was spacious in every way, a man formed by great and vital natural elements. When I first knew him he was more the noble lion (though with a black mane) than any other man I had ever met. It was this very leonine beauty, combined with his extraordinary sweetness of expression, that may have been the reason for the immediate rapport I felt. Passionate, fiercely loyal, his actions, his responses, his music sprang up from within his own nature like a volcano. No petty convention restrained this mighty force. It

Born in Moldavia in 1881, Georges Enesco was a student of Fauré and Massenet at the Paris Conservatory, and already a noted violin soloist at the turn of the century. He mastered all the major musical forms and conducted the principal orchestras of the world.

was both a natural respect and compassion for human life and effort and the chivalrous traditions of a cultivated feudal society which clothed his consuming love with the gentleness of a lamb.

Enesco's mind dealt in centuries. No human being I have ever known encompassed such wide measures of time and space. Generations of rugged peasants and conquering tribesmen seemed concentrated in his bearing and his gaze, and his memory held the collected works of all the great composers from Bach to Bartók. I mean that literally. There was truly no work that came up as an example that Enesco could not play immediately by heart at the piano. He knew the extremes of the simple life of the farm and the elegance of the court, as well as the spontaneous uncontrolled expression of the gypsy and the stylized, elegant, intellectually critical quality of the French. He was one of those great figures that emerged near the turn of the century from less happy countries, as did Janácek from Czechoslovakia or Szymanowski from Poland. Enesco was a great patriot, yet true to his day, he spoke impeccable English and trusted only the British flag at sea.

Enesco's playing conveyed a pulse and emotion which no mere authority or even clarity of conception can ever achieve alone. He never lost that verve or accent, those colors of vibrato from white to ultra-violet,

In the village of Certele in northern Rumania, the arrival of Easter and springtime is an occasion for celebration. It is from such traditions that Georges Enesco sprang.

the subtle varieties of slides never used out of context, the flashing bow, which are all the heritage of the Rumanian gypsy violinist. However disciplined his knowledge of composition, it never lost that magic element of improvisation. He was bent on communicating the sacred fire. In his Third Sonata for violin and piano, which my sister Hephzibah and I have often performed, every note, shade, color and accent is written out, so that any idiot-trained violinist can end up sounding like a true gypsy. To his credit I must add that, noting how I would never use the same fingering twice, he advised me to make a final choice as being wiser and safer for public performance, and suggested I might also make the acquaintance of the metronome.

The insight Enesco conveyed was an organic fusion of reason and intuition. No musician in my experience has achieved as defined and chiselled a synthesis as he. Once when I was fifteen, after I had studied, on Enesco's advice, with Adolf Busch, he asked me why I began the Bach Fugue in A Minor so loudly, with such authority. Since I had assumed Busch's opinion as my own, I answered that all fugues had to begin loudly because the theme was being announced and would now be developed. Enesco was patient and proceeded to explain that whereas some fugue themes could indeed be stated authoritatively, there were others like this one which began rather tentatively in the minor, though with a secure rhythm. He felt Bach himself would have begun them in a mood of search, launching the great design with just one thread, not expecting it to bear the whole weight of what would eventually become the tapestry. Being a stubborn child, I did not capitulate immediately, nor did I want to betray Adolf Busch. Enesco simply suggested I think about it and decide for myself. Of course he was right.

The music of Bach is in fact extraordinarily resilient. You can play it in a dozen different ways and it will continue to yield its magic. Enesco had that capacity for evoking each note as if it were created afresh. Many years later I happened to mention to him the operas of Mozart. He said, "Perhaps you will now learn to play Mozart as he should be played, and understand that every note he composed was like a syllable, a definite gesture, meaning something quite specific." As a boy I learned from Enesco that all the works of a master may have a bearing on any one of them. We cannot stop until we have taken hold of the composer's very manner of thinking and feeling and made it our own.

For proof of Enesco's phenomenal memory, equalled by his ability to learn, I can think of no better story than the incident to which I was witness one day in 1927 just after I had begun my studies with him. Maurice Ravel arrived at Enesco's apartment unannounced, interrupting our lesson. He had brought with him the manuscript of his brand-new

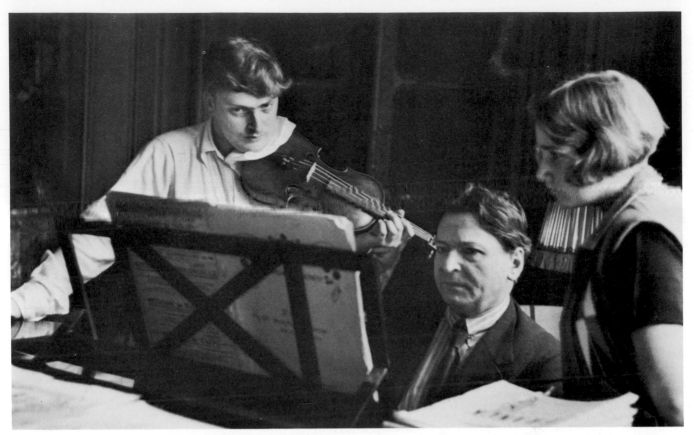

violin and piano sonata, the ink not yet dry, one might say, and he wanted to try it out right away. Ravel's publishers, Durand et Fils, in the correct French way then still customary, wanted to hear the work before deciding to publish it. Even Ravel had to obey, and he was anxious to have them hear it that very evening. Enesco apologized to my father and me most courteously, asking us to be patient while he rehearsed the work, adding that he would resume my lesson afterwards. With Ravel at the piano, he played the sonata through at sight, carefully and almost flawlessly. It is a difficult work and a long one, with interesting touches of jazz and blues that attracted so many composers in Europe at the time. When they were done, Ravel pronounced himself delighted and prepared to go. Enesco stopped him, saying, "No, let's try it once more, just to be sure." This time Enesco put his part aside and played the whole work from memory. My father and I were dumbfounded, as was Ravel. There are aspects to such gifts, which Enesco shared with Bach, Mozart and a few others of our own time, that seem to defy rational explanation.

Though Enesco never begrudged the time given freely to colleagues or to performing, his true love was composition. His works deserve to be better known, above all his opera *Oedipus* on which he worked for so long, carrying the huge score with him from engagement to engagement,

Yehudi Menuhin began his studies with Georges Enesco in 1927. In 1936, the year this photograph was taken, Enesco's opera Oedipus *was premièred at the Paris Opera.*

spending his nights bent over the staves. I admired him as a conductor for the way he made the act of performing music so rewarding for all the participants. Human beings need beauty as much as order and meaning, as Kreisler and Enesco taught me. They tuned their senses to the long heritage of their people, and through them I learned that art is communication, because through their art I came to know their people. It is a lesson worth remembering, as we consider that music is a vital key to the understanding of the people of our time.

Over the past half century, music in the West has almost split in two, or perhaps in four, changes which have affected the music of the rest of the world. While the terms classical or serious are often applied to music, it is also true that the avant-garde has steadily distanced itself from the traditional. This has happened in the popular field as well. Traditional jazz, folk music and show tunes are a long way from hard rock, punk rock,

The Original Dixieland "Jass" Band, recruited and organized by New Orleans musician and promoter Papa Jack Laine, became in 1917 the first generally accepted jazz band in America and Europe, recording and touring extensively. Yet for some time the rule in music was also "separate but equal."

Louis Armstrong (1900–1971) was the first internationally acclaimed black solo jazz star, remaining a favorite for over forty years. The poetry of his trumpet solos has never been surpassed, and his ability in his prime to improvise was legendary. Here he is in 1930, soon after leaving the shelter of the King Oliver Band.

astro rock. Signs of a possible reunification have begun to display themselves in the past few years, both in popular and in concert music.

In the years just after World War I, jazz quickly became established worldwide as the language of urban popular music. We have already followed the rise of ragtime, unmistakably the parent to jazz, along with the blues. Like ragtime, jazz travelled along the Mississippi River, flourishing in New Orleans, St. Louis and Kansas City, as well as in Chicago and New York. The origin of the term jazz is obscure; the word is certainly African, has sexual connotations, and was originally spelled *jass*. The jazz band was in part a scaled-down version of the marching bands which had already become popular in New Orleans and elsewhere before the turn of the century. In its most practical form, the jazz band consisted of not more than half a dozen musicians, each contributing his share to a communal improvisation. Larger jazz bands did not disappear, and those led by Paul Whiteman and Fletcher Henderson in the 1920s set a trend which continued into the thirties. Brilliant solo artists attracted a devoted following, notably Louis Armstrong whose trumpet improvisations became celebrated throughout the world, in person and on his early recordings with King Oliver. The vocal origins of jazz were maintained by such outstanding blues interpreters as Bessie Smith. From the beginning, jazz was an art uniting Americans north and south, and it soon drove out the sentimental turn-of-the-century ballads, transforming popular music as swiftly as rock has altered the music of our day.

As with rags, the driving energy of jazz came equally from black and white musicians. But it took an all-white group, the Original Dixieland Jazz Band in 1917, to begin spreading the word on a commercial basis. Their recordings remain the first true jazz discs, despite rumors of the existence of cylinders by the legendary black trumpeter Buddy Bolden, whose penetrating tone could be heard in New Orleans halfway across Lake Ponchartrain, it is said. Part of the fascination of jazz is to be found in the fact that it restores to music the freedom of improvisation, raising that skill to a level where it becomes the subject matter of the music. Mozart and Beethoven were content to restrict the free flights of their performers to the cadenzas of their concerti. In jazz all the players take the basic tune and embroider its harmony and melody as freely as possible without ever losing their sense of ensemble.

The classic jazz group consists of clarinet, trumpet, trombone, piano and drums. It is an ensemble whose conventions are as well established as those of the medieval consort. The trombone has sometimes been called the tailgate, as early jazz groups often travelled by flat-bed truck to play at dances, and the trombonist would sit with his legs dangling over the lowered tailgate to obtain better support for his heavier instrument. A banjo, double bass or saxophone might enrich the ensemble from time to time, but the standard jazz quintet is as classic as the string quartet.

Of course jazz itself was once considered bold, experimental and dangerous. It was denounced from church pulpits and by newspapers as a corrupter of youth, just as the waltz had been in the century before, and rock music more recently. Both rock and jazz have the same bite as ragtime from which they came. Ragtime and jazz hit Europe hard. Even Igor Stravinsky wrote pieces with rag touches, such as his *Circus Polka*. In country after country people came to jazz by the millions, to play it, to dance to it, to buy recordings of it. Jazz became America's major cultural export along with the movies, and a few expatriate writers; but jazz seemed to be just what people needed to help them forget bad times.

Jazz rode onto the concert stage thanks to the talents of George Gershwin, an intense, feverish young man, never really comfortable unless he was sitting at a piano. He was always at the very center of a

party. As with the music of Enesco, Gershwin's is a unique amalgam of two traditions, and it undoubtedly helped to make jazz more widely accepted. The speed with which jazz spread across the world was incredible. It happened because of recordings, because of that latest thing called radio, and because of the variety and dynamic quality of the American spirit. The music of the New World has proved to be the irresistible force, and musical tradition has not been the immovable object.

My feeling is that jazz, like Stravinsky, is music in tune with the age which gave us mass production. We submit ourselves to its beat as we do to the rhythm of work. Songs to accompany work, to steady its rhythm and ease its occasional monotony, are an old use of music. Dance tunes have always been infectious, making our feet move despite ourselves. But the character of such music has changed from age to age, culture to culture. The rhythm of mass production is perfectly exemplified by Chaplin's last silent film *Modern Times*. In music it is a quality which Africa brought to the West, each individual concentrating on keeping his place in the repetitive rhythm, no matter how complex the web becomes.

Besides the rhythm of mass production, jazz also corresponds to a widespread perception of the present world, that of a uniform mass moving as

In 1927 Al Jolson filmed The Jazz Singer *for Warner Brothers ana sound movies were born. On the set the microphone was placed above and forward, out of sight of the noisy cameras hidden in bulky soundproof boxes, which also enclosed the operator.*

one to a single generating force. That is not a false instinct, for the lunar tides and solar cycles affect us all. But jazz skimmed the ground swiftly like a dry grass fire, in many places sweeping away the existing local musical speech.

As the vigor of the New World grew, the vigor of Europe was dissipated, buried under excess. The rooms, the clothes, the food had all become too dense, detailed, laden with decoration. It was the same with European music, especially harmony. In Vienna, which had been the musical capital of Europe for more than a century, one man began looking for a fresh way out of the dilemma, as Debussy had done in Paris. That man was Arnold Schönberg. Born only a few weeks before Fritz Kreisler, in 1875, Schönberg had begun as a devoted disciple of Wagner, Strauss and Mahler, and even of Brahms. But Schönberg encountered the music of Debussy, of Scriabin, as well as the theoretical writings of Matthias Hauer, and his view began to alter. He began to think of the twelve notes that make up the octave as separate independent entities.

After producing works like *Verklärte Nacht* and the *Gurrelieder*, which are the summation of the chromatic style, Schönberg suddenly broke off into something new. It took him some time to arrive at a stable theory but

George Gershwin (1898–1937) helped American music to bridge the gap between white and black, popular and classical. His tragically premature death can be compared to that of Mozart or Schubert; after **Porgy and Bess** *he seemed on the verge of a breakthrough into new territory.*

already in such works as *Pierrot Lunaire* and the *Five Pieces for Orchestra*, written at the end of the first decade of the new century, he offered up an entirely new harmonic system, leaving harmony as we had known it far behind.

Until this time Western music had remained solidly locked to the concept of the triad, the familiar sound of the major and minor chord, a form of Euclidian logic. Standard harmonic logic was based on the home key or tone and on the two notes most closely related to it, the fourth and fifth above. A key could be established by playing in sequence the major triads built on one-five-one, or the softer one-four-one (called plagal). If the composer wanted to establish a key beyond any possible doubt, especially if he had wandered far afield, say from C into F-sharp major, once back home he would sound out the triads one-four-five-one. Schönberg threw all that out.

Edmond Kapp's portrait (1931) of Arnold Schonberg suggests a gentler side to the Viennese master, while displaying his unusual grip on the conductor's baton. Between 1913 and 1921 the composer fell virtually silent as he concentrated all his energy on the formulation of the twelve-tone system.

Curiously enough Schönberg wanted to recapture the same clean line, the one he so honored in Bach and the whole Austro-German tradition running back to the seventeenth century. Taking his cue from the keyboard with its equal temperament, Bach's principle of the equality of all the keys, he applied it instead to all of the twelve semitones. It was rather like our democratic ideal of equality before the law. He decided that these notes were all to be interchangeable, free to be arranged in whatever pattern he chose, without regard to previous harmonic and key relationships. He built his new system on the principle of what he called the tone row.

A tone row is an arrangement of the twelve semitones in a particular sequence. Under Schönberg's rules, no note in a row could be repeated until all twelve had been used up. Melodies were derived from this row, and so were the harmonies. It all sounds like some silly game. Eventually entire compositions could be built from a single row, the first one so constructed being Schönberg's Piano Suite op. 25, written in 1924. One might suppose that this notion was based on the idea that every note is entitled to the pursuit of happiness, that overall harmonic control was being rejected. Pure democracy, like pure communism, implies no social structure at all, but rather a benign anarchy where it is taken for granted that everything will find its proper and equal level. But we must be careful not to confuse the vocabulary of freedom with the vocabulary of notes. We might do better to compare the notes to the alphabet. It may be extraordinary that man has succeeded in expressing so much with twenty-six letters (more in Asian languages), but not even the poet has raised the alphabet to the level of language, nor decided that every letter shall have equal usage.

Schönberg's twelve-tone system seems to me to offer a similar proposition which we can accept for purposes of argument. It was an extraordinary adventure, for Schönberg was asking the most fundamental questions about the nature of music in the West since the invention of harmony nearly a thousand years earlier. His mature music makes unprecedented demands on the human ear. The structure emerges most clearly by visual analysis. I know there have been similar periods in music in times past, and Wagner's *Tristan* is often cited as comparable, for it was given up as being unperformable at first. Yet by the 1880s, twenty years after its première, it was accepted as a regular part of the opera repertory in Germany, France, England and the United States. To my mind the German word *Augenmusik*, meaning music for the eye, may be applied to much of Schönberg. I feel the real composer knows the sound he plans to make beforehand, just as the author first imagines his words. The use of paper, of sketching and revising, is a use of the eye to assist the ear, but not to supersede it. I do not exclude the possibility that many twelve-tone composers do set down what they "hear," but I have been exposed to the reverse often enough to believe that the difficulty is widespread. Clearly, audiences have not been willing to make the effort, by and large, in the sixty years or so since Schönberg introduced his twelve-tone system.

All this is the more remarkable when you examine a work like his Suite for Piano op. 25. The row upon which it is based ends with four notes which we would spell B, C, A, B-flat. In the German form of musical spelling, where B becomes H and B-flat becomes B, a practice running back to the Middle Ages, those four notes spell H, C, A, B. Run them backwards and they spell "B-A-C-H." It is a most touching gesture, included like a talisman, as if Schönberg were seeking Bach's blessing. The signature device was used often by the old master himself, just as he made a practice of running his themes backwards or upside down. It is heartening that Schönberg should have been so anxious to have us perceive him as part of that tradition, while believing that he had at last found the solution to the dilemma of Western harmony. In 1923 Schönberg wrote:

> Frankly I have so far for the first time found no mistake, and the system keeps on growing of its own accord, without my doing anything about it. This I consider a good sign. In this way I find myself positively enabled to compose as freely and fantastically as one otherwise does only in one's youth, and am nevertheless subject to a precise definable aesthetic discipline.

How very self-assuring and dogmatic that is, while aspiring to be true to every artist's dream.

Schönberg did see himself as part of the tradition, merely taking the next inevitable step. But I see him in a larger context. In him we are confronted by the dilemma of the equality which man seeks to impose on the inequality of nature. For those twelve notes of the octave are in fact not equal, not in nature. The tone row that tries to make them so is, to my mind, an arbitrary idea. Granted, Schönberg wanted to free the composer from old rules, which had been abused. What he did was to set up rigid new ones, for that is the only way his mind knew how to work. There is an obvious contradiction between the arbitrary and the free, and yet they so often depend on one another.

For some time now modern music has been described as dissonant, and no doubt many of you have felt in sympathy with this opinion. The fact is, you are right. Dissonance became the definition by which modern music knew that it really was modern. For Schönberg, the very idea of consonance and dissonance, the old idea of a harmonic center, became meaningless. He felt that the harmonic order should be imposed each time by the composer. But Schönberg in his way opened up our ears and gave us a taste of something new which subtly altered our musical experience.

Music and society in the West had together reached an unprecedented state of crisis. It was the old conflict between freedom and order, between old and new, raised to the level of open rebellion. The best proof of Schönberg's harmonic dilemma, and that of the composers who have followed in his path, is that they all deliberately attempted to avoid the strong natural intervals of the fourth, fifth and octave. Instead they stress the minor second and major second, intervals which are furthest from those we call perfect. These abrasive sounds help to prevent twelve-tone music from displaying any sense of harmonic center. Yet I wonder if we can really totally escape from the natural attraction between notes, any more than we can escape from our center of gravity except by leaving the earth altogether. What remains forever fascinating to me is that touch of genius in man which finally allows him to express himself, to break through any self-imposed bonds, however tight. We will see this in the music of Alban Berg, to my thinking Schönberg's most gifted disciple, for Berg took the new rules and turned them to great advantage.

Music is a two-way street, and while American jazz went abroad, Europe sent many of its most gifted artists to North America. Among them, besides Schönberg and Stravinsky, was Edgard Varèse, a Frenchman from Burgundy, that rich source of so many medieval musicians and much great wine. Early in Varèse's career his friend and mentor Claude Debussy had said to him, "You have the right to compose what you want. The music emerges and it is yours. Rules do not make a work of art." Varèse went many steps beyond Debussy, almost reinventing musical sound itself. At his first American press interview Varèse said:

> Our musical alphabet must be enriched. We need new instruments, and they must not remind us of things we've already heard a hundred times. Instruments are, after all, only a temporary means of expression. Musicians should take up this question seriously with the help of machinery specialists.

America let Varèse make his music even if she didn't understand it. The critics and public alike asked him constantly what it meant, but he would only answer:

> The music is not a story, it is not a picture, it is not a philosophy. It is simply my music. Listen to it, don't describe it. Music being a special form of thought can express nothing but itself.

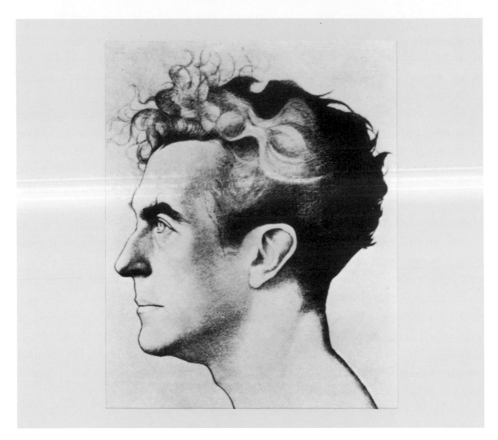

Edgard Varèse was at the height of his creative powers when this portrait was made in 1925. The original silverpoint is by Joseph Stella.

Beethoven could not have put it more aptly. It was exactly what he meant when, by way of replying to the same question about his *Eroica* Symphony, he sat down to the piano and simply played the first eight bars. It was his entire answer.

Varèse is known for works such as *Octandre, Ionisation, Hyperprism* and *Ameriques*. These succinct statements are a law unto themselves, built out of no past, whether harmonic, melodic or rhythmic. Although he lived until 1967, Varèse was at his most productive between the age of thirty-five and fifty-one (1921–1937). His period of near silence thereafter is comparable to that of Sibelius, who lived over thirty years without composing, or Rossini who remained nearly mute for forty. What we can say about Varèse is that his sharp, bitter, incisive music cuts to the bone of civilization. It is music suited to the glass-walled canyons of our modern cities, asking us who we are, and what music is, in as fundamental a way as the music of Schönberg. Varèse is looked upon by an entire younger generation of avant-garde composers, from Cage to Stockhausen, as the father of the really new music of our day. Stravinsky's musical language, however radical it appeared at the time, is seen now to lie within the tradition, whereas that of Varèse, like that of Ives, is without precedent.

This brings me to the heart of the problem facing music in our time. From the very beginning of human life, one of the purposes of music has been to give us pleasure. The other is to tell us the truth. The same applies to all the arts, of course, and our experiments within them are natural enough, being part of the learning process. But the label "disagreeable" is fairly new, and began being applied to some kinds of music only by the nineteenth century, for instance to Beethoven's. More recently some have applied the label to rock music, perhaps the first time this has been said of a form of popular music. It has occurred to me that perhaps one of the reasons we do not like some music, or some modern art, is precisely because sometimes we do not like ourselves, or the world around us, or our society. In Ancient Greece beauty and truth were wedded to each other. Today we recognize that some truths remain hopelessly, unredeemably ugly, as indeed they always have been. Artists who were responsible for some of these troublesome revelations, Picasso and Stravinsky, did return for a while to more familiar forms, within the neo-classical movement. But Schönberg and Varèse stuck to their guns, and their music has not yet been generally accepted by the public. It is the longest period we have known in which music considered important by some has been rejected by so many. What a change from the time five hundred years ago when Tinctoris said that music more than forty years old simply wasn't worth hearing. Today we often seem to say instead, "Out with the new and in with the old." Mind you, Edgard Varèse's *Ionisation* served recently as the background to a male dance solo in the Broadway musical hit show *Dancin'*. Varèse would have smiled to think that his once difficult score was now being played nine times a week by a pit band, and exceedingly well at that.

Over the years I have tried to bring new works into existence by commissioning new composers to write for me. The Sonata for Solo Violin of Belá Bartók in 1944 was one of the first. The violin concerto *Due Canti e Finale*, by the South African composer, Priaulx Rainier, is one of the more recent. I feel the performer has an obligation to recognize and play new works and, better still, to bring new music into existence by virtue of the promise of performance. We must constantly be ready to modify our own taste by refreshing it with the taste of others. If taste is only valid for the individual, it can quickly become prejudice, whether that of the artist or of the audience. All of us sometimes have difficulty opening ourselves to new experiences, but we must learn to take some music on trust until we know it better. I have always tried to become acquainted with unfamiliar music through those who love it most. We are not obliged to like all music, or all art, but love is the most compelling of all human sentiments, and when we encounter it we should attend.

The decadent frenzy of Berlin in the twenties is superbly captured in this painting by Otto Dix, part of a tryptich, evoking the bitterness and disillusion which became a part of the musicals of Kurt Weill and Bertolt Brecht.

The dilemma of our day is the complex tug of war between the intellectually abstract and the organically sensual. We can surrender to either or strive for synthesis, substituting balance for energy. The ideal is a point somewhere between. Europe is a delta country, constantly mixing mind and heart. In Freud, Schönberg and Einstein we find a maximum of discipline joined to a maximum of intuition. Real control lies in total identification but too much analysis may cloud intuitive sources, a problem with which contemporary music has been struggling for over half a century. For me, the music of the avant-garde has moved too far in the direction of analysis, of measurement and structure, at the expense of true freedom, whereas pop-rock has gone overboard the other way, for pure sensual impact without adequate development. In both cases it is the finer nuance of feeling which suffers.

In fairness to artists, whose role it has always been to break through barriers, even of their own making, I should point out that in this century the idea of the audience has changed drastically. Today the arts are supposed to belong to everyone. That is not a bad idea in principle, except that all skills are improved by practice, and a broad understanding of any art cannot occur without applying some effort. "I don't know anything about it but I know what I like!" turns out on closer examination to be a dubious proposition. I say the audience may know what it likes but it cannot know what it *might* like, and here is where the integrity of the purveyor comes into play. We must all be receptive to new experiences that enrich our old preconceptions, to the original voices in our midst. Artists at every level have long recognized that it is part of our function as human beings to make the best use we can of what we find around us.

Clearly the twenties were not a time of balance, and while serious composers experimented, popular music encouraged a plunge into exotic new experiences. In Germany, especially, the mood was almost hysterical, a bitter, biting spirit compounded of disillusion and nostalgia which the music of Kurt Weill captures to perfection. But the mood was not to last. Adolf Hitler came to power, and many artists fled, among them Weill, whose Berlin musicals with Bertolt Brecht had become tremendous hits. *The Threepenny Opera*, first produced in 1927, had become the sarcastic model for many later off-Broadway shows and postwar cabaret musicals. Weill's scores contain something of the mocking spirit of the Weimar Republic between the wars, and this persists in his American musicals. Weill never lost his sense of haunted yearning, of something never to be fulfilled. Cole Porter is probably the American composer closest in spirit to Kurt Weill, but there is such an unquenchable streak of joshing good humor in Porter that even the most acid lyric or shifty harmony emerges with wit and compassion. Cole Porter's heroes and heroines are fully realized, confident, especially in such musicals as *Kiss Me Kate*. Weill's are perpetually unsure, nowhere more so than in *Lady in the Dark*.

The movies brought other European composers to America. It was natural for Hollywood to make room for foreign talent; the industry was built by men from the old country. They wanted music they knew in their films, and Erich Wolfgang Korngold was one of those who helped to

On the day of party victory at the polls, September 1, 1933, Hitler's storm troopers marched through the streets of Nuremberg, Germany's most perfectly preserved medieval city. Six years later to the day, Hitler attacked Poland, and in the war Nuremberg was almost entirely destroyed.

provide it. In Vienna his opera *The Dead City* won him acclaim as a second Richard Strauss. Korngold put all his classical training to use in devising scores for swashbuckling epics and tear-stained tragedies. It was a trend that had started with the nickelodeon, where classics were pressed into the service of popular entertainment, only this time it was not the original but a pastiche.

Writing music for films is a highly professional task, a discipline for which not all composers have the gift. Movie music has also been regarded as low-grade work, as writing a screenplay may be seen as less worthy than writing a fine novel. The money is good, but the soul is poorer. Perhaps that is one reason why so few major composers have been drawn to films. Copland, Prokofiev, Walton and Vaughan Williams are notable exceptions. Most do not wish to take the time to master the skills,

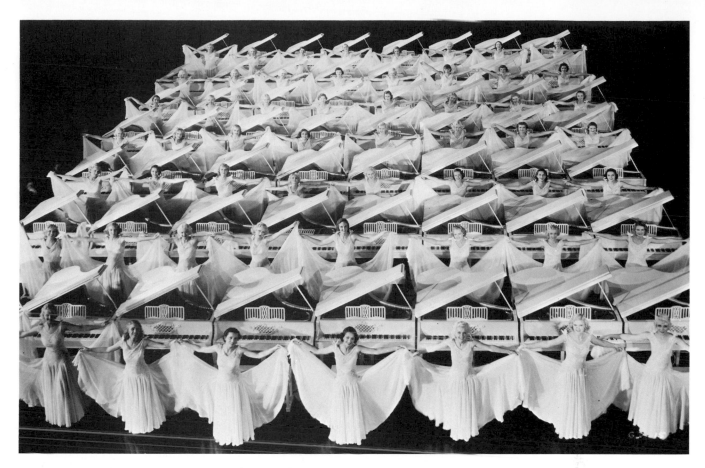

and film producers are not much inclined to give them the opportunity anyway, knowing it will be difficult to meet their standards. Not many composers who see themselves as part of the tradition of Beethoven and Bach respond easily to the idea that they should provide "seventeen seconds of mounting fear" in one section and "one minute ten of young romance tinged with regret" in another. Composers like Lully or Purcell would have had no difficulty with the task, for that was in a sense what they did for a living. As for Wagner, his music dramas are scored like films, assigning themes to each character, mirroring every change in emotional tension, and his composing techniques have adapted themselves well to the movies.

I am occasionally surprised that audiences will accept the classical musical style of the West in films when they sometimes resist it in its original form. This is linked, of course, to the notion of culture for everyone. I do not believe it is necessary for every music lover to mount the slopes of the Bach Chaconne, or even to bathe in Rachmaninoff, yet throughout this century the movies have shown that huge audiences can relate to a musical language which is not that of the immediately

Busby Berkeley became Hollywood's master of film choreography, often photographing his dancers from above in shifting patterns like bits of glass in a kaleidoscope. In Golddiggers of 1934 *he arranged sixty-five white baby grands (two not visible) in the apotheosis of the keyboard.*

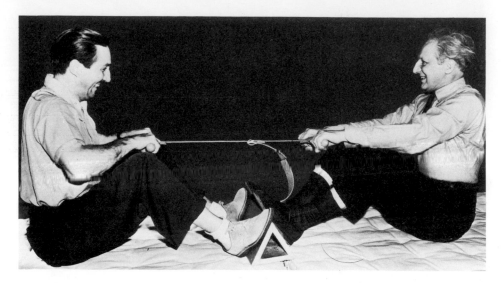

popular. However, that has not stopped the gap from widening, nor the popular side of the industry from concentrating on producing the latest hit while so many serious composers remain unheard by a wide public.

It is now that we come to grips with another change in our century, the concept of culture for everyone. The avant-garde may have been deliberately avoiding contact with the general audience, but the definition of an audience was undergoing a major transformation everywhere in the world, with the help of the media. Two musicians, conductors of first rank, made a particular contribution to the role that movies and radio were to play in America's musical life: Leopold Stokowski and Arturo Toscanini. Stokowski's knowledge of recording techniques was far in advance of that of his colleagues. He experimented constantly with the set-up of his orchestra in the concert hall, as well as in the recording studio. In 1936, Stokowski left the Philadelphia Orchestra and moved to Hollywood to make his career in films, "a higher calling" was the way he put it. He brought with him a degree of experience which made him a match for the best studio sound men, often to their chagrin. Stokowski made an appearance in *The Big Broadcast of 1937* and then starred in a remarkable film with Deanna Durbin, *100 Men and a Girl*.

Stokowski's greatest film venture, far bolder in its implications, continues to merit study by critics and filmmakers. This was his collaboration with Walt Disney in the creation of *Fantasia*. The result may also be questionable in some respects, but it remains a remarkable achievement, not least for its breakthrough in handling movie music reproduction long before the day of stereo or quadraphonic sound.

Stokowski knew the visual value of the conductor, for the audience as

In Hollywood, Leopold Stokowski encountered Walt Disney, who thought it would be fun to make Mickey Mouse the star of an animated short based on The Sorcerer's Apprentice. *That was in 1938. Two years later they brought forth* Fantasia, *the most revolutionary musical film ever produced. Here the two masters meet over an exercise footboard.*

well as the players. In *Fantasia* he appeared in silhouette, alone on a high podium at the beginning and close of each work. His crowning gesture to Hollywood came when Mickey Mouse as The Sorcerer's Apprentice made an epilogue appearance, climbing the steps to the podium to shake hands with Stokowski. For the first half of the century Leopold Stokowski epitomized for most Americans what the symphony conductor should look like, how he should behave, and in large measure he helped to popularize the symphony orchestra in North America.

If Stokowski was, *sui generis*, transcribing works of Bach for a Straussian orchestra, placing them under a hydraulic press, then Arturo Toscanini must be described as force of nature. He was already seventy-one when he took over the NBC Symphony in 1937, confessing he was afraid he might be too old for the job. He held the post until he was eighty-seven.

The story of the Toscanini years at NBC is memorable for many reasons. American network radio was barely a decade old when he came, the Depression still held the country in its grip. When Toscanini approached his new orchestra for his first rehearsal he was as nervous as a tyro making his debut and sweated profusely. The inaugural broadcast on Christmas night was heard by millions—one of the listeners was President Franklin D. Roosevelt, then at the start of his second term. It was the artistic and public relations coup of the broadcasting industry.

In a day when the transistor is king and pocket radios go along on beach picnics, alpine climbs and desert safaris, it is not easy to recapture the time when radios were imposing pieces of living room furniture, oracles enshrined just as TV sets are now, occupying a place as important as the hearth once held. What could be easier than to hang a microphone in front of a performance and transmit the results to the nation? Major networks in Europe and America had standing orchestras of some fifty players to back up dramas or provide light interludes. But only NBC had Toscanini.

There has been so much stress on the visible presence of the conductor that it is hard to convey the force of Toscanini's personality, borne over radio to the listeners. But it was undeniably there every Sunday from 5 to 6 P.M. Conducting is an intensely personal expression, which is why the same orchestra will sound so different under various leaders. Stokowski and Toscanini unsuccessfully tried an exchange of podiums between Philadelphia and New York in the thirties. The two orchestras had become extensions of these opposed personalities.

That the symphony conductor should be an object of veneration is a recent development. It was born in the nineteenth century, the age of the individual, as orchestras began to grow in size. Virtuoso conducting is

The few who were able to secure those precious free invitational tickets to Arturo Toscanini's broadcasts with the NBC Symphony between 1937 and 1954 can never forget the quiet, precise intensity of his supple conducting style.

usually regarded as having begun in France with François Habeneck, Louis Jullien and Hector Berlioz, all active in Paris and London from 1816 to 1869. But the art came to full flower in Germany and Austro-Hungary. In the latter part of the nineteenth and early twentieth centuries four names stand out. These are Richard Wagner and Franz Liszt, and their younger followers Hans Richter and Arthur Nikisch. Richter and Nikisch came to dominate orchestra style in Europe by the turn of the century. Richter worshipped the written score. Nikisch was freer and one of the first to conduct without a score. Leopold Stokowski, who had substituted for Nikisch in Paris in 1908, modelled himself after that elegant stylist, abandoning the use of the baton. Arturo Toscanini was a conductor in Richter's mold, engaged in combat with the orchestra to win the day for the composer, firing the volatile Latin temperament to white heat.

Culture for everyone is a noble idea, but the arts were not always thought of in this way. Ghislebert's cathedrals may have served the people, yet they were made to the specifications of the masters of the church. Michelangelo painted on the ceiling of the Sistine Chapel for his patrons. Monteverdi created his operas for the nobility of Mantua and the patricians of Venice. Mozart and Beethoven wrote for an elite in Vienna, and Chopin for an educated circle in Paris. Until recently their music was available only to those who could afford to hear it performed, often in wealthy private homes or expensive concert halls. The only alternative was to learn to play it for yourself. The winds of populism have been blowing through the world for quite a long time now.

The movies and radio helped accelerate the spread of cultural literacy, a process which had begun with the printing press. Moreover, our lives are no longer so clearly divided between those who work and those who play; and it is a good thing, for the vitality of a culture depends on roots sunk deep into the daily lives of us all, whereas its structure and its flowering depend on those who have the gifts and the time to formulate it. In any case culture is not an end product but part of a continuous cycle. We can see this clearly in Indonesia, where classical and popular music are one and the same, as in India. Here the teaching of music proceeds by direct example, as it has for centuries.

It was in the 1930s that Western musicians began to be increasingly aware of a brilliant, cultivated music from the Indonesian islands of Bali and Java, the melodious percussion of the gamelan orchestras. Mountains of recording equipment had been taken into the field by specialists who returned with sounds of the kind Debussy had heard in Paris in 1889. Gamelan music is a collective art belonging to a culture in which virtually everyone takes part. Each town and village is fiercely proud of its own conception of the gamelan. The family of gamelan gongs and xylophones ranges from deepest bass to brightest treble, some suspended alone, others arranged on long racks and played by half a dozen men in a row, each controlling only a few gongs, like bell-ringers. The instruments of Java and Bali come in several forms, from the tuned metal bars to those of bamboo and wood, some made to be shaken and carrying names like *Anklung*. A gamelan orchestra generally comprises at least a dozen players, but the number may exceed thirty. The identity of an Indonesian village is deeply tied to its gamelan orchestra, like American home towns with their baseball teams.

The movie musicals of the thirties offered escape, and idols of the screen (many now forgotten, for instance Irene Ware) helped an entire generation forget its troubles (and sometimes collect free dishes at Wednesday evening double features).

The virtuosity of a Balinese gamelan ensemble must be seen as well as heard to be believed and understood. The unity of many hands moving through swift and subtly changing rhythms is an art comparable to any virtuoso orchestra in the world.

Culturally the islands still retain links with the mainland, as revealed in their decoration of the gamelan instruments. Bali in particular shows a love of this art comparable to the most elaborate Western Renaissance art of decorating lutes and virginals. Stands supporting gongs and tuned bars are carved and gilded with the most fanciful animal and plant shapes. The music of Bali is notable for rhythmic counterpoint, a subtle art passed on by careful, patient example. The delicately curved metal hammers flash among the bars so swiftly that we hardly see the intertwining of separate lines by various players. A teacher will sit across from a student with one instrument between them, showing his pupil how to master his part, as they both carefully damp each note with the left hand after it is sounded. Once a sequence is secure, well memorized, the teacher will play his own contrasting part on the same instrument. For a Western musician it is astounding to see the teacher easily playing with the notes in reverse order from the norm, the lowest notes to his right and the highest to his left.

These Indonesian forms of music and dance derive strength from a combination of conviction and historical experience. They have persisted in the face of change and invasions of other cultures and faiths, articulating the way Indonesians feel about their identity as a people.

Music has always had this power. In a sense it is a form of nationalism, for the music of Bali is unmistakably distinct from that of its neighboring island of Java—prouder, more aggressive, less sinuous. It is a cultural asset belonging to all the people, and has helped to shape their lives for generations.

Style is an elusive thing and every conscientious musician spends a lifetime pursuing it. In the end each must find his own way. Students all over the world are learning Western music as our own young people seek to understand the music of other cultures. The improvement in the training of musicians is one of the most notable developments of our century.

The purpose of music in education is *not* to produce a ready-made audience with "well-informed" tastes; it is decidedly not the object to produce a market for specific goods; it is to produce a musical climate both open-minded and critical, to produce musical skills and crafts, and to encourage human beings to be humane. Albert Einstein played the fiddle well enough to take part in chamber music at home, but luckily he never dreamed of a concert career. Relativity also exists between human

In many Balinese villages, all the men take part in the Ketchak *or monkey dance, part of the telling of the* Ramayana *legend. Its syncopated rhythms are as powerful a part of the Balinese tradition as the dancing by young girls of the classic* Legong.

lives. What music does for all of us, at its best, is to sharpen our sense of intuition, while at the same time sharpening our analytical and critical faculties.

At the Yehudi Menuhin School in Stoke D'Abernon, Surrey, we have tried to set a quiet example extending well beyond the simple making of music. In this international school we have students from every continent and denomination. Each morning they all come together to share in a common experience. Part of it will be musical, as they may sing or play instruments, or listen to a recording. Part of it will be philosophical, the reading of a short text from a book; it may be something from the Bible, but it may also be a poem or an excerpt from Saint-Exupéry. This is followed by a minute or so of silence. After the music and the central thought, the silence is a concentration of the moment of listening to one's self and listening together that cements the sense of community and the purpose of life at the school.

Finding an authentic personal voice has been the Western composer's problem for a long time. One American who has taken part in the struggle of the twentieth century is Aaron Copland, one of his country's most honored composers, and one who has spoken with an uniquely American voice.

Students from the Yehudi Menuhin School are now enrolled in many leading conservatories around the world. Their generation will carry on the spirit exemplified by Kreisler and Enesco.

MENUHIN Composers have always needed roots, a link with their environment, with their past, their people. What are the roots you found that enabled you to compose music which is so American in flavor?

COPLAND First of all I was born in Brooklyn. That gives you a start.

MENUHIN I was born in the Bronx. B is a revered letter in the musical alphabet: Bach, Beethoven, Brahms, Bartók—and now Brooklyn.

COPLAND It may not be a brilliant start. But I got it into my head that one of the great attributes of French music was that it sounded French, German music sounded German, the Russians wrote music that sounded Russian. It seemed to me odd in the early 1920s that a country like the United States, with its own kind of life and civilization, couldn't write serious music that would reflect my country in the same way.

MENUHIN But the Russians have been on their soil for a long time. Germans developed a way of thinking that went with their literature and their way of life; the French likewise. The United States offered such a bewildering variety of cultures.

COPLAND Remember Walt Whitman and Emerson, typically American figures in the arts.

MENUHIN But wasn't that a New England phenomenon? Yet you composed *El Salon Mexico*.

Born November 11, 1900, two years after Gershwin, Aaron Copland is world-acclaimed as the dean of American composers. He has found a uniquely personal solution to joining together the popular and the serious in music.

COPLAND It was another phase of the same desire. After using American folk tunes, it seemed easy to handle Mexican or Spanish materials.

MENUHIN But is Spanish any more American than Elizabethan or Appalachian?

COPLAND Appalachian is closer to Brooklyn, and I could feel more natural with it. Now Walt Whitman couldn't have been European or written as he did if he hadn't been born in this country. He lived in Brooklyn a long time.

MENUHIN How would you define "feeling American?"

COPLAND Just ask any American. A certain liveliness, a freshness of temperament, perhaps.

MENUHIN Isn't it also an ability to identify with people of other origins?

COPLAND That's true. Think of the popular composers, the folk materials, and the contribution of the Negro in creating spirituals and jazz. The whole world recognized that this was a contribution to light music. I couldn't see why we couldn't also write our symphonies and operas and give them a flavor that would seem as American. Gershwin succeeded with *Rhapsody in Blue* and *An American in Paris*, from the standpoint of jazz. I wanted to spread it to New England hymnody and give it a chance to be expressive in a symphonic way.

MENUHIN You wedded that to the European tradition, the discipline of counterpoint. You studied with Nadia Boulanger.

COPLAND I spent three full years with her and felt like a very lucky young student when I found her.

MENUHIN I was thinking of Ernst Bloch who also tried to be American. He spent a lot of time studying native Indian chants, and fondly imagined that he put them in his *American* Symphony. I feel that they are Jewish melodies, though they could be Slavic, Moorish or otherwise.

COPLAND Well, he wasn't born in Brooklyn.

MENUHIN There is another aspect of the American essence we should consider, and that is the imaginative, almost aggressive, technology which has become so far-reaching. Our best minds work in technology more than in architecture.

COPLAND We have youngsters working with electronic music, putting it on tape.

MENUHIN At this moment it still seems to me like doodling with a new toy.

COPLAND You're asking for pretty speedy work. The business of producing electronic sounds that resemble music is awfully new. I think the main thing is to encourage the public to keep an open mind. It is weaned on a comparatively small segment of the great music of the world. There is lots of room to increase the repertoire. I think the public gets an overdose of the great masterpieces.

MENUHIN I feel the same way. The United States is growing so rapidly, sometimes I feel the music of Beethoven and Brahms is almost an anomaly.

COPLAND You don't really mean that. I couldn't go that far.

MENUHIN Nonetheless, it is music of a different period in the history of man, a totally different conception of life. To what extent is it valid?

COPLAND It is valid for the time in which it was written. If it weren't it wouldn't interest us.

MENUHIN Are the people who live it escaping from their civilization?

COPLAND They may not be in tune, but the field of music is much greater than some care to admit, and that's a great mistake.

MENUHIN I do think we find a great deal of good will. The other night I played the sonata Bartók wrote for me. It was in a small Long Island town. A friend of mine overheard someone say, "I suppose we should like that." But they liked Beethoven's *Kreutzer* Sonata much more.

COPLAND It's an old disease. We do depend on a more knowing minority to listen with both ears, to try to hang on to what new composers are doing. We can't hope for the general public to stay with us, but gradually the musical idiom does change.

MENUHIN In some circles there is a fashion for listening to new music which one does not understand. It isn't always rewarding.

COPLAND It can't always be rewarding. If you are going to fool around with the unknown, you're bound to get some worthless stuff. Those of us who enjoy the search are willing to take the chance.

MENUHIN One can't have it both ways. When we first listen to Chinese, the most beautiful poem will not tell us anything.

COPLAND If you feel free to use an idiom that seems natural to you, to say things that are not quite so obvious, if you write a really tough piece that lasts half an hour, you know in advance that such a piece cannot have a broad audience. There are pieces by Beethoven which are more difficult for the public to latch onto. I think we composers distinguish in our minds those pieces which are meant for the mass public and those meant for a more cultivated listener. Of course, we love to encourage cultivation among all our listeners. I wrote a book called *What to Listen for in Music* and it pleased me when I felt that I had helped somebody get closer to music. Each person has his own capacity; we all have our limits.

MENUHIN There are contemporary works which at first hearing—or perhaps second or third—I still cannot quite grasp.

COPLAND I could easily name a few to which I have the same reaction.

MENUHIN Do you avoid the triad, the traditional harmony?

COPLAND Heavens, no! But there is no reason to confine yourself to them since music has developed to such an extent. We have come a long way in the last two hundred years, and I would want to take full advantage of that. Stravinsky and Schönberg really invented a new kind of language that has extended our understanding of what music might be.

MENUHIN Yet Stravinsky has popular appeal, not at first perhaps, but it didn't take all that long. I'm sure that if Bartók had lived another few years he would have enjoyed popularity.

COPLAND He was a sad little man. I spent an afternoon with him and came away rather depressed.

MENUHIN He didn't communicate with his fellow man except through music. He had an almost violent contempt of the ordinary. Whatever he said or did was essential. It may have been his illness which made him so economical. Now what do you think about current pop music, the shouting and ear-splitting noise which commands such vast audiences?

COPLAND We don't have to worry about it, it is temporary. Something else will come along to take its place.

MENUHIN These last few years we have seen different audiences grow for the serious versus the popular music. Are there any bridges?

COPLAND Many young people come up after my concerts, and from their enthusiasm I can tell they're not strangers to the lighter music, but it doesn't get in the way of their love for serious music. Don't forget that anybody turning a radio knob can hear music they never knew existed. Music is available to young people in a way it was not when I was eighteen.

MENUHIN Is there a work you would like to be known for?

COPLAND I've been asked that in the past and it's like asking a mother, "Which one is your favorite child?" You might know, but it wouldn't be fair to the other children to say whom. It looks as if the work which has attracted people the most is the ballet I wrote for Martha Graham, *Appalachian Spring*.

MENUHIN But it may not be the one you most value.

COPLAND No. I would love to think that was my *Piano Fantasy*. The work lasts half an hour without pause, which is a long time. I wish it were in the same category, but I just know by its nature that that is too much to hope for. You like your works for different reasons, some because everybody seems to like them and you just join in, others beause they are like a neglected child about whom nobody seems as enthusiastic as you had hoped they would be. Those you feel most tender about.

MENUHIN What a charming answer.

American composers of great distinction such as Aaron Copland are now represented in concert programs all over the Western world—Elliott Carter, Roger Sessions, Leon Kirchner, are among the best known. Canadian composers, too, such as Murray Schafer and Harry Somers have

made their mark. It is not easy to recall the time in the mid-twenties when it was generally supposed that there was no such thing as American music, apart from jazz and popular songs.

Throughout this century the American way in popular music has come to focus more and more on "the latest." The trend has been growing since the times of Stephen Foster and Victor Herbert. The dance bands that played their melodies had become larger, inspired perhaps by John Philip Sousa's example, and also because for so long bigger was better. In the thirties popular orchestras such as those organized by Benny Goodman, Glenn Miller and the Dorsey Brothers established the "big band" era. North Americans were seeking to amalgamate their European heritage into a musical idiom belonging uniquely to this continent, where so many different kinds of people coexisted for the first time under unfamiliar conditions in a new land. In our time, this has given way to the super-amplified assault of the rock band, in which half a dozen players can sound like five hundred.

It has taken me longer than I care to acknowledge to admit the human mind's extraordinary ability to make the beautiful serve the ugly. I

The big band sound belonged to many originators, none more than Benny Goodman who artfully blended his brilliant clarinet solos with the performers in each section of his band. Among those who started with Goodman were Gene Krupa, Lionel Hampton, Teddy Wilson and Harry James.

remember sitting in our country house in California in 1939 just before the outbreak of the war, and hearing Hitler on short-wave radio addressing a huge crowd in Danzig. I felt it was a broadcast from a madhouse. The *Horst Wessel Lied* chorused by a million voices sounded like the climax to an unholy union. Its power was pitiless.

I believe from my experience in visiting the Soviet Union that the commandeering of music there has been less evil than naive, turning the expression of a vital people into patriotic platitudes. I have heard oratorios to Lenin that were all solemnity and dramatic trappings, in fact modelled in form and content on every detail of the *St. Matthew Passion*. The sentiment may be admirable, but the object seems to us inappropriate. The beauty of music lies in part in its placement at a point equidistant between reality and abstraction.

The epitome of this human artistic dilemma is found in the music of Alban Berg, who with Anton Webern, his fellow student under Schönberg, completes the holy triumvirate of twelve-tone music. Berg constantly treads on both sides of the dividing line between the anti-tonal world of his teacher and the traditions of Vienna where he came of age, reminding us that this school always looked to Gustav Mahler as one of its mentors. There are recurrent hints of recognizable harmony in the midst of his most rigorous twelve-tone writing, for instance in his *Lyric Suite* for string quartet where he quotes Wagner's *Tristan* theme. In his two operas *Wozzeck* and *Lulu* he makes use of traditional methods of construction, such as sonata form, passacaglia, theme and variations. His last musical work was a Violin Concerto finished in 1935. Berg dedicated the work to the memory of a young girl who had just died, for whom he cared deeply. The work is a larger farewell to a world he loved which he did not suspect he was to leave himself within a few short weeks.

It took me some time to come to terms with the Berg concerto. When I first tried it I could sense its historical importance and a genuine sincerity of purpose. But there was also artifice in the coda where he makes repeated use of the Bach chorale tune "Es ist genug" (It is Enough). At first I did not like to hear that noble chorale, with its unusual harmonization of a melody that begins by spanning an augmented fourth, used in this way. I was unsympathetic to the whole twelve-tone system as well, feeling that Berg had used it in order to escape from his own romantic character which he could no longer bear, imposing it upon his music like a screen, to become something he wasn't. Over the years I have come to feel somewhat differently, and although the work is not a favorite, I find its

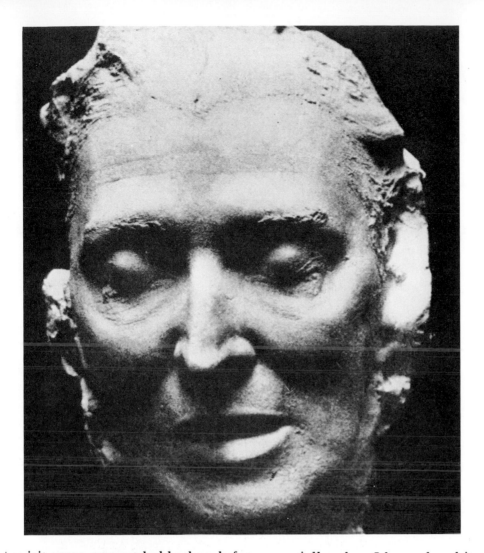

spirit more approachable than before, especially when I have played it with Ansermet and Pierre Boulez. I have always felt one should go first to someone who loves a thing one doesn't understand in order to break through.

Under Boulez I finally found it possible to give a performance of the Berg concerto with which I was satisfied and I think I came to understand Berg's use of that Bach chorale better too. Berg is less concerned with identifying himself as part of a tradition. His mastery of the classic forms was already amply demonstrated, and his virtuosity in handling twelve-tone writing in such a way as to retain a sense of connection with tonality is in some respects his most important contribution to the method. In the concerto's poignant close, the last statement of the chorale hanging in the air and our memory, the violin climbing up and up, Berg lets go of the known past and admits the unknown future. It is the struggle of each of us as individuals, in this century, and always.

Alban Berg died on Christmas Eve, 1935, and this death mask was taken the next day. He was only fifty, and had finished his violin concerto barely four months before. His second opera, Lulu, *on which he labored for seven years, was left incomplete. With Berg, the Romantic era launched in the nineteenth century was nearing its close.*

Junk-heap or compost-heap, that is the question: whether music has lost its way, or whether it may flower anew. John Cage questions the validity of music itself, Steve Reich treats it as process, Muzak makes it into subliminal filler. Technology transforms both the making and mass marketing of music. Canadian pianist Glenn Gould argues that the recording has replaced the concert hall. Popular music is transformed from the sentimental ballads of Sinatra to the driving beat of Presley, the emotional intensity of the Beatles and the street roughness of the Rolling Stones. Young people begin to rediscover the music of the more distant past and of other cultures; and the role of sentiment returns to both classical and popular music. Béla Bartók is the epitome of the uncompromising artist, one who nonetheless does not lose touch with his roots in the soil and the people.

8. Sound or Unsound

WE LIVE IN CONSTANT DANGER of destruction; each generation must redefine the term for itself, anxiously measuring growing risks and benefits against progress and its price. We also live in a time of artificially heightened sensations, and we are consequently subject to manipulation more than ever before. Past civilizations have held music sacred; it gave a sense of beauty which man could glimpse, a perfection to which man could aspire. In our time music has largely lost that role, becoming instead part of the ubiquitous process of exploitation.

Certain things I hold sacred. I know that to a bee, the rose is not an object of beauty but a source of food; yet to both the bee and to me, the rose is sacred, if we mean by sacred a gift to be cherished and on which we depend. In the same sense, music is beauty for me. The value of real music lies in its ability to knit us together as whole beings.

Fortunately nature will not allow us to exploit her domain indefinitely; before we destroy the last tree and ocean, we will no doubt have annihilated ourselves, and nature's cycle will begin again. Similarly, we will destroy our sense of hearing before we destroy music. The ecstatic experience is necessary, but nature has ways of preventing excess. The Whirling Dervish falls in a trance, brought to a halt by lack of oxygen before he is wholly exhausted, and wakes refreshed. It is part of his ritual, his encounter with ecstasy.

As you read these lines, somewhere in space a collection of the world's music, the music of man, is riding aboard Voyager I and Voyager II. These messenger rockets were launched from Cape Canaveral in Florida in

The site of the launching of so many rockets, including the manned moon landings, is now falling into disuse as space exploration gears up for the next phase of space stations and interplanetary travel.

David Bowie is a founder and durable star of the movement known as "glitter" rock, a perennial in a field noted for its quick shift of allegiance from one luminary to another. His recent music shows an interest in styles ranging from West Indian reggae to African drumming.

1977, and carry on board not only instruments, but video-recorded pictures and sounds from our earth and its people with elaborate instructions on the operation of playback equipment, written entirely in pictographic signs, as universally comprehensible as our invention will allow. After these manmade satellites sail past Jupiter and Saturn, sending back data on the earth's huge companions, the huge gravitational pull of these planets will scoop them up and fling them onward into the void. It is fitting that a human message should be aboard, a gesture somewhat similar to a shipwrecked sailor heaving a bottle out to sea. Fifty thousand or perhaps a million years from now Voyager I and II may be intercepted by another form of intelligent life. We may speculate on the reactions of the listeners to the samples of plainsong, the rhythms of Chuck Berry, a Bach fugue, a Beethoven symphony, a nose flute, Stravinsky's *The Rite of Spring* or Gershwin's *Rhapsody in Blue*, sent aloft as representative of the music of man.

All the technologies that enable us to propel our message through the universe have been developed within the past one hundred years. These technologies are geared to sight, hearing, and to our linear mode of thought. We don't know whether other forms of life on distant planets will be sensitive to the same vibrations. Our message has gone out to the unknown, unimaginable receiver.

I find equally poignant the prospect of human expeditions into the vastness of space, lasting decades, perhaps several lifetimes. What music will they take along to remind them of life on earth? And if the spaceship is self-sustaining for several generations, when all living memory of earth has vanished, what will that music communicate to those on the spaceship? Will space-humans create another music of their own? Robbed of contact with earth, the sounds carried on air, the waves of the ocean, the force of gravity itself, will they lose touch with creative desire? What will become of the pagan in all of us?

In music, as in much else since the end of World War II, a dilemma seems to arise from an ever more bewildering, fragmented consciousness, with no reliable guideposts to the future. Music itself seems to have abandoned the organic, the biological need for sensual satisfaction and our spiritual need for the metaphysical. Electronic music is an example, a form of music which runs the gamut from the output of a sophisticated synthesizer to the assembly of audio fragments on tape. In Canada, the Canadian Electronic Ensemble performs on a quartet of synthesizers—the latest state of the technological art—producing tones ranging from a whispering confusion of birds to sounds more deafening than a thunder-

clap. These instruments are the outcome of work done in the fifties and sixties at centers in Germany, France, and the United States, though their aesthetic content at times resembles that of a computer data printout sheet. It is worth pointing out that the four players who form the Canadian Ensemble were skilled brass instrumentalists before they took up synthesizers.

Electronic music is an abstraction, a move away from the organic to the inorganic, representing a conception of the universe reduced to distances, pulsations and structures. Recently some electronic instruments have begun to develop a flexibility which approaches that of natural instruments, in that the performer has scope for direct and spontaneous sound production. Edwin Roxburgh, a brilliant English composer and former student from that veritable womb of great contemporary composers, Nadia Boulanger, conceives works for solo instruments with electronic commentary dependent on the actual free, live solo interpretation. Watching the young people of the Canadian Ensemble rehearse, I was

The quartet known as the Canadian Electronic Ensemble performs a wide repertory of their own original compositions, some improvised, others completely planned in every detail, using the latest state of the art in computer-synthesizers.

struck by the range of sounds they could produce with so little apparent effort. This seemed to me a music appropriate to an age of travel to the moon and Mars.

At the computer center of the University of Toronto, research is being conducted into instruments used for notating electronic music. It is remarkable to see a piece of equipment that displays all the symbols of Western musical writing, that permits their selection and arrangement in sequences of the composer's choosing, and their immediate playback with all the characteristics of timbre and amplitude designated. Western music has struggled since the Middle Ages with the problem of equating notation with sound. In our century, we have visual structures whose dazzling complexities seem to have little or no relationship to the sounds they are expected to generate.

What the computer cannot do is breathe, as the notes on paper do not breathe. Life must be infused into them by the performer. The computer is like a mechanical player piano, with a broader range of colors perhaps, but able only to give back what has been fed into it. Moreover, the sound does not vibrate naturally, as does a column of air in a pipe; a loudspeaker is activated through direct electrical impulses. It is a sound without human warmth. Composers may find it a useful tool to check tonal combinations, and instruments may yet evolve whose spontaneous capacity equals that of the modern orchestra. But the instrument is only as good as the player.

Not only is technology learning how to manipulate the elements of abstract sound and notation, it is also able to reproduce synthetically virtually every musical sound we can produce naturally, except, of course, the crucial and most important element—the vital force between (and during) each note. Electronic instruments are in the same stage or condition as all keyboard instruments, including harpsichord, organ and piano, relative to the violin or the human voice. Their designers are ingenious, but they are thus far unable to devise a means of transmitting a vibrating, constantly changing impulse. These instruments can be operated, but they are at present impervious to human expression. We will still have to ask, "Where is Bach?"

One musician who has been questioning music in still more fundamental ways is the American experimental composer, John Cage. Influenced as a young man by the music of Bali and Java, as well as by the experiments of Varèse and Schönberg, Cage took off in a direction all his own. He re-examined the phenomenon of sound itself, as well as all of the

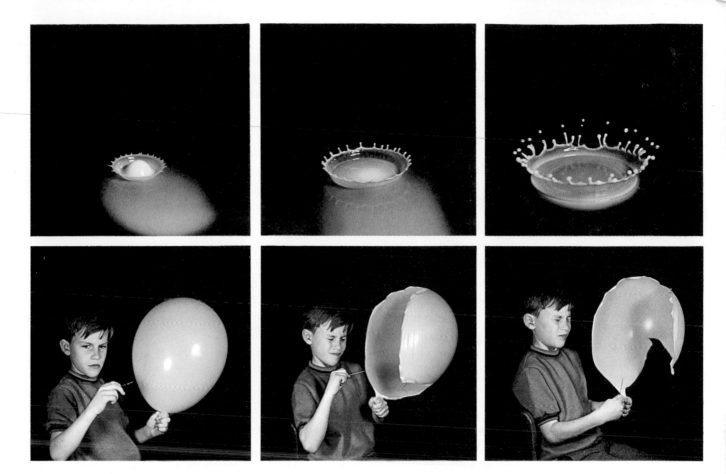

conventions which clung to Western music. Cage's pieces in the 1940s for "prepared piano" have become famous. Screws, nuts, bolts, strips of paper and felt, thumbtacks, paper clips, marbles and other buzzing, rattling, damping objects were introduced on or between the piano's strings and on the hammers. In order to hear the resulting sound—like that of a small harpsichord—one had to stand close because these foreign objects reduced the piano's natural volume. If the performer played too vigorously, they would simply fly about or be ejected (an aesthetic result interesting in itself of which Cage would not necessarily have disapproved).

More recently, Cage gave a performance in Cambridge, Massachusetts of an event he called *Harvard Square*. He brought a piano onto the traffic island in the center of the square, and a crowd soon gathered. Cage started a stopwatch, closed the keyboard lid and folded his hands. The crowd waited. After a specified time, determined by consulting the *I Ching*—a Chinese lexicon relating wisdom and practical philosophy to numbers and the occult—he opened the lid and stood up. The audience applauded as Cage took his bows. And what was the performance? It was nothing other than the ambient sound of Harvard Square traffic, casual conversation, footsteps and other noises.

The stop-motion camera can reveal to us unsuspected patterns in time, too quick for the naked eye to perceive, from the sculptured splash of a falling milk drop to the popped balloon unwrapping itself around the very air it had held compressed.

Such behavior in another time and place might have led to medical treatment, police arrest or communal prayer for the salvation of his soul. But John Cage is undismayed by the controversy he sometimes causes, and his soul remains full of cheer.

I suppose John Cage is really trying to open up our ears, to teach us to listen to unstructured time. Time can seem to flow quickly or slowly; when we are waiting for something to happen it can seem endless, but it speeds up alarmingly when we are caught in the middle of an event we cannot control. Events in time each have their own individual pattern, one which is not always immediately apparent. Sometimes time itself is the barrier, just as we cannot see ourselves with the perspective of the future. The growth of a flower is imperceptible, while the beauty of a drop of milk falling into a dish, like the beat of a hummingbird's wings, is too fast for the naked eye to register. But the moving picture camera can expand or contract time, accommodating our limited senses, allowing us to look into the heart of things.

When we listen to music or play it, one of our satisfactions lies in the recognition of its pattern. Events in nature happen in their own time, but with music the composer sculpts time, giving it shape and weight, making it flow faster or slower, imposing it on us. Whether it is a simple dance rhythm or the larger pattern of a symphony or an Indian raga, music takes us into its own time, inhabiting us like a spirit, an alter ego. Dance music lightens and lifts; a funeral march weighs us down. Music takes over; we become its captives. At least that is what we have come to expect. But a composer like John Cage is not simply encouraging us to listen more closely. He challenges us to ask whether we and the music we make, and indeed whether all human achievements, are not merely accidental events in a random universe. I cannot accept this passive view of life; but there is no doubt that Cage does force us to re-examine music, just as we re-examine our sense of hearing. He leads us to ask: "Is music sound or un-sound?"

In our time, composers have invoked the entirely random, carrying one of Cage's ideas to a length even he has not yet explored. Chance or "aleatoric" music, as it has come to be called, was the rage in the sixties and early seventies, taking a variety of forms (or rather avoiding them). Some composers like Karlheinz Stockhausen, who was born near Cologne in 1928, struck a compromise between the planned and the random, composing works whose parts were transposable in time sequence; for instance, his *Momente* which drew considerable attention in 1962–63. The Greek composer Yannis Xenakis, born in 1922, has

written works with the help of a computer. The idea of freedom in performance is hardly new; the cadenzas to Romantic concerti or opera arias were often taken *a piacere* as license to depart entirely from the text.

By tradition and training I belong to the school which subscribes to the idea that music must be heard and willed, by both composer and performer, before it can be sounded. However, I recognize that aleatoric music may provide interesting interludes in composed works. These episodes are usually severely circumscribed in time, texture, pitch, rhythm and dynamics. "Chance" music apparently has even gone so far as to have a treble staff painted on a goldfish bowl, while the performer tried to sound the notes inspired by the fish swimming casually by. I have thought of fleas or jumping beans on music paper; however, I find such a rejection of consciousness and the past entirely alien. I believe we should gladly acknowledge today what we knew or experienced yesterday, for otherwise everything must constantly take us by surprise, and we can have not the remotest concept of a possible future. The mind has a great capacity to protect itself, to survive an accident or shock by not remembering moments of fear or pain, but that is quite another thing. Shaped sound is an echo of human existence, music is an echo of the mind and heart, and the two are combined in an act of will. Chance music is largely an abdication of artistic responsibility, though a fascinating game, and, moreover, it can be interesting to discover just how much of it is really "chance."

The multiplicity of Steve Reich's family of xylophones and other musical intruments has a kinship to the gamelans of Indonesia, the style vigorous as on Bali, and submerging the human voice within the whole as on Java.

At the opposite end of the spectrum is the genre known as "process music," a phenomenon of the seventies, whose style has been pioneered by performer-composers like Philip Glass and Steve Reich. This music is not based on the old European convention of articulated melody, harmony and rhythm, but focusses on subtle shifts of small details within a total web, a minimal counterpoint demanding total concentration on the part of both performers and listeners. Born in 1936, Reich has trained the cadre of able performers who take part in his music. The first impression of this music is that the same phrases are simply being repeated over and over. On closer listening, it becomes clear that slight changes are being introduced by each player as the music progresses. Similar techniques are part of the music of Indonesia and of the *riti* player in Senegal.

Steve Reich has studied African drumming in Ghana, and Balinese gamelan music at the University of Washington. Daily, he would record and replay his lessons, sometimes at half or one-quarter speed, in order to transcribe the learned patterns, taking each rhythm and line apart. His *Music for Mallet Instruments, Voices and Organ* written in 1973 shows us the results. "Process" music is not easy to accept for those trained in the European tradition, but, fortunately, music around the world can never be governed by a single aesthetic.

A form unlike electronic music, chance music or process music originated in France after World War II called *musique concrète*, where efforts were made through the technology of recording to incorporate the sounds of nature, of machines, of speech, into a musical texture. Any sound could serve as an ingredient, as raw material for a composition, from the fragmentary reading of a poem to the clatter of dishes in a basin, or even a musical sound from a piano or guitar. These sounds could also be played in reverse, on tape, made to run faster or slower, transposed and transformed by reverberation or damping, contrasted at any dynamic level regardless of their natural relationship.

Edgard Varèse was certainly aware of this movement when he began his own work in audiotape collage in the late 1940s. He was one of the first to attempt the combination of live musicians with pre-taped sounds. Later his *Poème electronique*, made entirely on tape, was the talk of the 1958 Brussels World's Fair, and is undeniably the legitimate child of the union between electronic music and *musique concrète*, consummated in the fertile imagination of this unique artist. Not even Stockhausen's remarkable *Hymnen* (1971) caused the stir brought about by Varèse in such a large popular context. Now that Pierre Boulez, born in 1925, has taken over the new experimental music center at the Centre Pompidou in Paris, perhaps Varèse's musical child will grow to unexpected maturity.

Of course, the mechanization of life has been going on ever since the first farmer hitched oxen to a plough. We wax romantic over the imagined sound of horses' hooves on cobblestones, but these were all manmade sounds, from the horseshoes, to the cobbles, to the town walls themselves throwing back the echo. It must have made a fearful racket. The city of Paris was in some ways noisier in earlier centuries than before its boulevards were widened in the nineteenth century to permit the easier passage of troops on parade. The great cities were once the refuge of the composer, for they could still afford seclusion and quiet. Today composers have all but abandoned them.

We may have blurred the definition of music in our day, but we can be certain of one thing: our world grows louder each year. I believe that the generation born since World War II is the first for which the machine is a totally natural part of daily existence. The furor over the noise of the Concorde is merely symptomatic of a larger malaise of noise pollution, the effects of which may be quite as insidious as the chemical wastes

The Canadian pianist, Oscar Peterson, represents a tradition of jazz improvisation which has been part of the music of North America for more than fifty years, and the standard he sets has drawn the deserved praise of every critic.

which hang in the air of our big cities. I believe the human ear is in danger. I have been in a rope factory where the level of sound was quite incredible, causing a serious hearing loss among workers over a period of time. For years now, high amplification has been the essence of rock music. I need not repeat the statistics already so widely reported of the incidence of deafness among teenagers.

Manmade noise destroys the relative sound proportions of man in nature, making us impervious to natural cycles; conversation dies; noise kills the natural content of the mind. Music may change in order to keep pace with a swifter lifestyle, but fortunately we cannot listen to music any faster or slower than its own pace—for it will not let us.

Electronic amplification is obviously here to stay and is not necessarily all bad, for indeed without it we could not enjoy music in our homes so easily. I have had occasion to play the violin with some microphone boosting, and it can be a boon beyond description out of doors, or in a hall with bad acoustics. The real test lies not in a crude battering ram of sound, but in the ability of a single tiny strand to make thousands hold their breath. In fact, I have found that if one is losing the audience (an event to which few players admit), it is best to play more softly still. Pop musicians actually play softly a good deal of the time and let the loudspeakers do the work.

There are those who have insisted that art is superfluous to life, and again those others who contend that life has no meaning without art. My view is that life is art, and that living is in fact the greatest and most difficult of arts. Perhaps musicians have a slight advantage in that they must both listen to themselves and be listened to. It is important that what they say be wise and compassionate, strong and tender. In this conception of living as art, there are no absolutes, but there are standards; and it is in measuring up to these that we can find our greatest satisfactions, our finest aspirations.

The establishment of a high standard in concert music runs back hundreds of years, but it was in the field of jazz that it became part of popular music, especially from World War II onward. Jazz is a particularly democratic form of music, one in which each individual makes his spontaneous contribution, joining with others in an agreed common framework. Invention is the heart of this art and the virtuosity developed in the twenties and thirties now led to startling developments. Soloists like John Birks "Dizzy" Gillespie on trumpet and Charlie "Yardbird" Parker on alto saxophone were among those who heard an interior sound and brought forth "bebop," parent to progressive jazz; Ella Fitzgerald was the vocal star of this style. Others, such as Thelonious Monk, Cecil

Taylor and Dave Brubeck on piano, Miles Davis on trumpet and Archie Shepp on saxophone, learned indirectly from the experiments of concert music, from impressionism to atonality. Big bands led by Woody Herman and Stan Kenton enlarged the virtuosity of large ensemble playing.

The constant cross-fertilization between popular and serious forms of music is a pattern traceable to the Middle Ages. The flow has usually been from grassroots to exotic hybrid. In jazz since the war the flow has been the other way. An important hint had been provided early by Benny Goodman performing the Mozart Clarinet Quintet with members of the Budapest Quartet as far back as 1937, then commissioning Béla Bartók to compose *Contrasts* for him in 1941, and Aaron Copland to create his Clarinet Concerto in 1946. After the war the fraternity of jazz performers was far more cosmopolitan, mixed readily with classical musicians, and borrowed many ideas. By the early sixties John Coltrane on soprano saxophone provided a series of performances and recordings which carried jazz to new frontiers, drawing on the atonal, the world of chance and meditation, the endless vistas of renewal of which music has always been capable.

A similar pattern is reflected in the popular music of Latin America. The craze for the mambos of Tito Puente and others swept northward in the 1950s, bringing with it a rhythmic freedom learned in part from the explorations into native sources by such classical composers as the Brazilian Heitor Villa-Lobos and the Mexican Carlos Chavez. There are today progressive varieties of samba and tango, many taking the songs of Carlos Jobim as a point of departure. The continent has also seen the rise of native performers such as Los Indios Trabajares who applied modern arranging techniques to traditional Maya and Inca melodies. In much of this music the range and variety of percussion instruments is far greater than in North American jazz orchestras, an African flavor surviving more strongly there; yet this very feature has allowed Latin American music to capitalize on many of the rhythmic breakthroughs of Stravinsky and the technical innovations of Varèse, though the process is one of unconscious osmosis, not deliberate imitation.

The crisis which occurred in concert music in this country, beginning with Schönberg and Stravinsky and proceeding to the experiments of our own day, is mirrored by an equally serious crisis affecting popular music, even more divisive than the split which took place when jazz began replacing sentimental ballads just after World War I. That crisis is the development of pop-rock music, a phenomenon which has been the dominant force in urban popular music since the mid-sixties, and whose reign in England and North America is even longer. Youth has always

Elvis Presley began to make feature films when barely out of his teens. This scene from Loving You (1957) recreates his phenomenal ability to seduce audiences of young people.

needed its heroes, and during the thirties and forties, America's young people found them in Bing Crosby and Frank Sinatra. Gifted with bewitching voices and personalities, these singers produced new disciples, mobs of ecstatic youngsters, responding to the appeal of these stars, whom commercial interests quickly learned to exploit.

It is reasonable to ask which came first, the public, ready for communal entertainment or the idol who provided it? Rock and roll emerged in the 1950s with Elvis Presley as its deity. This music originated in a mix of black and white traditions, rhythm and blues grafted onto country and western, and perhaps a touch of folk protest. With Elvis it was the aggressive, taunting sexual performance as much as the music which drove fans to hysteria. Elvis became the delight of the young, the despair of their parents. The Beatles, four boys from Liverpool who, musically, grew up far from home in Hamburg's notorious *Reeperbahn* district, irrevocably altered the course of pop music in the sixties. Their music is

more original than Elvis's, and its very nature, evolved in isolation from the mainstream, will probably ensure its longevity. The Beatles were closer to the California flower children, offering companionship and compassion rather than sex as bait. Elvis on the other hand points directly to Mick Jagger and the Rolling Stones, asking surrender rather than seduction. The distance between *Here, There and Everywhere* by the Beatles and *I Can't Get No Satisfaction* by the Stones is staggering.

Most will agree that the Beatles remain the deepest influence on the continuing world-wide rock music phenomenon. Their songs have

The Beatles always maintained a strong sense of theatrical presence, and could even afford to "send up" their own image (as they did in their feature films A Hard Day's Night *and* The Yellow Submarine*). Here they pose at the entrance to the offices of their company, Apple Corporation.*

entered the general repertoire, a tribute which can be paid to few others except Presley. Like his, their early sound was raw; later the lyrical ballads of Paul McCartney and driving energy of John Lennon, from *Please Please Me, The Yellow Submarine* to *Eleanor Rigby* and *Sgt. Pepper's Lonelyhearts Club Band*, altered the direction of popular music making. American groups such as The Jefferson Airplane and the Grateful Dead, masterminded in the sixties in San Francisco by promoter-entrepreneur Bill Graham, would not have dreamed of ignoring the Beatles' inventive contributions to an ever volatile medium. Ringo Starr brought an element of brash, self-mocking good humor; George Harrison espoused the sitar, which with the group's benefit concerts for relief to Bangladesh helped to create a wave of Indian awareness among Western young people.

Rock is now nearly a generation old, and despite the Beatles' breakup in the seventies, the style and songs they created continue to influence the growth of rock. In England their psychedelic followers include Pink Floyd, Cream and The Who, and their storytelling gifts were continued by the Incredible String Band. Even the Rolling Stones, archetypes of the aggressive counterculture movement in the U.S., went through a period in which their music was derived from the warmer love-in style of the Beatles. It is probably not unfair to say that there would be no punk-rock, glitter-rock or astro-rock without them, as there might have been no Altamont or Woodstock, where hundreds of thousands gathered in 1969;

The growth of the younger generation's new collective consciousness reached a culmination at the 1969 Woodstock Festival, whose reverberations are still felt today.

and surely without the example of the Beatles' films and personal lifestyles, there would not be the lavishly staged and costumed rock concert extravaganzas of recent years.

Part of the appeal of rock and roll lies in its sense of community participation. Young people, as always, need the security of their peers about them—at dances, in record stores, and above all, at public performances, where the hysteria of adulation is part of their outlet. This has long been true for opera divas who had their claques whom they sometimes paid. In the nineteenth century fashionable young aristocrats fell over themselves to pay homage to dancers like Marie Taglioni and Fanny Elssler. The crowd of fans at a rock concert is visible proclamation of collective identity.

Much of contemporary rock and roll is the music of disillusion, of a generation set adrift from the past. It is no wonder that young people created their own culture, rejecting the hypocritical world handed to them by a generation standing accused of bringing untold agony to life on this planet. The postwar birthrate had soared dramatically everywhere in the West, and industry seized upon the new audience, appearing to satisfy its wants; for young people are often confused and gullible. After all, we gave them the example; and they, in turn, are obliged to develop their own brand of "hypocrisy"; we seem forever condemned by fate to pretend to be what we cannot be. Were they able to forgive their forebears, it would be a first step towards honesty. And although young people may well know what they like, they can have little idea of what they might like, given the chance.

The only time I experienced something akin to the adulation of a crowd of some two hundred thousand people—fellow Jews—was in Bucharest just after World War II, where I came not only as a disciple of Rumania's adored Georges Enesco, but also as an American and a Jew. There were at that time some four hundred thousand Jews in Bucharest who had escaped to Rumania from all parts of Europe. King Michael was still on the throne, though Russia was at work behind the scenes to oust the old order. There was plenty of good food and wine, a crush of cars in the streets, a sense of well-being returning. But what I recall most vividly was the crowd in the street waiting for me, particularly when walking to the nearby synagogue. We could hardly get through, ever, at any time of day or night. The people were full of affection and warmth, but the situation really became tedious. Finally, the management put up a police barrier. I hated it. But just as rock stars must, I felt that the borderline between admiration and the desire for contact was shrinking; when the

Ron Wood and Mick Jagger of the Rolling Stones explode into action during their flamboyant public performances, driving their audiences to a similar frenzy.

impulse of the fans to take away a shred of something personal as a souvenir can so suddenly turn into a free-for-all.

I have had one direct encounter with the Rolling Stones. In 1976 I received word that one hundred tickets to the Stones' opening performance at Earl's Court were at my disposal to be sold as a benefit for my school. I felt this would be the right time to see what the Stones were like, and I did want to thank them for their gesture. We arrived at Earl's Court behind schedule, when the warm-up groups were finishing. I had already been told a good deal about the atmosphere surrounding the Stones, what kind of people they were. We arrived in great style in the huge black car which had been provided for us, driving right into the garage behind Earl's Court where we joined other cars of like extravagance. Though we were some distance from the hall, I heard what sounded to me like a premonition of hell.

We edged up the narrow stairs into the arena while the sound grew like a thunderstorm. I wanted to listen for the musical content, but for me the sheer volume obliterated that possibility. For the first time I experienced real physical pain hearing music. Of notes, pitches, musical design, I could distinguish little. It seemed to me quite unlike the music of the Beatles which has a real melodic quality, whereas this was aural overkill: a sheer sound wall. Under such overpowering circumstances, I understood how deliberately the whole madness is engineered. It aims to numb all aware senses, to leave no choice but to surrender and participate. I did neither—I left after ten minutes. The Rolling Stones are trying desperately to generate and liberate emotion, but as they know little of those disciplines and structures through which emotions are transformed into art, they can only generate hysteria. Their music is more like the elimination of structure, dissolving everything back to crude clay. It is a form of self-glorification, demonstrating how much people need to drown their identities.

I may have difficulty relating to rock, but I am an American and there is a touch of jazz in my blood. In recent years I have had the immense joy of performing with Stéphane Grappelli, the Frenchman whose way with a violin has already made him a legend among European jazz buffs. Grappelli is a superb artist, already immortalized by his records with the gypsy guitarist Django Reinhardt (*The Third Man*) and with the Quintet of the Hot Club of France. As for the jazz musicians who are part of Grappelli's ensemble, they are the salt of the earth. Together we have played Gershwin, Cole Porter, Jerome Kern, joining complementary talents in performances which yielded much mutual pleasure.

The marriage of musical worlds once thought of as separated by the equivalent of a Berlin Wall has always appealed to me, and my performances with Grappelli have brought me as much joy as those with Ravi Shankar. More recently still for *The Music of Man* television series, I had the joy of meeting with the French-Canadian country fiddler Jean Carignan in a work composed for him by André Gagnon. In this duet, the Vivaldiesque phrases allotted to me reminded me of the way builders of past ages would use material from old buildings, bits of columns, marble facings, to assemble new ones. It is a cultural scavenging which Bach might have sanctioned, for he appropriated the music of Vivaldi and others. Sometime I would like to be able to perform with the Canadian

pianist Oscar Peterson, surely one of the most distinguished musicians of any age, whose inventive virtuosity is the envy of his peers, unique in his sheer domination and subtle understanding of his instrument. He represents the peak of a tradition which has existed in North America throughout this century.

Music in our time has been threatened from a number of quarters, of which the mass media and the experiments of the avant garde are but two. Electronic pianos and organs are commonplace, some used by rock groups at nerve-testing levels. Walter Carlos produced his best-selling record *Switched-on Bach*, with the Moog synthesizer—a veritable electronic orchestra, one layer at a time. Perhaps the most appalling of these creations is the electronic "sweetener" used in preparing pop music recordings. It simulates artificially the sound of dozens of violins playing a saccharine obbligato in a higher register over the driving beat.

French-Canadian country fiddler Jean Carignan has been a star performer for forty years, a rival to the best that Nashville can produce, and a source of pride for his people in Quebec.

This is a cheap way to avoid engaging musicians, and as corrupting as artificial fruit flavors, debasing our natural taste. Our world has become a sounding board for manmade sounds, amplified to suffuse and suffocate us; urbanized populations are divorced more and more from the sounds of nature and the living performance of music. We may seek to cover up the artificial sound environment with Muzak, but I feel that man should object to the invasion of his sovereignty and privacy by the constant stream of music which pours out of amplifiers like gas warfare. It is but a short step from there to the infiltration of subliminal messages, influencing our choice of products and services, perhaps even our political and social views, an idea which has in fact been tried out.

Second only to Muzak on my list of musical abuses is the television commercial. It is bad enough that these visual capsules promote their products as panaceas to make one feel younger, more attractive, more successful. Most are placebos anyway; but too often, besides catchy jingles, these messages exploit the power of the voice to persuade. Imagination does the rest, for we live, sacrifice and die by our imaginations. Commercials seduce us with the voices of sirens.

Technology and World War II did contribute at least one important new instrument to the world of music: the steel drum. That extraordinary human resourcefulness which can turn almost any surface capable of giving out some form of resonance into an instrument for music is a process as alive today as when Siberian cave men made flutes and percussion out of mammoth bones. The secret of the steel drum's manufacture is a story of communal trial and error whose details have become blurred by claims and counter claims. The process has been perfected to the point where it can be formally taught, as at the Pan Unlimited School in Port of Spain, Trinidad.

The steel drum band has become not simply a popular entertainment, but is inextricably intertwined with the calypso tradition. At first the music was made only by and for the poor—a West Indian troubadour might sing for his food and board—and was considered not quite respectable. These songs also expressed the people's attitudes toward the colonial world, the cost of living, world events or simple nonsense rhymes.

During World War II the West Indies were used as a refueling base for warships, so steel drums were in plentiful supply. The empty oil barrels would have rusted to junk if it were not for human curiosity and ingenuity. Since then this spontaneous music has made its way almost as ubiquitously as American jazz. We hear some of its infectious lilt in the now popular reggae music, and young Westerners have taken up the steel drum almost as avidly as the African or Latin-American bongo drum.

More recently, musicians have not hesitated to take hold of the resources offered by technology, particularly the dramatic improvements in the quality of recorded sound. As audiotape has become the standard initial medium, following its introduction in the late 1940s, the possibility of constructing note-perfect recordings through tape splicing has become a practical reality. In the 1950s and '60s this technical capacity was undoubtedly overused, and some recordings made in this way began to give off a synthetic flavor. In the 1970s the recording industry has tended to move, in the classical field at least, toward the "long take," sessions in which whole movements of symphonies or sonatas, entire acts of operas, are taken down without a break, in order to preserve the living, breathing flow of the performance.

It has even happened while recording Beethoven's Sonatas no. 7 and 10 with my sister Hephzibah that I have completed an entire work, playing it three times without a break in the morning, like a concert performance, and doing the same in the afternoon. When we were done we simply told the producer to pick the best one. Recordings made in this way to me have something immediate and compelling in them, which is lacking in recordings pieced together. Audiotape is a wonderful safety net, but acrobats are not re-engaged for the following season if all they do is fall off and climb back up. Of course an obvious mistake should be corrected, for it can be tolerated in the concert hall as a passing disturbance, but if it were perpetuated in a disc, it would no longer appear accidental.

Among the artists who have wrestled with the problem of recording, none has done so with more brilliant, provocative results than the Canadian pianist Glenn Gould. Now that he is retired from the concert platform (his last public performance was in 1964), he has devoted himself to a unique career in the media of recordings, radio and television. His artistic integrity and searching spirit are of that high order to which every musician would do well to aspire. At the same time, Gould has frequently taken positions on artistic matters which are at odds with many of his colleagues, in issues of interpretation as well as recording technique. It has been my pleasure to perform with Glenn Gould a number of times in the recording studio, and we talked not long ago about the difficult question of reality versus versimilitude in recordings.

GOULD (completing the playback of a Bach gigue, recorded "close up") Now, Yehudi, you've got to admit that you would not be likely to encounter a sound like that in the concert hall.
MENUHIN I would still recognize your playing. Whatever you've added electronically does not add to the clarity and perfection, or the relationship of the voices, which is your inherent way of playing.

GOULD The point is that, if I were to play that piece in a concert hall, as I have done many times—in fact, it used to be one of my party pieces—I would not be free to select the perspective we just heard; it represents a tight, clinical, X-ray-like view of that work, precise and at the same time intimate, which enables me to dissect it in a special way. On the platform, I would be forced to accept a compromised perspective—one which would be more or less equally acceptable to the listener down at the lip of the stage and to the standee up beyond the far balcony. I don't need to tell you that, ultimately, one ends up with a perspective which is appropriate, if at all, only for the listener in row L of the orchestra.

MENUHIN Not having your extensive experience with the recording studio, I simply play and the hall does the rest. But doesn't all this technology for quadraphonic recording presuppose that the ideal listening point at home is one spot somewhere in the middle of the room? As soon as you have three people listening, two of them will be in the wrong place.

GOULD It is an absurd concoction when you think about it, because it means implicitly that in Germany the father will have the optimum seat, in America it will be the mother, in France the mistress.

Glenn Gould and Yehudi Menuhin meet over the huge console of a modern recording studio, under the watchful eye of CBC producer John Thomson.

MENUHIN I agree there is music written today which demands the metamorphosis you can achieve on these amazing consoles if it is to survive. But the music that concerns me, the single-voiced violin, even though I sometimes play two strings or even three, is not materially affected by the choices available on that console.

GOULD We've had this conversation before, Yehudi, and I suspect that what inhibits you from making full use of the technology is the fact that it compels the performer to relinquish some control in favor of the listener—a state of affairs, by the way, which I happen to find both encouraging and charming, not to mention aesthetically appropriate and morally right.

MENUHIN You must admit the pianist starts out with an instrument which is remote from him to a degree. The sound is made through mechanical connections, therefore the electronic side is yet another mechanical manipulation, which is acceptable considering the vast spectrum the pianist controls. But the violinist's approach is intimate, personal, and this machinery appears almost as an intrusion. I believe both attitudes are valid. Splicing the tape, for instance, is what you feel enables you to achieve perfection.

GOULD I believe this whole question of splicing is a red herring; I think it's become all mixed up—and improperly so—with the idea of "honesty" and "integrity." Naturally, it's antithetical to the concert process, where you go from first note to last, but that antiquated approach has nothing whatever to do with the major percepts of technology. It matters not to me whether I am "successful" in creating a performance through one take, or whether I do it with 262 tape splices. The issue is simply not important.

MENUHIN You are building a structure corresponding to your vision and anything that helps is legitimate. But take the Beatles, who started out playing in public spontaneously; by the time they became accustomed to crutches which enabled them to record tracks separately and put them all together, to add notes and take them away, they could no longer play in public because the public expected something else, having become accustomed to this form of recorded creation.

GOULD In a sense, that is also what happened to me. I found I was competing with my own recordings, which nobody can do really. My recordings represent my best thoughts.

MENUHIN I refuse to believe that. I've heard you play and I know that if you wanted to you could carry off a performance in the concert hall which would be as staggering as anything you do in the recording studio.

GOULD But doesn't it come down to this: if an actor wants to deliver a proper "To be or not to be," he may do it in the context of the play *Hamlet* or he may do a travelling routine in which he reads excerpts, as Sir John

Gielgud used to do. In any case, he doesn't have to run through the first two acts in his head in order to find the appropriate tone for that soliloquy.

MENUHIN The point is that he must know the work as a whole inside of him, to know what it feels like even if he never performs it. There is a point beyond that, and that is that I often find greater satisfaction in reading a score rather than hearing a performance. You first have to hear it in your mind before you can play it.

GOULD But how do you explain the strange notion that the musician who sometimes happens to be a recording artist should be subject to different laws from the stage actor who may on occasion appear in films. It is quite legitimate for the film actor to have a series of emotive moments that appear to be in real time. The interior may be shot on a Hollywood lot, if such things still exist, and the exterior in Tierra del Fuego, yet the relationship between the shots is seen as perfectly logical. Yet if you explain to people that this is precisely what you do in making a record that satisfies your best thoughts on a work, they think it's fakery, cheating.

MENUHIN I think it is a confusion of two different worlds. The one is accustomed to living a thing through, which is the final result the public wants and considers real. Those who use techniques to enhance the dramatic effect would look upon the concert performance as old-fashioned, not taking advantage of the available means, and perhaps shoddy because people are satisfied with something less than perfect. Let us say a film about a mountain climber can be done in sections, a mock-up mountain can be used. The actor can take it easy, and probably won't want to go up anyway. But there is another risk, the danger to the climber who actually goes up the mountain and cannot do it in bits and pieces. He's got to do the whole thing as a consecutive effort.

GOULD Yes, but it seems to me, Yehudi, that what technology is all about is the elimination of risk and danger. I suspect that this is where we really part company, because I don't think one should deliberately cultivate situations that have built-in elements of risk and danger, not if they can be removed by superior technology. That is the problem of the concert hall where things can fall apart, the horn can crack, and so forth.

MENUHIN Has technology really reduced risk and danger, apart from music. Isn't there a risk of losing the sense of life, the sense of risk itself?

GOULD Obviously, technology has its own dangers, but I think the purpose of technology is to give the *appearance* of life.

MENUHIN Are you satisfied with the *appearance* of life only?

GOULD Well, a recorded performance is not exactly real life.

MENUHIN So we have to live on two different levels. When we satisfy a natural urge we can't do it in bits and pieces. It has its own built-in timing. You can only stretch it to a point.

GOULD I can't agree. If your ideal "To be or not to be" is something you carry around in your head, you might well repeat it to yourself one line at a time. Why, then, should you not assemble it as a composite, taking advantage of the benevolence that technology permits, the blanket of charity that it throws over everything you do?

MENUHIN I doubt this blanket of charity would evoke from the piano such playing as yours from anyone but you, with all the help it can give.

GOULD Compliments aside, why do you resist the idea that it is possible to cut in on a particular note and say: "That is the mood, the tenor, the emotion behind that note?" It really needs only the context which one carries about in one's head.

MENUHIN On the other hand, once you've made the recording, are you sure you aren't ignoring your listener to an extent? Are you sure he is listening to it with the same devotion and concentration as he would in the concert hall? He might be interrupted by frying bacon. In the concert hall there is something compelling; besides, certain types of music are communal experiences, for instance the *St. Matthew Passion*. The whole congregation was meant to feel and react as one.

GOULD "When two or three are gathered together," I suppose. But it seems to me there is no greater community of spirit than that between the artist and the listener at home, communing with the music. I would even go so far as to say that the most important thing technology does is to free the listener to participate in ways that were formerly governed by the performer. It opens up options he didn't have before.

MENUHIN That still doesn't invalidate the concert hall, the experience of which is essential, and remains the standard against which everything else is judged.

GOULD Nonsense, Yehudi. It was the standard until something else came along to replace it, which is exactly what the recording did; and the recording, surely, is now the standard against which the concert must be judged.

MENUHIN If no one is ever going to climb a mountain again, and we have to be satisfied with films about it, where are we?

GOULD We are without people who can climb mountains, which I think is a profoundly good thing. It will save any number of deaths per year.

MENUHIN No, you mustn't say that. You'll make up with ignoble deaths on the road.

GOULD If I had the technology to prevent them, I'd do that too. I'm sure it will come. But the point is that the listener becomes something more than a consumer, he becomes a participant. For example, I've been doing some solo piano recordings, when the repertoire is appropriate, not with two or four tracks but with eight—the idea being to find a way of merging many perspectives, which are all miked simultaneously, but differentiated subsequently, and subjected to rather cinematic techniques. For example, one perspective might involve a "shot" taken from inside the piano, jazz-style, with the mikes virtually lying on the strings, while another might relate to a "shot" involving back-of-the-hall ambience. The advantage is that you can combine these perspectives in a kind of acoustic choreography and do so, moreover, after the fact, when you've put as much distance between yourself and the recording session as possible. You then prepare a master plan—not unlike a film director's shot list—and, in the right music—Scriabin, for example—it works exceedingly well. I'm sure that Scriabin, with his mystical theories about a perfumed union of the arts, about transcendent mountain-peak experiences and all that sort of thing, would not disapprove.

MENUHIN It is true the piano does lack somethings which a studio can lend it. The piano has one quality over its whole range, whereas the harpsichord can give at least three or four combinations. The violin has four strings. Bartók in his *Melodya* starts off on the G string, then the next phrase is on the D, then the A, then the E. He rises and goes back down. Each of these strings has a totally different quality. It would be gilding the lily to enhance still more the contrast between those strings. But with the piano, I admit that you need techniques which give each section of a work a different perspective.

GOULD I wasn't thinking of that primarily, though what you say about the relationships between the two instruments is certainly true. What I was thinking of, rather, was that we always proceed on the assumption that a piano sits, in recording terms, midway between the left and right speaker. It has often occurred to me that no one, including those who work in "quad," has thought very much about the question of perspective. I admit that it might not be appropriate to use multi-perspective techniques on Haydn quartets or Bach fugues, but it's fascinating, in late-Romantic repertoire, to mix the perspectives as one would stops on the organ. One can, for example, get great clarity—great proximity—and combine it with great range—great depth—and those two things are normally antithetical to both concert hall and to conventional recording.

MENUHIN I'm sure you've added immeasurably to the aesthetics of music, for the piano is a static object. It needs redemption of some kind, and you have redeemed it more than anyone else possibly could.

Glenn Gould proceeded thereafter to perform two Scriabin preludes, op. 57, *Le Désir* and *Caresse Dansée*, in that impeccable fashion unique to

him, note perfect and superbly evocative. Given the choice between a beautiful performance with a tolerable mistake and one which is perfect but lacks that electric vitality, I will always choose the first. But my encounter with Glenn Gould has made me more conscious than ever of aspects of microphone technique which have developed over the past half-century, and the difference between the recording and the actual performance. The simple solution, and still the best solution, was to hang one microphone in the middle of a hall, and if the acoustics were good, the results could sometimes be astonishing, as we can still hear in Fyodor Chaliapin's unforgettable *Boris Godunov* excerpts, recorded during an actual performance at Covent Garden in London in 1928. Yet that very recording demonstrates one of my beliefs, that the live performance can never disappear. The public comes to see and hear the performance happening at that time, incandescent and galvanizing. I remember Chaliapin's *Boris* well. What no recording can convey, even that marvelous one by Chaliapin, is the smell of sulphur. There is simply not the same order of involvement with the *performance* of the music, though the musical experience may nonetheless retain great intensity.

Whether art should imitate life, or rather sublimate and exalt it, is a question which has bedevilled artists and the public ever since the cave paintings. Italian opera composers of the late nineteenth century spoke of *verismo*, taking their themes directly from the lives of the people. Yet the spectacle of a tenor singing "Vesti la Giubba" is as far from real life as a Byzantine icon. In our time, providing we do not regard the machine as the source of ultimate truth, we may yet have the best of both worlds. The printed page gives us the notes, the phrasing, the speed and dynamics, but if it is to make sense in performance, we must rely on our knowledge of other human beings, of the composer and his thoughts and of musicians who receive and transmit his message. It helps the performer to know that Beethoven had profound opinions about humanity, was fearless in calling for justice, and also could show great tenderness. And an artist tells us as much about himself through the way he performs, as he does about the composer.

In recent years in the United States, music has raised its voice in protest, sounding the aspirations of many. The divisions between the races have been painfully visible for so long. America had already ostracized Paul Robeson for his refusal to bow to authority as much as for his political beliefs, surely one of the saddest moments in American social history, depriving black and white Americans alike of the gifts of one of their most passionate spokesmen. If the spiritual "Nobody Knows the Trouble I've Seen" expresses the resigned despair of bondage, no hymn has aimed

Bob Dylan's songs burst upon the sixties, and critic Ralph Gleason called him "one of the great warning voices of our time." Along with singer Joan Baez, he represents the committed artist seeking to transform his society.

Rostropovich . London 1965

higher or possesses greater simplicity than "We Shall Overcome." The sight of thousands of black and white men and women marching with linked arms, chanting the words which carry the same message of dignity that we hear in the sonorous voice of the late Dr. Martin Luther King Jr., was an inspiring spectacle brought powerfully to millions by television.

In the sixties, a time of profound dissent over national and social goals as the agony in Vietnam grew ever more intense, Americans responded to another hymn, "Blowing in the Wind," written and sung by Bob Dylan, a performer whose career started in the cafés of Greenwich Village:

How many roads must a man walk down
Before you call him a man?
How many seas must the white dove sail
Before she sleeps in the sand?
. . . The answer is blowing in the wind.

The form of the song is simple and strophic, like so many by Schubert, and the melody barely spans an octave. But Dylan's images are specific, universal, and deeply emotional. A cry of conscience, this song became a national anthem for an entire generation.

The Russian cellist Mstislav Rostropovich has become a symbol of the artist's exercise of conscience, and was expelled by the Soviets for his support of the writer Alexander Solzhenitsyn. He is captured here in 1965 by Edmond Kapp.

The artist in our day cannot altogether escape his role in history or in his society. I have often thought of Dmitri Shostakovich, a timid and anxious person, struggling all his life within the state system without ever quite breaking through. I was surprised when I met Shostakovich for the first time at the Prague Spring Festival around 1947. His music breathed the passion and fire of war and heroic sacrifice, but he himself appeared pale and anxious. It is sad that a man who had such genius and so much to say was not able to reach the very apogee of his capacity because of political disapproval. Great honors were accorded him and he had to live up to them, ending his life in such terror that he trembled constantly. He was a fine composer who might have achieved even greater heights elsewhere or at another time. Shostakovich proves that music is infinitely flexible and can adapt itself to any purpose, but human beings cannot. Here was a great spirit surviving through sheer brilliance.

I mentioned earlier having once heard an oratorio to Lenin in Moscow, celebrating him as a saint. In the oratorio the narrator described events in Lenin's life, and one in particular caught my attention. The baritone sang of the time Lenin entered a factory and a woman worker was so overcome that she fainted; yet so ardent was her admiration that she recovered in time to present him with flowers as he left. It was all perfectly serious, with choruses like Bach chorales, the same aura of reverence for a symbol, as if this were a biblical setting. It is true that Bach used cantata and oratorio movements with new words as occasional music for court weddings or princely homecoming odes, and Handel took his opera-composing techniques whole into the creation of his dramatic oratorios, celebrating characters and events from the Old Testament instead of Roman rulers or the mythical gods of Ancient Greece. Yet these composers paid tribute either to a distant past or to a living presence. The blend of the two in the oratorio to Lenin struck me as touchingly naive, though the music itself was professionally constructed and not all that bad.

In much the same spirit the communist Chinese have been using music to sell a heroic view of mission to their people. Much of "modern" Chinese theater and ballet is kitsch, bereft of originality. It is what my wife Diana likes to call "basement *Spartacus*," referring to the heroics of that lamentable work, created by the Bolshoi Ballet, which succeeds in surpassing the epics of Cecil B. deMille. Yet behind all of this lies an idea which has genuine value, namely that nobody should consider himself superior to the taste and mentality of the people. In time, great art will again be produced by the Chinese, though not while it is assembled by collectives and committees, or dictated by infallible policy, to glorify the coming of electric power or to give thanks for the completion of a hydro-

electric plant. This is what accounts for the tawdriness of so much ideological music. It is made by politicians reproducing what they imagine the people will like, rather in the same manner as Western TV networks produce situation comedies and police dramas.

A phenomenon especially characteristic of recent decades is that of the artist creating a personal expressive language as a vehicle for his conscience. In the continuing conflict between old values and new, one American artist has managed to tread the fine line with great skill, the choreographer and dancer Martha Graham. After Isadora Duncan and the Diaghilev Ballet Russe, no single artist has had such an effect upon the dance and its music in this century. Just as Diaghilev recruited Stravinsky, so Martha Graham induced many composers to write for her, among them Aaron Copland and William Schuman. She also introduced themes and physical movements into the dance which were the very antithesis of the forbiddingly disciplined ''ice princesses'' of the St. Petersburg school.

It is not too extreme to say that Graham altered the dance, as Stravinsky altered music. It was vital for Graham, long before our postwar era of sexual liberation, that the body regain its natural rhythms and movements. The old, idealized pas-de-deux had to yield to a freer conception. The barefoot dancing of Isadora Duncan may have been Graham's precursor, along with Vaslav Nijinsky, whose barely disguised, self-gratifying gesture as he lay face down on the scarf at the end of *The Afternoon of a Faun* shocked even blasé Paris. Because Graham's approach to dance was revolutionary, she was forced to develop her own training program for

The revolutionary cultural spirit of China has abated somewhat since the normalization of relations with the West, and collective ballets such as this may in future give way to a new flowering of the always fertile Chinese imagination.

Martha Graham's career as dancer and choreographer spans more than half a century, from the moment in 1930 when she danced in Leonid Massine's production of The Rite of Spring. *She has fortunately chosen to recreate many of her greatest works for younger performers, who will carry her tradition forward to another generation.*

her dancers. At the same time she was creating dozens of works, gathering around her artists, composers and designers. Perhaps in no other sphere is the vitality, dynamism and imagination of America more true to itself, while also allied to the older traditions of Europe, than through the dances of Martha Graham: a musical dance theater of unique proportions, revealing the intimate relationship between music and movement.

Despite the varied musical experiments of this century, there have been many artists who have not abandoned the values of the past, those most

likely to reach the hearts of the people, yet without speaking in an outdated language. Such a one was my dear friend Benjamin Britten, whose music always maintained a personal human voice, speaking what he felt to a public whose ear he knew. He is one of many composers who found inspiration in Oriental, Indonesian and Japanese styles, but his entire life work was given over to music which paid little or no attention to trends or fads. The voice we hear in *Peter Grimes*, the opera with which he first won world acclaim, may be more youthfully flamboyant than the one which ruminates in his last opera, *Death in Venice*, but it is unmistakably the same voice, passionate, consoling, eager.

I had the memorable pleasure of sharing many concerts with this devoted musician and sensitive man. Benjamin Britten is as native to England and the history and tradition of her music and her people as Beethoven is to Germany, and Bartók is to Hungary. He is a composer for whom words and ideas are of paramount importance, and his is the voice

Yehudi Menuhin and Benjamin Britten walk together in Germany in 1945 at the time of their joint concerts for the inmates of liberated concentration camps.

of his people. I first met him on the eve of a tour I was making of former German concentration camps, including Belsen. The crucible of World War II made an indelible contribution on artists by bringing them in contact with experiences which affected them profoundly (as they affected all our lives). The traumatic upheaval of war had made a deep impact on me, for wrenched out of a concert artist's routine, I had been thrust into a life where the unexpected and improvised became the rule, igniting a new excitement and stimulation.

Ben was so anxious to come to Germany with me that I naturally agreed, for here was an opportunity for me of making music with one of the most brilliant and sensitive musical minds which had ever appeared in the ranks of mankind. We never rehearsed, but took along a pile of music—sonatas, concerti, and small pieces. No one in the world has ever accompanied either voice or violin as Ben did, and with him I felt the power of music as it unlocked the hearts of those whom the Nazis had tried to reduce to brutish levels. For the first time in years these people felt human and over the years I have had the most extraordinary letters from those who listened to us at that time.

In Benjamin Britten I see the survival of that same spirit which shaped Purcell, the Elizabethan madrigalists, reaching back to Dunstable and "Sumer Is Icumen In." It is a deep love for the human voice, the natural breathing of the musical line, the organizing sense of rhythm. Over an active composing career of forty years, his output was prodigious, in a day when quantity is suspect. He never once wavered in his conviction that the purpose of his art was the communication of human feeling. He is part of that resurgence of English music from Sir Edward Elgar onward, a twentieth century phenomenon in which all Britons take justified pride, when contemplating the works of Vaughan Williams, Walton, Tippett and, more recently, Edwin Roxburgh, Peter Maxwell Davies and Lennox Berkeley, to mention only a few of the most distinguished names.

When beginning this book I referred to the work of Dr. Manfred Clynes, whose book *Sentics* I have read with profound pleasure for the many fresh questions it raises. He and Murray Schafer both lament the brutalization of the ear, and claim as I do that we must come to terms with our feelings, each of which Dr. Clynes says has a measurable shape; we memorize not only ideas but sensations, and these include our emotions. He helps us to restore our intuitive faculties and points out their operation in responding to the works of the composers we love. He has worked at charting pure "essentic" forms for each emotion and each composer, and his work proves that great composers knew the sentic cycles instinctively, reorganizing what was essential to the human being and giving it form. I find myself responding to Dr. Clynes's conclusions and am anxious to know more about what he promises to reveal concerning emotions we have suppressed.

In the seventies there has been a huge increase in demand among young people for music of every period and place. Often, the living culture of the day has grown up around the amateur, a word to be used in its true sense of one who loves. Through their breadth of interest, young people have the opportunity to evolve a less commercial sense of values and a greater awareness of the economy of life on a planet where coexistence with fellow creatures on land, in the seas and the air is essential.

A recent headline in the *New York Times* declared: "Sentiment Stages a Comeback in the Pop World," and performers like Nick Lowe and David Edmunds have introduced a lively sense of humor and parody into their straight uncomplicated sound. On the other side of the musical fence, the American composer George Rochberg, born in 1926, once a devoted follower of the post-Schönberg twelve-tone serial school, recently wrote a violin concerto for Isaac Stern, perfectly suitable for a virtuoso, a contemporary answer to the great nineteenth century models. The same composer's Third String Quartet, a long eclectic work, draws as freely on Mahler as on Stravinsky, while maintaining a personal tone. Rochberg has said that this work marked his time of turning: "By 1972 I had arrived at the possibility not only of a real and personal rapprochement with the past (which had become of primary importance), but also of the combination of different gestures and languages within the frame of a single work." In Finland, Aulis Sallinen, born in 1933, has written a distinctive Third Symphony which demonstrates that the younger generation of composers in that country need no longer be intimidated by the ghost of Sibelius. The musical experimentation of the fifties and sixties seems to be giving way to a return to music of the heart.

Now that so much musical variety is available, the standard European classical repertoire may seem like a run-down mansion, once very beautiful, but covered now with moss and inhabited by spiders' webs. Yet musicians continue to interpret this supreme heritage with understanding and passion. We may have abused the music of man by commercializing it, forcing it into strange molds; but it is always there, awaiting our response, reminding us that the survival of civilization demands restraint.

There are many university centers in North America, England and the European continent where large numbers of students are learning not only to master the music of our more distant past but, better still, are returning to the custom of making the instruments themselves. The revival of the recorder has made it a familiar friend, especially in England. But to that simple instrument has now been added an array of exotic-sounding instruments such as the rackett, busine and krummhorn, along with the lute, bandora and viol, now heard in the profusion of summer music festivals. Groups compete with one another as avidly as any members of the Society for the Preservation and Encouragement of Barbershop Quartet Singing in America. Vocal groups perform Ockeghem, Binchois, Victoria and John Dowland, whose bittersweet songs retain their extraordinary appeal. The members of the Toronto Consort maintain a summer program where students can obtain direct contact with the roots of their music, and many early music groups are active in London, somehow finding the means to survive throughout the whole year.

In Africa the local musical traditions are being re-examined in fresh ways. Negritude is the word coined in the past forty years to describe the burgeoning black consciousness of Africans, the spirit of which is echoed in the recently popular American slogan "black is beautiful." Two examples of the change struck me particularly in Senegal, one because of its well-intentioned incongruity, the other because of its genuinely original quality. I have mentioned the addition of the *kora* and the *balafon* to the Holy Mass, now chanted in Wolof, the most prevalent native language in Senegal, at the monastery of K'eur Moussa. More interesting still is the work being done by Lieutenant Julien Jouga and the choir he has trained in Dakar over the past twenty years.

This skilled musician has developed a unique repertoire for the choir, a music he has created out of the rhythmic and melodic traditions of the area, adapting them to contemporary needs and forms. It is frequently responsorial singing, in which Jouga will intone a phrase of proposal and the choir will answer or comment, a form of singing found throughout Africa. The rhythm and metre of this music fall in odd lengths following the pattern of the Wolof language. The singing is characteristically open-throated, and the verve of the performers is as infectious as their professionalism. Here an effort is being made to create an African music in the image of the twentieth century, in the spirit of negritude, and in the blend of races, tribes and beliefs which have lived together in the area for so long. It is a spirit which finds an outstanding spokesman in their poet-President, Leopold Sedar Senghor.

Many students of foreign native musical traditions have told me that it is possible to work and grow within another musical language, once thought to belong only to those born to it. The old dance forms of North India known as *bharata natyam* were practiced there by only a few specialists until just recently. Many American students have flocked to India to study there since the war, and this gesture of high respect has

begun to restore these traditions to favor in India itself. There is no doubt that interest in Indian music was popularized in the West by the Beatles, especially George Harrison, forming part of the "raised consciousness" movement to which the passion for Zen Buddhism belongs, and possibly also that for LSD. Thereafter, the sitar was recognized as a legitimate instrument in the West, and can even be found in some rock groups.

At the University of California, Berkeley, numbers of students take their class in Javanese gamelan and song very seriously. North American youth playing the music dedicated to sacred deities and myths, a pastoral ancestral music grounded in Hindu and Buddhist beliefs, is a reflection of the contemporary desire to "live it" rather than merely to study through books—to steep oneself in the very vibrations, the sounds which are invoked by a totally different civilization. This music is totally removed from pop music, whether punk or glitter or power, or any of the other spontaneous fashions. In a sense, America prepared itself for this situation by absorbing African, European, Central American and Eastern musical traditions; it represents the world of instant communication,

The choir formed by Lieutenant Julien Jouga in Dakar, Senegal has toured the nation frequently, and appeared in Paris and other European centers, as well as on recordings.

travel and opportunity, a mirror of the constantly changing ethos of worlds and people in collision, a veritable Tower of Babel. Out of this we must learn to teach, to make some new order, and therefore to understand each of the new or ancient exotic ways of being, and to live these cultures through their music.

In New York City we find another example of the exploration into the arcane. David Hykes, a film maker and student of Buddhism still in his mid-twenties, became fascinated with the music of Mongolia and Tibet, and particularly with the method of singing in which one voice is able to generate a fundamental tone together with a whole shifting series of overtones. One might think that Hykes would study this music at its source. He did, in a way, but not by travelling to Tibet. He secured some recordings, and listened to them over and over, determined to solve the mystery himself. He slowly began to test his own voice, and by trial and error found he could reproduce the same effects. It took two years, and the first time he actually succeeded he was so elated he immediately called in some friends to demonstrate what he had achieved. From this came the group Hykes calls The Harmonics Choir, whom he trained as he had trained himself. The mystical sound of their blended overtones casts a unique spell which belongs exclusively to them.

President Léopold Sédar Senghor is an articulate spokesman for the cause of an independent Africa. His poetry has been widely translated.

Throughout this book I have stressed the parallel and reciprocal relationship between folk music and *musique savante*, between improvised music or traditional music on the one hand and composed, structured music on the other. In the dissolution of lines of demarcation in this era of jet travel, television, and of satellites exploring outer space, we live in a cultural mêlée of East and West, of classical and popular. The burden of so much knowledge thrust upon us by literacy, education and modern communications has forced us to become the trustees of the repository of world civilizations, like some tired nightwatchman guarding a museum full of dead treasure. It is imperative that we should feel a connection with the living moment which springs from this very past, finding an expression which is a fusion of past, present and anticipation of the future. Music is as much part of creation as is the ocean, intangible yet tangible, visible and aural. Like the sea, it flows within us, speaking for our soul.

In no person is this cross-fertilization more pronounced than in Béla Bartók, the last of the great romantic composers. Profoundly rooted and attached to his native Hungary, thoroughly versed in the folk music of almost each village with its traditional songs going back hundreds of years, as well as in the folk traditions, rhythms and melodies of all the Balkan countries, of Turkey and the northern coast of Africa, he was at the same time the most disciplined, erudite of men and musicians. Intellectually and structurally his compositions rank with the greatest in musical history while, at the same time, they never lose the immediacy, the poignancy, the message, that total range of human emotion which is the heritage of living generations. Pride, pain, joy, serenity, meditation, humor—you will find all of these compellingly expressed in the music of Bartók from the shortest, most concise work of a few bars to the most extended symphonic and chamber music works.

Bartók's heart and mind belong to all mankind; at the close of his self-imposed exiled life in the United States, unable to bear the fascist totalitarian regime that had taken over his native Hungary, he was about to embark on a study of the Indians of the American Northwest, which would have enriched North American music beyond belief. It would also have given the Indians a vivid sense of their own culture, the most valuable elements of which would have renewed their self-confidence and their sense of human dignity.

In his Concerto for Orchestra, composed during his last years in New York, Bartók includes in the last movement a jaunty jazz tune. He was a man who was curious and profoundly analytical about every aspect of human expression, totally unprejudiced. Even more than Delius in Florida, he brought to the United States a contribution which left a deep mark on American musicians, but which only achieved a small fraction

In a remote corner of central Europe in 1908, Béla Bartók listens as a villager sings folk songs into his Edison cylinder recorder. He spent the rest of his life transcribing these carefully preserved recordings.

of what he might have done had he lived longer. While composing, he was at the same time working at Columbia University on the gigantic task of classifying all his folk material, an undertaking which has now appeared in print. His spirit was as suited to the painstaking work of compiling his massive catalogue as it was to fiery creation: it was as scholarly as it was forceful.

It was a great privilege to know Béla Bartók during the last three years of his life. In fact, he intended to spend the last summer with me in California, in 1945; but shortly before coming he had to give it up, for he was too ill with leukemia to be allowed to travel. For me the thrill of knowing Bartók was the realization that through his music and without any words, his heart had been revealed to me. The very first words we ever exchanged were after my accompanist and I played for him the first movement of his Sonata Number One for Piano and Violin. I had wanted him to hear it before playing it in New York and had arranged this meeting. Bartók, a man of few words, was already seated with the score in hand in front of the piano and with a pencil poised in the air like some terrifying schoolmaster waiting to catch a mistake.

Under the circumstances, no words could be exchanged. Although it sounds immodest, I like to remember his words when we had finished the first movement: "I didn't think works could be played like that until long after the composer was dead." For composers do not reveal their true hearts to the living. It is only through their music that they become known and understood, and if their music is a personal idiom, it takes a long time for interpreters to penetrate the very core of their meaning.

I was bold enough to ask Bartók to write a sonata for solo violin for me. I could have asked for a great concerto or a sonata with piano, but I wanted to impose the least possible burden upon him. It was the only way to help him financially; he was too proud to be helped except by giving himself. This sonata is no doubt the greatest work for violin alone since Bach.

The Sonata for Solo Violin is difficult, and although Bartók was present when I first performed it at Carnegie Hall late in 1944, I regret that I was not able to let him hear it in a truly finished interpretation, for over the years this music has come to speak to me, and I believe to all of us, in the deepest spiritual terms. The first movement is marked *tempo di ciaccona* in which Bartók looks back at one of Bach's monumental works for solo violin, translating it into the free but disciplined Hungarian idiom. There follows the fugue, perhaps the most aggressive, brutal music I was ever to play. The serene *melodya* follows, and to close there is the presto—swift, dancelike, elusive. I made some suggestions to Bartók

on phrasing, fingering, bowing, and other technical problems, many of which he accepted. But when at one point I asked him if he would alter one chord, which was especially awkward to play, he answered "No!"

As a young man Bartók travelled all over Hungary in the years from the turn of the century until the 1920s. At the time he started on his quest, most of these territories were ruled by the Austro-Hungarian Empire. Bartók carried with him a simple Edison cylinder recorder with which he collected Serbian, Croat, Slovenian and Hungarian folksongs, painstakingly notating them afterwards in his fine spidery hand. What Bartók learned in these excursions he put into his music, which always remained deeply rooted in the life of the people. It is a spirit heard in all of the works he wrote in America, in none more than the Third Piano Concerto, written in the final months of his life for his wife, the pianist Ditta Pasztory, completing it less than two days before his death. It was a gesture one can only compare to Michelangelo at ninety, refashioning his nearly completed, final *Pietà*, forced to let the chisel fall only weeks before relinquishing life itself. The orchestration of the final seventeen bars of

The young Béla Bartók at the dawn of his difficult, extraordinary career, photographed about 1905.

the concerto was completed by Bartók's devoted friend and disciple, Tibor Serly, a musician of great skill and intuition, who performed an even greater task in rescuing from oblivion the sketches for a Concerto for Viola which Bartók had dropped in favor of the final gift to his wife and companion. As completed by Tibor Serly, the Viola Concerto has entered the concert repertory as a fully mature masterpiece.

Bartók's music will survive the various experimental schools and even the great dodecaphonic composers in the same way that Brahms survived and will survive his contemporaries, Wagner and Strauss. I remember when Bartók interrogated me about how I had analyzed a recurring chromatic figure in the violin concerto. He said, "I wanted to show Schönberg that one can use all the twelve notes in a row in a thousand different ways and yet remain tonal."

Bartók was what I like to call a moderate fanatic. His passion was contained, his freedom disciplined. His music serves us as a higher conscience, asking ultimate questions. For we have seen that beauty and truth may assume many faces and many masks, but we need to make the effort to recognize them. We may lose something of the clarity of our definition of ourselves, yet rediscover in the process another kind of self, one which encompasses a greater truth, that of a total living experience in which death is a part of life, sorrow a modulation of joy, in our reach toward ecstasy and revelation. As the living cell must fulfill its destiny, following the dictates of its chromosomes, so, too, are we not ourselves spurred on by that star which illuminates the way to all our arts, propelled by a yearning which will not let us be, making possible masterpieces which we recognize to be expressions of a greater self?

We are told that Saint Francis of Assisi could attune his ear to the conversations of the birds, bringing to life the legend of Orpheus. To me, that same sense of communication with every living thing underlies all that Bartók wrote, linking our past with our future. I wish he could have lived to see us beginning to realize, as we have, the dangers of divorcing ourselves from nature, and our return to the essential values that this wonderful land has to offer. Bartók would certainly have taken full part, asking whether through self-refinement and endless effort we will be able to transform our experience into service to our fellow man and to our common environment. Bartók demands that we search for honesty, love and fidelity within ourselves, and reminds us that music will serve those who strive to live its harmonies.

Picture Index

Bibliography

I. GENERAL

Baines, Antony (ed.), *Musical Instruments Through the Ages*, Penguin Books, New York City, 1973

Barzun, Jacques, *Pleasures of Music*, University of Chicago Press, 1977

Bernstein, Leonard, *The Infinite Variety of Music*, Simon & Schuster, New York City, 1966

Brockway, Wallace, *The World of Opera*, Pantheon Books, New York City, 1962

Chailley, Jacques, *40,000 Years of Music*, Farrar Straus and Giroux, New York City, 1964

Chase, Gilbert, *The Music of Spain*, Dover Press, New York City, 1959

Ewen, David, *The Complete Book of Classical Music*, Prentice-Hall, Englewood Cliffs, N.J., 1965

Garvie Peter (ed.), *Music and Western Man*, J. M. Dent, London, 1958

Geiringer, Karl, Musical Instruments (2nd ed.), Oxford University Press, New York City, 1958

Gillespie, John, *Five Centuries of Keyboard Music*, Dover Press, New York City, 1972

Grunfeld, Fred, *Music*, Newsweek Books, New York City, 1974

Kupferberg, Herbert, *Opera*, Newsweek Books, New York City, 1975

Lang, Paul Henry, *Music in Western Civilization*, W. W. Norton, New York City, 1973

Lang, Paul Henry, *The Experience of Opera*, W. W. Norton, New York City, 1973

Mellers, Wilfrid, *Man and His Music* (4 vol.), Schocken Books, New York City, 1962

Menuhin, Yehudi, *Unfinished Journey*, Alfred A. Knopf, New York City, 1976

Prunières, Henri, *A New History of Music*, Vienna House, New York City, 1972

Robertson, Alec and Denis Stevens, *Pelican History of Music*: 1. Ancient Forms to Polyphony; 2. Renaissance and Baroque; 3. Classical and Romantic. Penguin Books, New York City, 1960, 1963, 1968

Sachs, Curt, *The History of Musical Instruments*, W. W. Norton, New York City, 1940

Schonberg, Harold C., *The Lives of the Great Composers*, W. W. Norton, New York City, 1970

Stevens, Denis (ed.), *A History of Song*, W. W. Norton, New York City, 1960

Strunk, Oliver (ed.), *Source Readings in Music History*, W. W. Norton, New York City, 1950

Weiss, Piero (ed.), *Letters of Composers Through Six Centuries*, Chilton Book Co., Philadelphia, 1967

Young, Percy M., *A Concise History of Music*, David White Company, New York City, 1974

II. ENCYCLOPEDIAS

Groves' Dictionary of Music and Musicians (Eric Blom, editor), St. Martin's Press, New York City, 1973

International Cyclopaedia of Music and Musicians (Oscar Thompson, editor)(10th ed.), Dodd Mead & Co., New York City, 1975

Oxford History of Music (Percy M. Buck, editor), Cooper Square Publishers, Inc., New York City, 1973

III. CHAPTER ONE

Backus, John, *The Acoustical Foundations of Music*, W. W. Norton, New York City, 1969

Blacking, John, *How Musical Is Man*, University of Washington Press, Seattle, 1973

Crump, J. T., and William P. Maher (editors), *Chinese and Japanese Music*, University of Michigan Press, Ann Arbor, 1975

Galpin, Francis W., *The Music of the Sumerians*, Da Capo Press, New York City, 1970

Jeans, Sir James H., *Science and Music*, Dover Press, New York City, 1968

Jones, Albert, *Africa and Indonesia*, E. J. Brill, Leiden, Holland, 1964

Lawler, Lillian B., *The Dance in Ancient Greece*, University of Washington Press, Seattle, 1964

Lippman, Edward A., *Musical Thought in Ancient Greece*, Da Capo Press, New York City, 1975

Sachs, Curt, *The Rise of Music in the Ancient World*, W. W. Norton, New York City, 1943

IV. CHAPTER TWO

Appel, Willi, *Gregorian Chant*, Indiana University Press, Bloomington, 1958

Arnold, Denis, *Giovanni Gabrieli*, Oxford University Press, New York City, 1974

Brown, Howard M., *Instrumental Music Before 1600*, Harvard University Press, Cambridge, 1965

Bulos, Afif Alvarez, *The Handbook of Arabic Music*, Librairie du Liban, Beirut, 1971

Coates, Henry, *Palestrina*, J. M. Dent, London, 1938

Holroyde, Peggy, *The Music of India*, Praeger Publishers, New York City, 1972

Idelsohn, A. Z., *Jewish Music in Its Historical Development*, Schocken Books, New York City, 1967

Munrow, David, *Instruments of the Middle Ages and Renaissance*, Oxford University Press, London, 1976

Reese, Gustave, *Music in the Middle Ages*, W. W. Norton, New York City, 1940

Reese, Gustave, *Music in the Renaissance*, W. W. Norton, New York City, 1959

V. CHAPTER THREE

Arnold, Denis, *The Monteverdi Companion*, W. W. Norton, New York City, 1972

Bebey, Francis, *African Music*, Lawrence Hill & Co., New York City, 1975

Bukofzer, Manfred, *Music in the Baroque Era*, W. W. Norton, New York City, 1947

Harley, John, *Music in Purcell's London*, D. Dobson, London, 1968

Hill, William H., *Antonio Stradivari*, Dover Press, New York City, 1963

Lang, Paul Henry, *George Frideric Handel*, W. W. Norton, New York City, 1966

Prunières, Henri, *Monteverdi*, Dover Press, New York City, 1972

Raynor, Henry, *A Social History of Music*, Schocken Books, New York City, 1972

Scott, Ralph H. E., *Jean Baptiste Lully*, P. Owen, London, 1973

Westrup, Jack A., *Purcell*, J. M. Dent, London, 1965

Wechsberg, Joseph, *The Glory of the Violin*, Viking Press, New York City, 1972

VI. CHAPTER FOUR

Biancolli, Louis, *The Mozart Handbook*, Greenwood Press, Westport, Conn., 1975

Blom, Eric, *Mozart*, Farrar Straus & Giroux, New York City, 1962

Brown, Maurice J. E., *Schubert*, Da Capo Press, New York City, 1977

David, Hans T., and Arthur Mendel (editors), *The Bach Reader*, W. W. Norton, New York City, 1945

Einstein, Alfred, *Mozart and His Times*, Alfred A. Knopf, New York City, 1958

Geiringer, Karl, *Johann Sebastian Bach*, Oxford University Press, New York City, 1966

Geiringer, Karl, *The Bachs: A Family Portrait*, Boston University Press, 1953

Geiringer, Karl, *Haydn* (2nd ed.), Doubleday & Co., New York City, 1963

Lang, Paul Henry, *The Creative World of Beethoven*, W. W. Norton, New York City, 1971

Lang, Paul Henry, *The Creative World of Mozart*, W. W. Norton, New York City, 1963

Marek, George R., *Beethoven*, Funk & Wagnalls, New York City, 1969

Pincherle, Marc, *Antonio Vivaldi*, W. W. Norton, 1957

Wechsberg, Joseph, *Schubert*, Rizzoli International, New York City, 1977

VII. CHAPTER FIVE

Barzun, Jacques, *Berlioz and the Romantic Century* (3rd ed.), Columbia University Press, New York City, 1969

Berlioz, Hector, *Evenings With the Orchestra*, University of Chicago Press, 1973

Calvocoressi, Maria, and Gerald Abraham, *Masters of Russian Music*, Alfred A. Knopf, New York City, 1936

Chissell, Joan, *Schumann*, Farrar, Straus & Giroux, New York City, 1967

Critchley, Macdonald, and R. A. Henson, *Music and the Brain*, William Heinemann Medical Books Ltd., London, 1977

Ehrlich, Cyril, *The Piano: A History*, J. M. Dent, London, 1976

Einstein, Alfred, *Music in the Romantic Era*, W. W. Norton, New York City, 1947

Gál, Hans, *Richard Wagner*, Stein & Day, New York City, 1976

Gavoty, Bernard, *Chopin*, Charles Scribner's Sons, New York City, 1977

Geiringer, Karl, *Brahms*, Allen & Unwin Ltd., London, 1968

Hume, Paul, *Verdi*, E. P. Dutton, New York City, 1977

Marek, George R., *Gentle Genius: The Story of Felix Mendelssohn*, Funk & Wagnalls, New York City, 1972

Nettl, Paul, *National Anthems*, Frederick Ungar Publishers, New York City, 1967

Newman, Ernest, *Wagner as Man and Artist*, Vintage Press, New York City, 1960

Pulvey, Jeffrey, *Paganini, the Romantic Virtuoso*, Da Capo Press, New York City, 1970

Raynor, Henry, *Music and Society Since 1815*, Schocken Books, New York City, 1976

Searle, Humphrey, *The Music of Liszt*, Williams & Norgate, London, 1954

Wechsberg, Joseph, *The Waltz Emperors*, G. P. Putnam's Sons, East Rutherford, N. J., 1973

Weinstock, Herbert, *Tchaikovsky*, Alfred A. Knopf, New York City, 1946

VIII. CHAPTER SIX

Barzun, Jacques, *Music in American Life*, Indiana University Press, Bloomington, 1962

Bierley, Paul E., *John Philip Sousa: American Phenomenon*, Appleton-Century-Crofts, New York City, 1973

Cowell, Henry and Sidney, *Charles Ives and His Music*, Oxford University Press, New York City, 1955

Debussy, Claude, *Debussy on Music*, Secker & Warburg, London, 1977

Gelatt, Roland, *The Fabulous Phonograph*, Macmillan Publishing, New York City, 1977

Highwater, Jamake, *Ritual of the Wind: North American Indian Ceremonies, Music and Dance*, Viking Press, New York City, 1977

Howard, John Tasker, *Stephen Foster*, Thomas Y. Crowell, New York City, 1953

Lang, Paul Henry, *Stravinsky*, W. W. Norton, New York City, 1963

Lockspeiser, Edward, *Debussy*, McGraw-Hill, New York City, 1963

Marek, George R., *Richard Strauss: The Life of a Non Hero*, Simon & Schuster, New York City, 1967

Palmer, Christopher, *Impressionism in Music*, Charles Scribner's Sons, New York City, 1973

Schafer, William J., and Johann Riedel, *The Art of Ragtime*, Louisiana State University Press, Baton Rouge, 1973

Shattuck, Roger, *The Banquet Years*, Random House, New York City, 1968

Vlad, Roman, *Stravinsky*, Oxford University Press, New York City, 1967

Walter, Bruno, *Gustav Mahler*, Alfred A. Knopf, New York City, 1959

IX. CHAPTER SEVEN

Blesh, Rudi, *Shining Trumpets: A History of Jazz* (2nd ed.), Alfred A. Knopf, New York City, 1958

Copland, Aaron, *Copland on Music*, W. W. Norton, New York City, 1963

Copland, Aaron, *What To Listen For In Music*, McGraw Hill, New York City, 1957

Feather, Leonard, *Encyclopedia of Jazz*, Horizon Press, New York City, 1960

Gould, Glenn, *Arnold Schönberg*, University of Cincinnati Press, 1964

Lentz, Donald, *The Gamelan Music of Java and Bali*, University of Nebraska Press, Lincoln, 1965

Lockner, Louis Paul, *Fritz Kreisler*, Macmillan Publishing, New York City, 1950

Panassié, Hugues, and Madeleine Gautier, *A Guide to Jazz*, Greenwood Press, Westport, Conn., 1956

Peare, Catherine Owen, *Aaron Copland*, Holt Rinehart & Winston, New York City, 1969

Reich, Willi, *Alban Berg*, Vienna House, New York City, 1974

Rosen, Charles, *Arnold Schönberg*, Viking Press, New York City, 1975

Rushmore, Robert, *The Life of George Gershwin*, Thomas Y. Crowell, New York City, 1966

Slonimsky, Nicholas, *Music Since 1900* (4th ed.), Charles Scribner's Sons, New York City, 1971

Tudor, Andrei, *Enesco*, Foreign Language Publishing House, Bucharest, 1957

Varèse, Louise, *Varèse: A Looking-Glass Diary* (vol. 1), W. W. Norton, New York City, 1972

Whitall, Arnold, *Music Since The First World War*, J. M. Dent, London, 1977

X. CHAPTER EIGHT

Appleton, Jon, *The Development of Electronic Music*, Prentice Hall, Englewood Cliffs, N. J., 1975

Baraka, Imamu Amiri, *Black Music*, William Morrow & Co., New York City, 1967

Bartók, Béla, *Essays*, St. Martin's Press, New York City, 1976

Boulez, Pierre, *Boulez on Music Today*, Harvard University Press, Cambridge, 1970

Cage, John, *Silence*, M.I.T. Press, Cambridge, 1968

Cott, Jonathan, *Stockhausen: Conversations*, Simon & Schuster, New York City, 1973

Ernst, David, *Musique Concrète*, Crescendo, Boston, 1972

Helm, Everett, *Bartók*, Thomas Y. Crowell, New York City, 1972

Kendall, Alan, *Benjamin Britten*, Macmillan Publishers, London, 1973

Lipscomb, David M., *Noise: The Unwanted Sounds*, Nelson-Hall Co., Chicago, 1974

Macmillan, Keith, and John Beckwith (editors), *Contemporary Canadian Composers*, Oxford University Press, Toronto, 1975

McDonagh, Don, *Martha Graham*, Praeger Publishers, New York City, 1973

Mellers, Wilfrid, H., *The Twilight of the Gods: The Music of the Beatles*, Viking Press, New York City, 1974

Nyman, Michael, *Experimental Music: Cage and Beyond*, Studio Vista (Cassell & Collier), London, 1974

Palmer, Tony, *All You Need Is Love*, Grossman Publishers, New York City, 1976

Payzant, Geoffroy, *Glenn Gould*, Van Nostrand & Reinhart, Toronto, 1978

Pickering, Stephen, *Bob Dylan Approximately*, David McKay Co., New York City, 1975

Reich, Steve, *Writings About Music*, New York University Press, New York City, 1974

Schafer, R. Murray, *The Tuning of the World*, Alfred A. Knopf, New York City, 1977

Wagley, Charles, *The Latin American Tradition*, Columbia University Press, New York City, 1968

Index